INTERNATIONALIZATION AND MANAGING NETWORKS IN THE ASIA PACIFIC

ASIAN STUDIES SERIES

Series Editor

Professor Chris Rowley,

Cass Business School, City University, London, UK; Institute of Hallyu Convergence Research, Korea University, Korea
Griffith Business School, Griffith University, Australia
(email: c.rowley@city.ac.uk)

Elsevier is pleased to publish this major Series of books entitled Asian Studies: Contemporary Issues and Trends. The Series Editor is Professor Chris Rowley of Cass Business School, City University, London, UK and Department of International Business and Asian Studies, Griffith University, Australia.

Asia has clearly undergone some major transformations in recent years and books in the Series examine this transformation from a number of perspectives: economic, management, social, political and cultural. We seek authors from a broad range of areas and disciplinary interests covering, for example, business/management, political science, social science, history, sociology, gender studies, ethnography, economics and international relations, etc.

Importantly, the Series examines both current developments and possible future trends. The Series is aimed at an international market of academics and professionals working in the area. The books have been specially commissioned from leading authors. The objective is to provide the reader with an authoritative view of current thinking.

New authors: we would be delighted to hear from you if you have an idea for a book. We are interested in both shorter, practically orientated publications (45,000þ words) and longer, theoretical monographs (75,000e100,000 words). Our books can be single, joint or multi-author volumes. If you have an idea for a book, please contact the publishers or Professor Chris Rowley, the Series Editor.

Dr Glyn Jones
Email: g.jones.2@elsevier.com

Professor Chris Rowley
Email: c.rowley@city.ac.uk

INTERNATIONALIZATION AND MANAGING NETWORKS IN THE ASIA PACIFIC

Edited by

NIPAWAN THIRAWAT

CP
CHANDOS
PUBLISHING
ELSEVIER
An imprint of Elsevier • elsevier.com

Chandos Publishing is an imprint of Elsevier
50 Hampshire Street, 5th Floor, Cambridge, MA 02139, United States
The Boulevard, Langford Lane, Kidlington, OX5 1GB, United Kingdom

Library of Congress Cataloging-in-Publication Data
A catalog record for this book is available from the Library of Congress

British Library Cataloguing-in-Publication Data
A catalogue record for this book is available from the British Library

ISBN: 978-0-08-100813-3 (print)
ISBN: 978-0-08-100885-0 (online)

Publisher: Glyn Jones
Acquisition Editor: Glyn Jones
Editorial Project Manager: Ana Claudia Garcia
Production Project Manager: Debasish Ghosh
Cover Designer: Greg Harris

CONTENTS

CONTRIBUTORS

C.R. Graves
The University of Adelaide Business School, Adelaide, SA, Australia

E. Phijaisanit
Thammasat University, Bangkok, Thailand

P-S. Seet
Edith Cowan University, Joondalup, WA, Australia

O. Sivarak
Mahidol University International College, Nakhon Pathom, Thailand

A. Tejapaibul
Fiscal Policy Office, Ministry of Finance, Bangkok, Thailand

N. Thirawat
Mahidol University International College, Nakhon Pathom, Thailand

S. Tulayasathien
Fiscal Policy Office, Ministry of Finance, Bangkok, Thailand

N. Udomkit
Mahidol University International College, Nakhon Pathom, Thailand

PREFACE

The role of Asia-Pacific companies including international activities conducted is still considered a relatively new issue in comparison to existing information and literature, which is mostly focused on the analysis of companies from developed countries. This book includes case studies and empirical evidence from works by researchers and experts on network management and international business expansion, emphasizing in-depth analysis of activities, policies, and strategies of Asia-Pacific companies.

Furthermore, debate is incorporated to provide information to readers on applications of business networking, internationalization theories, and best practices, as well as to develop policy recommendations and discuss the role of the public sector in supporting overseas expansion of the private sector. This book will attract readers and individuals (those in academia as well as practitioners) who are interested in exploring and understanding the successful internationalization strategies of Asia-Pacific firms and interactions between the public and private sectors.

This book illustrates a different focus and contents from other books in international business. This book includes many interesting topics related to both network management and internationalization in the Asia-Pacific region. For the first time these two topics are combined and integrated into a single book, with special emphasis on developing countries. It also highlights internationalization and networking strategies of firms from Asia-Pacific countries.

I am grateful for extensive support on the collaboration of this book, which could not have been completed without the valuable time, constructive comments, and professionalism of the contributors.

CHAPTER 1

Introduction

N. Thirawat
Mahidol University International College, Nakhon Pathom, Thailand

This book consists of two interesting and important topics about network management and internationalization in a single book, which has never been published before. In most books, topics are separated, such as the book being specifically on the topic of network management, whereby international expansion issues would only be within a subheading related to international business.

This book aims to provide knowledge and a better understanding of relevant conceptual frameworks as well as practical guidance on how to manage networks and internationalize successfully. Further, this book proposes policy recommendations and discusses the impact of trade and international investment policy, both at national and regional levels, on business operations of companies in the Asia-Pacific region. The role of Asia-Pacific companies in the global market and the role of governments in supporting international activities of these companies are reviewed.

Asia-Pacific countries are selected as the main context of this work because the Asia Pacific is a region with a high growth rate and has received great attention from researchers, businesses, and governments of various countries over the past 10 years. However, existing literature on international business activities and strategies of Asia-Pacific firms and dynamic relationships between the public and private sectors is still scant.

This book is the combination of theories of network management and internationalization, applications of these theories, case studies, empirical evidence, and linking the public and private sectors in expanding businesses overseas together in a single book. This book is recommended for academics, businesspeople, students, members of the general public interested in international business and management of networks, policy makers, and government officials.

This book is organized topically. Each chapter of the first part of the book focuses on regionalism and its implications, internationalization theories and strategies, as well as the global supply chain in the Asia-Pacific region. This book consists of internationalization theories and empirical evidence, with

Internationalization and Managing Networks in the Asia Pacific
http://dx.doi.org/10.1016/B978-0-08-100813-3.00001-8

case studies of Association of Southeast Asian Nations (ASEAN) multinational companies and other Asia-Pacific firms that have succeeded in expanding abroad, such as Singaporean, Taiwanese, Thai, Malaysian, Indonesian, Japanese, Chinese, and Australian companies. These help provide guidelines of analysis for the adaptations these companies made to internationalize successfully, market penetration strategies used for the ASEAN Economic Community (AEC), and international expansion of Asia-Pacific companies across countries in Asia and other continents.

The second section emphasizes the relationship between internationalization and networking of Asia-Pacific firms, theories and analysis related to network management, the power of business networking, as well as the significance and role that business networking plays in propelling organizations toward international business, especially in the Asia-Pacific region. Moreover, it includes relevant theories and applications to assist in identifying key stakeholders in the AEC. This section contains various fascinating headings, such as networking strategies and internationalization of Asia-Pacific firms and contemporary issues in internationalization.

This book differentiates itself from other books where it provides advice to the public sectors within Southeast Asia on formulating and implementing policies. It also includes the role of the public sector in supporting international business activities of the private sector, consisting of many ASEAN companies and analyzing both national and regional policies, such as the AEC.

The second chapter discusses the development of the AEC, exploring obstacles faced in economic integration on the regional scale. This chapter also looks into the effects on businesses in the regionalization era, proposing Southeast Asian companies take advantage of business opportunities that arise from reduced trade and investment barriers. This chapter focuses on the importance of information and communication technologies and improvement of information and communications technology infrastructure and human resources, as flexibility and innovation will determine countries' competitiveness globally. Southeast Asian industries with the potential to grow include telecommunications, e-commerce, banking, health, logistics, education, and the Internet of Things. New perspectives on the changing context of competitiveness in the integration of the AEC will be presented throughout this chapter, highlighting important economic development factors in the digital age and dependency on collaboration between ASEAN members, which will lead to both national and regional gains.

Chapter 3 highlights the importance of foreign direct investment (FDI) in ASEAN's economic drive. ASEAN member countries are both FDI recipients and direct investors, a virtue from foreign investment policies and freedom of investment both nationally and regionally. This chapter discusses the ASEAN Comprehensive Investment Agreement and compares variations on investment promotion policies: a tool to enhance international competitiveness. Chapter 3 will suggest benefits from the liberalization of investments and investing in ASEAN member nations, with emphasis on flexible policies corresponding to differing needs, dependent on the degree of social and economic development in each nation. At the same time, this chapter proposes policies to boost competitiveness of ASEAN nations.

Chapter 4 examines the main theories explaining the internationalization phenomenon, together with detailed case studies relevant to each theory. This includes the study of the dynamic internationalization process for multinational companies, which was initially conducted by Uppsala University's academics who formulated the Uppsala model. The Uppsala model illustrates the systematic and progressive course of internationalization that firms proceed with, through sporadic export, independent intermediaries, foreign trading branches, and foreign trading and production branches. In 1993 Dunning published his eighth book, entitled "The Globalization of Business." In this book, he identifies the three key aspects of firms' internationalization that are the vectors of the eclectic paradigm, further classifying the motives of internationalization into four categories: resource seeking, market seeking, efficiency seeking, and strategic asset seeking. Network model and institutional theory as well as resource-based view theory are also highlighted. The case companies include BANPU, Creative Technology, Daewoo Motor Company, Constellation Brands New Zealand, Charoen Pokphand Group, Siam Cement Group, Lion Group, Toyota Group, Li & Fung Group, Pohang-Yeongil Port, Boost Juice, Indian Pharma Multinational, and small-sized businesses in Sri Lanka.

In the fifth chapter I explain internationalization strategies, including case studies collected from Southeast Asian multinational companies. From the exploration of literatures, I identified categorization of internationalization theories in terms of market entry, research and development, technological transfer, product variations, product and price mix, businesses' branch model, and product branding. Strategies were also categorized into business types, such as regional exporters/importers, global exporters/importers, multinational companies, and outsourced manufacturing and design companies. I suggest alternative strategies to be coupled with internationalization strategies, and illustrate case studies from ASEAN multinational companies such as Charoen Pokphand Foods, Frase and Neave

Company, Krungsiam Beverage, PETRONAS, Trias Sentosa Tbk PT, Air Asia, Proton, Thoresen Thai Agencies, Pho24, and Thai Smile Airways to explain internationalization theories in different dimensions.

Chapter 6 presents the global supply chain in Asia, the definition of global supply chains, the integration of communication technology within the supply chain, the importance of the supply chain, Asia's supply chain, and future trends. Case studies illustrate specific business models. Advancements in communication technology have been an asset to large businesses as they expand worldwide with the motive to seek valuable opportunities. As a result of changing technologies the world is becoming smaller as people become more interconnected and supply chains lengthen and become more sophisticated. It becomes increasingly necessary for businesses to take an interest in the integration of their supply chains so they can become competitive and successful in the global arena. In doing so, Asia's economy and gross domestic product to population will grow faster than in other parts of the world. Asia will become the world's future economy. Understanding future trends in Asia will support the supply chain in conducting businesses to their best ability.

Chapter 7 illustrates the importance of networks for the internationalization of Asia-Pacific companies, as well as increased global competition, which has pressured companies toward organizational development. Internationalization theories help companies access international markets by gathering information on other markets and business opportunities, and also reduce restrictions on resources. Furthermore, they assist in determining directions on market expansion. This chapter gathers network principles and debates their roles and uses in internationalization. Examples from case study firms in the Asia Pacific are also included.

Chapter 8 studies the possible impacts of involvement from different external networks on the possibility of internationalization by small and medium enterprises (SMEs). The researcher finds that Australian SMEs not only utilize the owner's and senior management's network, but also benefit from information and connections with external partners to promote internationalization. The researcher finds evidence that SMEs must access networks and external investors' and advisory boards' resources in internationalization. The researcher finds that policy makers and industry groups play a significant role in facilitating SMEs to develop network strategies for internationalization.

In Chapter 9 I revisit relevant literature on network management strategies implementable in Asia-Pacific companies going global. Various types of networks are presented in this chapter, such as networks between multinational companies and SMEs, general business networks, formal and informal business networks, intrafirm global production networks, intercompany global production networks, and cluster and ethnic networks. The benefits gained from networks are explained in this chapter, coupled with case studies from multinational enterprises in India, Thailand, Japan, China, Taiwan, New Zealand, Australia, the Philippines, Singapore, and Malaysia.

I expand on internationalization problems and obstacles faced by Asia-Pacific companies in Chapter 10. Theories and new ideological frameworks on internationalization obstacles are also illustrated here. I categorize obstacles faced in internationalization into two main categories: internal and external obstacles. Internal obstacles can be categorized further into financial, resource, management, operational, marketing, and knowledge issues, whereas external obstacles can be categorized into process, governmental, environmental, and innovative issues. These not only limit business activities internationally, but also constrict companies in becoming truly internationalized.

The final chapter concludes this book. It provides concluding remarks on Asia-Pacific firms' internationalization and network management, including some directions for managers, investors, and policy makers.

CHAPTER 2

AEC and the Changing Economic Landscape: Issues, Prospects, and Potentials

E. Phijaisanit
Thammasat University, Bangkok, Thailand

2.1 BACKGROUND AND OVERVIEW OF AEC

The Association of Southeast Asian Nations (ASEAN) was established on Aug. 8, 1967, in Bangkok, Thailand, with five founding nations: Indonesia, Malaysia, the Philippines, Singapore, and Thailand; together they are known as the ASEAN 5. Being an open and inclusive regionalism, more countries within the region, namely Brunei Darussalam, Vietnam, Lao People's Democratic Republic (Lao PDR), Myanmar, and Cambodia, joined at a later stage, making up the present-day 10-member ASEAN. The ASEAN charter comprises three pillars: (1) ASEAN Political-Security Community (APSC), (2) ASEAN Economic Community (AEC), and (3) ASEAN Socio-Cultural Community (ASCC). The goal of the formation is to accelerate economic growth within the region, promoting mutual assistance and development in the fields of commerce, technology, education, regional peace and stability, and socio-cultural bonding and progress. Among the three charters, AEC is perceived as the more prominent in transforming the economic landscape within and across the regions.

At the end of 2015, AEC was officially established, thereby further integrating the regional economies. AEC is based on four pillars. The first pillar envisions a single market and production base where there will be free movement of goods and services, and freer movement of skilled labor, investment, and capital. Dismantling tariffs and relaxing labor movements for eight professions are examples of some of the initiatives undertaken. The second pillar reinforces the first by promoting regional competitiveness through the development of innovation, hard and soft infrastructure, linkages, and connectivity. The third pillar aims to support small and medium enterprises in order to make AEC more inclusive. Lastly, the fourth pillar seeks to enhance the competitiveness of ASEAN and increase its role at a global level.

Internationalization and Managing Networks in the Asia Pacific
http://dx.doi.org/10.1016/B978-0-08-100813-3.00002-X

ASEAN is a community endowed with tremendous potential and opportunity, making up a gross domestic product (GDP) of USD 2.57 trillion (ASEAN, 2015). Despite being a relatively young regional bloc, ASEAN has become one of the most attractive regions for trade and investment. One distinguished feature that makes ASEAN very attractive is its population, which accounts for over 600 million, second only to China and India. This implies that AEC possesses a large pool of human resources as well as potential customers for businesses. With the formation of the single market and production base, coupled with freer movement of a skilled workforce and capital, entrepreneurs in ASEAN will be able to mobilize their resources more efficiently. Freer flows of skilled and semiskilled labor will mitigate issues pertaining to the shortages of the workforce within the region. Regional and foreign firms, particularly multinationals, that look for lower labor-intensive production costs will be expanding into member countries with higher population density (e.g., Vietnam and Indonesia) as trade and investment barriers are removed. Such foreign investment creates employment along the supply chains, which eventually benefit the host countries. In addition, the integration of the economies implies a larger market. With zero tariff barriers and a growing proportion of the middle- and upper-income population, business enterprises will enjoy a larger market for their products. However, this also implies a higher degree of competition because extra-regional firms can also expand into the domestic market.

ASEAN can be characterized by its rather heterogeneous composition. Nevertheless, this heterogeneity makes the community unique. One indicator of the diversity is reflected in the Global Competitiveness Report 2014–15 by the World Economic Forum (2014). Each member of ASEAN is at a different stage of economic development, yet there are business potentials to be realized by firms within the region. For instance, factor-driven economies tend to rely more on their resource endowments with limited technological innovations. They enjoy the advantages of being labor abundant, which supports the nations' lower wage level. This implies opportunities for large firms seeking host countries with lower wages to establish plants in the region. Similarly, efficiency-driven economies are to enhance their productivity through improvements in education, training, the financial market, and the goods and labor market. For innovation-driven economies, they will rely on the development of technological innovations to catch up with competitors in the market. Countries in the latter stages seem to enjoy increased productivity. However, these countries can encounter difficulties such as increasing costs of production due to a higher level of wages and shortage of unskilled labors for some tasks. Thus diversity among the member countries can be thought of as *complementarity* in the sense that one country's strength can offset the other's weakness, thereby reinforcing the community's competitiveness at a global level. With diversified competitive advantages, all member countries can mutually benefit from each other in various dimensions: socially, economically, and politically.

2.2 REDUCED BARRIERS AMONG ASEAN COUNTRIES AND BUSINESS IMPLICATIONS

With huge efforts to integrate the ASEAN economies, plausible impacts resulting from the changing economic landscape should be taken into account. Some significant initiatives undertaken to fulfill the objectives of the AEC are discussed herewith. These initiatives have, to some extent, already reshaped and can potentially alter the nature of conducting businesses within ASEAN as well as the rest of the world.

2.2.1 Goods Market

The impact of AEC is very much pronounced in the case of the goods and commodity market. The initiative to liberalize intra-ASEAN trade or to establish the ASEAN Free Trade Area (AFTA) was made by eliminating both tariff and nontariff barriers. Under the Common Effective Preferential Tariff (CEPT) agreement, countries in ASEAN are required to limit the duties imposed on a long list of products to 0%–5%. Other nontariff barriers like quotas are also removed. The agreement was made among the ASEAN 6 first in 1992, which extended to cover Vietnam in 2006, Lao PDR and Myanmar in 2008, and Cambodia in 2010. However, there are certain commodities that the respective governments may wish to exclude from market liberalization for the purpose of protectionism in the newly opened economies. Such commodities, which remain unaffected by the CEPT agreement, are on the Sensitive list (protected for a long period of time) or General Exception list (excluded from the agreement). The coverage of commodities with zero tariff rate suggests dramatic progress in terms of coverage for the ASEAN-6, whose coverage has almost reached 100% since 2010. Nevertheless, the new members, Cambodia, Lao PDR, Myanmar, and Vietnam (CLMV) lagged behind when the coverage reached the 50% level in 2012. Tariff rates have been reduced to the average level of around 0.54%. Regarding the export and import commodity profile, most of the items in trade are electronic devices, mechanical parts, and raw materials such as mineral fuels, rubber, iron, and steel.

From the perspective of most firms, good market liberalization can be a double-edged sword. On one hand, firms can increase sales volume by expanding into foreign markets and thereby reaching more customers. From the population of over 600 million in AEC, around 60% belong to the middle- and upper-income groups. The growth of the middle-income population in the region opens up business opportunities in household durables, education, and health care services. Hence firms, especially those producing consumer durables (refrigerators, televisions, air conditioners, and electronic devices), will greatly benefit from the market expansion. Other advantaged groups are firms producing food and beverages, and those in the retail business. Some prominent markets in AEC with a growing number of middle-class individuals are Indonesia, the Philippines, Malaysia, and Thailand. CLMV economies still need to increase the purchasing power of their middle-income group, while Singapore and Brunei are exceptions owing to their small population. On the other hand, firms should also take into account that the middle-income individuals in AEC differ from those in the Western world whose purchasing power is relatively higher. Firms need to produce high-quality commodities at affordable prices. In addition, there is pressure on businesses to work on new products to maintain their competitiveness under the new environment. Entrepreneurs are pressured to develop their products to fit the needs of both domestic and foreign customers and, at the same time, keep up with the competitive forces through the creation of technological innovations.

Extra-AEC trade in goods is also important as it accounts for around 75% of the region's total trade. Owing to this significance, agreements have been made with the dialogue partners, including Australia, New Zealand, China, India, Japan, and South Korea. Such initiatives are expected to strengthen the economic power of the regional bloc. Nevertheless, ASEAN business entrepreneurs are entitled to better conditions and fewer restrictions under the agreements made. Therefore, well-aware ASEAN firms can benefit to the fullest from the advantages of being in a regional bloc.

2.2.2 Service Market

Besides the liberalization of good markets discussed previously, ASEAN countries undertook some initiatives to liberalize trades in service as well. This further assisted in creating a more competitive single market and production base. Liberalization of trade in service is important because it is the main driver of the AEC economy and helps business enterprises achieve a more efficient delivery of services. Moreover, the service sector contributes to approximately 40%–50% of the GDP for ASEAN, according to the ASEAN macroeconomic database. Thus business firms can reap greater benefits from both the goods and services markets. Liberalization of trade in services will boost growth and eventually increase ASEAN's competitiveness, thereby attracting foreign investment.

Several sectors indicate good potential to benefit from liberalization of service. Notably, the ASEAN Framework Agreement on Services (AFAS) aims to remove all restrictions on trade in services for five priority service sectors (i.e., air transport, e-ASEAN, health care, tourism, and logistic services) by allowing foreign (ASEAN) equity participation up to 70% in service sectors. Furthermore, there are the Mutual Recognition Arrangements (MRAs) for freer flow of skilled labor in eight professions, which include architectural services, accountancy services, engineering services, surveying qualifications, medical practitioners, dental practitioners, nursing services, and tourism professionals. At present, eight packages of commitments have been implemented under AFAS. With each package, ASEAN countries have negotiated to create a freer trade in services in several economic sectors and mode of supply. The aim was to liberalize all modes of supply by 2015.

The impact of liberalization in the service sector is rather complementary to that of the goods market. However, the effect will be more prominent on the economies that rely heavily on the service sector for growth. For instance, Singapore's service sector contributed to around 74.9% of the GDP in 2013. Similarly, the service sector contributed to a considerable portion of the GDP for the Philippines, Malaysia, Indonesia, and Thailand as well (57.7%, 50.2%, 42.6%, and 45.5%, respectively). With a more efficient delivery of services, firms can provide higher quality of services and goods to consumers. MRAs signed in favor of the eight professions will allow better job opportunities. From the employers' perspective, there will be an ample supply of more competent employees who have attained the occupational standard mutually set by the ASEAN countries. However, foreign workers of the eight professions are subject to the domestic regulations governing that particular occupation. For instance, foreign doctors seeking employment in Thailand will be required to pass the licensure examination. Pressure imposed by MRAs for medical professionals removed the barrier to entry, as previously the licensure examination was conducted in the Thai language. This, to some extent, is expected to mitigate the issue of the shortage of medical professionals in Thailand. With Thailand's projection of becoming a medical hub, foreign doctors can serve a purpose, with Thai doctors devoting more time to domestic patients. Thus businesses related to these eight professions will benefit from a larger pool of the qualified workforce. Nevertheless, as in the goods market, entrepreneurs should be aware of increasing competition because firms in other countries also have access to similar opportunities.

Another important area with much business potential is logistic service. Despite the fact that most member countries in AEC already possess efficient connectivity via air transport, land transport within the region still lags behind. Governments of the ASEAN member countries have become aware of the significance of transport management, linkages, and connectivity. Various mega-infrastructural projects have already been proposed and undertaken to improve the efficiency of land transport. Some examples are ASEAN Highway Network, Singapore Kunming Rail Link, and India-Myanmar-Thailand Trilateral Highway (ASEAN, 2012). Not only will these transport facilities increase the efficiency of overall business performance (faster delivery, increase in trade, etc.), but growth of infrastructure will also lead to urbanization of cities at the borders, further creating employment opportunities and improvements in the standard of living.

Besides the enhancement of physical connectivity, ASEAN countries have also prioritized the information and communications technology (ICT) sector in their liberalization efforts. This is because the physical connectivity of ASEAN economies remains inadequate. There is a need to reinforce the sector with more efficient Internet connectivity. The ASEAN ICT Masterplan envisions a vibrant, inclusive, digital economy. Therefore efforts have been made to create ICT infrastructure in Cambodia, Myanmar, and Lao PDR to empower people with knowledge and awareness of modern technology. This is also to encourage business firms to explore the benefits of ICT in product innovations to improve quality of life. The ICT sector plays a very significant role by interconnecting people, goods, and software. It helps ASEAN transform into a digital economy under the concept of the "Internet of Things." Business firms in retail e-commerce, health care, transportation, energy, and even agriculture see potential gains from applying modern ICT in their normal functioning to create a seamless network of business operation. For instance, many banks offer mobile applications that customers can access through any portable device, allowing them to conduct transactions at home. With efforts to make e-payment more secure, combined with the growth of Internet users and social media, firms in retail e-commerce can benefit from market expansion. The physical connectivity discussed previously also aids in the delivery of goods. Being a paradigm-shifting agent, ICT can enhance business performance significantly.

Moreover, tourism is the service sector that will benefit from both MRAs and the development of transportation linkages. In 2013, total tourist arrivals in ASEAN accounted for around 98 million people, which comprised 44% from intra-ASEAN and 56% from extra-ASEAN. Malaysia had the highest share of intra-ASEAN visitors (47.3%). Given these statistics in the background, tour operators within ASEAN will have greater opportunities in serving intra-ASEAN travelers, as governments have already lifted restrictions on visas for ASEAN travelers. For extra-ASEAN tourists, a plan for a single ASEAN visa has been made to facilitate foreign travelers in the future. Thus travel agents and the hotel business can be expected to prosper as a result of rising demand coupled with improved efficiency in the standard of services, physical infrastructure, and human resources.

2.2.3 Investment

It is undeniable that initiatives undertaken to establish AEC will eventually increase the role of ASEAN in the global economy. With greater opportunities in ASEAN, more employment opportunities will come along and eventually this will bring about a higher standard of living and purchasing power of ASEAN people. An increase in consumption is expected to translate into economic growth. ASEAN is gradually on its path to becoming a robust regional bloc. This will attract more foreign direct investment (FDI) from other parts of the world. Foreign investment will improve not only the manufacturing sector, but also other sectors, such as services, telecommunications, logistics, education, health care, and banking. According to the ASEAN FDI database for 2014, FDI inflows in the region reached USD 136.18 billion, 10.4% higher than the FDI inflows posted in 2013. The flows of intra-ASEAN investment were highest for Lao PDR (55.2% of the total intra-ASEAN), while Singapore succeeded in attracting FDI from abroad (60.4% of total extra-ASEAN). Intra-ASEAN investments, despite being on an increasing trend, were still lower than those of the extra-ASEAN. Most of the FDI to ASEAN came from the EU and Japan.

It is evident from the investment trends that ASEAN has been successful in attracting FDI both from outside as well as within the region. Freer flow of investment will further facilitate the business performance of ASEAN and drive the region through enhanced competitiveness. One of the most evident responses of the governments in ASEAN is the establishment of special economic zones (SEZ). In general, SEZ are set up by the government with the aim of developing that particular area by attracting firms to set up production units through implementation of supportive schemes such as tax and nontax incentives and the development of basic infrastructure. Such policy drive contributes in drawing investment into the economies. Thailand can be considered one of the economies that has succeeded in establishing SEZ. Thai SEZ are majorly located in the border area: Kanchanaburi (close to Myanmar), Chiang Rai, Mukdahan, Nhong Khai and Nakhon Phanom (close to Lao PDR), Sa Kaeo (close to Cambodia), and Songhla and Narathiwat (close to Malaysia). According to the Board of Investment of Thailand, trade values between Thailand and these four economies in 2010–14 grew continuously to an average of THB 900,000 million (Board of Investment, 2015). This figure will definitely increase in the future. The establishment of SEZ provides perfect opportunities for firms using labor-intensive techniques of production, as they can access the pool of the labor force in neighboring countries. Related business along the supply chain (logistics service, distributing firms, etc.) will also gain from SEZ. These possible benefits are not only limited to domestic firms and people in the locality, but also to foreign participants. The growth of SEZ eventually attracts more foreign investment into the economy. Investment in warehousing, distribution channels, and other related services near the borders will further boost economic activities.

2.3 DIGITIZATION AND IMPLICATIONS FOR THE AEC

In the era of digitization, ICT plays an indispensable role in almost every kind of business sector. The ICT sector has transformed people's way of life, which in turn affects how firms should adapt business strategies to improve their potential of tapping into the market. With the boom of the Internet industry in the last decade, people have altered their lifestyle from communicating with each other via traditional channels to receiving and accessing information across the cyber world. Communication is becoming more drastic with the growth of the Internet. Information is available at the fingertips at almost zero marginal cost. The growth of social media like Facebook and Twitter has caused people to spend greater amounts of time on the Internet. Inevitably, the growth of social media will be infinite. Thus business firms in ASEAN and elsewhere should realize this trend and make use of modern ICT to reach larger customers via advertisement on social media. ICT can lead to more efficient delivery of service and overall competitiveness of the business sector. Acknowledging the significance of the ICT sector, ASEAN countries have taken various initiatives in the past, many of which pertain to liberalizing the ICT sector with the aim of supporting other business sectors so ASEAN firms can compete globally. The future of business rests upon the vision of the digital economy, smart cities, and the Internet of Things (IoT), which would certainly transform the business landscape for firms in the retail e-commerce, health care, education, transportation, and energy sectors. As an elaboration of the previous discussion on the service sector in AEC, this section continues further to reflect the current situation of Internet connectivity in ASEAN and the initiatives related to the ICT sector that have been undertaken toward the establishment of AEC.

To recall, the major context of the AEC revolves around combining economies into a single common market where member states collaborate and complement each other in terms of economic, political, and social aspects. In this respect, ICT constitutes one of the priority sectors that received significant attention among policy makers, as enhanced communication technology, particularly in the form of the Internet, can boost the performance of information-based industry as well as all other industries. For instance, the Internet facilitates trade in goods and services, and supports investment. As people become more interconnected via the Internet, information flows more smoothly and thereby enhances firms' ability to expand the market at a lower cost. Thus, improved Internet connectivity not only promotes the flow of information, but also reduces transaction costs for almost all types of business firms. However, the current setback arises from the considerable digital divide among ASEAN countries. Thus the main objective of ASEAN's initiatives in the ICT sector is to mitigate the digital divide by creating a robust infrastructural base. In addition, the effort seeks to promote interconnectivity and interoperability of communication networks to facilitate all sectors of the economy (ASEAN, 2011).

2.3.1 The Digital Divide in ASEAN

As mentioned previously, ASEAN countries suffer from a digital divide. The Internet penetration rate, which is the number of Internet users adjusted with the total population of that country, indicates the proportion of the population that can access the Internet. Brunei, Singapore, and Malaysia are in the top three, with Internet penetration rates of 81%, 78%, and 65%, respectively (ASEAN, 2010). This suggests that the ICT sector in these countries has high coverage because the majority of the population can access the Internet. On the contrary, there is a very conspicuous difference among ASEAN members, with Lao PDR, Cambodia, and Myanmar having low Internet penetration rates of 8%, 1.3%, and 0.2%, respectively. For ASEAN as a whole, the Internet penetration rate suggests that, on average, only 20% of the ASEAN population can access and use the Internet. Thus initiatives aim at digital inclusion to minimize the digital divide within the country among the haves and the have-nots, and also among the industrial and emerging economies.

At a glance, the difference in the development of the ICT sector in each ASEAN country can be partly reflected in the countries' GDP per capita. In other words, countries with a high level of GDP per capita tend to have higher Internet penetration rates. Thus, Lao PDR, Cambodia, and Myanmar will need to step up with the others in the region by improving their infrastructural base. On the demand side, Internet penetration rates can be improved by providing mobile phones at lower and more affordable prices. With the growth of wireless communication networks, landline telephone networks are no longer a prerequisite in accessing an Internet connection. Fortunately, several initiatives under AEC have facilitated the flow of investment into the ICT sectors of these three economies. In 2013, Norway's Telenor and Qatar's Ooredoo were the first two foreign companies selected by Myanmar Posts and Telecommunications to invest and develop the mobile network in the country. It is projected that 97% of the population will be provided with cellular 3G service by 2019 (ASEAN, 2014). Cambodia has solved the issue of connectivity by developing a robust mobile network instead of fixed-line telecoms with large companies like Vietnam's Viettel Metfone and the domestic firm Smart Mobile. Viettel Metfone also entered Lao PDR's telecommunication sector (ASEAN, 2014). Nevertheless, one may be misled that countries with high Internet penetration rates provide more opportunities. Another dimension that cannot be left out is the demographic composition of Internet users. Despite having high Internet penetration rates, Brunei and Singapore contribute to less than 4% of all online users in the region. Clearly, Indonesia, the Philippines, Vietnam, and Thailand represent a large proportion of Internet consumers in the region (ASEAN, 2010).

There are some takeaways up to this point. First, a higher Internet penetration rate will result in a more efficient flow of information among people, which would benefit business firms in all sectors. Second, in addition to the Internet penetration rate, demographic composition is also important, as firms need to know the nature and characteristics of their potential customers. Third, improving connectivity is not sufficient in itself for the ASEAN digital economy. A digital economy requires an interconnected platform of various networks.

2.3.2 Interconnectivity and Interoperability: From Internet Economy to Digital Economy

ASEAN countries can be better off in two aspects: economies of scale and economies of scope. In the economic sense, economies of scale imply reduction in average costs owing to the expansion of output, while economies of scope owe to the variety of output. Firms can achieve economies of scale through enhanced connectivity. For instance, as more and more people can now access information on the Internet, firms can reach their potential customers more easily through advertisement in social media or publicity in online news. This improved linkage provides cost advantages to firms in terms of volume. However, to integrate ASEAN economies, there needs to be interconnection of different technological networks together, making them interoperable.

Economies of scope require linking software and applications of different networks together, making them interconnected. One example to illustrate interconnectivity and interoperability is the feature present in current social media sites. Facebook, Twitter, YouTube, Google, Instagram, and other popular social media outlets are normally interconnected. Users are put at ease to sign in using just a single account. Social media is also interoperable in the sense that it can be accessed from any device: home computer, workplace laptop, or mobile devices. A similar feature is also present in services offered by entertainment and electronic businesses. Consumers can purchase a membership to movies on any device without having to leave home. Film resumes from where it was paused. Another example is cloud computing technology, where users can retrieve information saved in the cloud on any device.

Business firms and governmental agencies in ASEAN countries are working in a similar direction to interconnect systems pertaining to business and social welfare to achieve greater efficiency and improved quality of life for all. In business, one of the most significant issues concerns the online mode of payment for goods and services. This requires interconnectivity and interoperability to provide convenience for customers, which would further facilitate the liberalization of trade that ASEAN aims to achieve. There are many examples of such innovations that aim to enhance the social welfare of the people in ASEAN. The Traffic Information Collection and Delivery System is one of the projects under the ASEAN Smart Network Initiative. The project aims to mitigate congestion on roads in metropolitan Bangkok. Cameras and sensor devices collect data related to car navigation and GPS. This information is stored in the database center and transmitted to personal computers, radio stations, smartphones, and car navigation systems. With this interconnectivity, travel time tends to be shortened, as people receive real-time information about traffic and can choose alternative routes in case of accidents or traffic congestion.

2.3.3 ASEAN ICT Masterplan

To meet the goals of AEC by the end of 2015, the ASEAN Telecommunications and IT Ministers proposed a 5-year plan under the name "ASEAN ICT Masterplan" in 2010. The masterplan was expected to deliver four main outcomes: (1) ICT as an engine of growth for ASEAN countries, (2) recognition for ASEAN as a global ICT hub, (3) enhanced quality of life for people of ASEAN, and (4) contribution toward ASEAN integration. The formation of AEC cannot be truly completed without enhanced interconnectivity and interoperability, as the ICT sector drives ASEAN economies, employing more than 11.7 million people and contributing to around USD 32 billion or more than 3% to ASEAN's GDP as of 2011 (ASEAN, 2011). These figures are expected to increase further.

The ASEAN ICT Masterplan envisioned an inclusive, vibrant, and integrated ASEAN by empowering and transforming the ICT sectors of all the member countries. To achieve its goals, the masterplan rested upon three pillars, which required three foundations. In brief, economies were required to build a strong foundation in three aspects: infrastructure, human capital, and bridging of the digital divide. Following this, the economies could move on to building three pillars: promoting trade and investment in the ICT sector, uplifting the quality of life of people through ICT, and keeping the engine going through innovation. Singapore, Malaysia, Indonesia, Thailand, Vietnam, and the Philippines have a relatively well-established ICT sector, while Myanmar, Cambodia, and Lao PDR need to develop their infrastructural base to move closer to the rest of the ASEAN economies. In all, initiatives are aimed to develop the ICT infrastructure and human resources, promote accessibility and innovation in the industry, and establish a safe and healthy regulatory environment. All these contribute to the formation of AEC's single market and production base.

A part of the AFAS mentioned earlier, which aims to liberalize trade in services, addresses the ICT sector under the name E-ASEAN. E-ASEAN was signed by all ASEAN members in 2000 with the aim of strengthening the competitiveness of the ICT sector, reducing the digital divide among members, promoting cooperation between public and private sectors, and liberalizing trade in ICT products and services. Under the E-ASEAN framework, ICT refers to the infrastructure, hardware, and software systems that are used to process and disseminate information as products or services. E-ASEAN aims to (1) facilitate the establishment of the ASEAN information infrastructure by enhancing interconnectivity and interoperability between each country's system; (2) boost e-commerce by creating trust through implementation of laws and regulations, ensuring a secure mode of payment and protection of personal and vulnerable data; (3) facilitate trade and investment in ICT products and services by signing MRAs covering ICT sectors in order to create a unified international standard; (4) establish an e-society by imparting awareness and knowledge about ICT among small business owners, workers in the ICT sector, and civil servants; and (5) enhance delivery of government services by using modern applications to facilitate the linkage between the public and private sectors. When these are fully realized, the overall competitiveness of ASEAN will be raised, as ICT plays a significant role in almost every sector of the economy.

2.3.4 ASEAN Smart Network Initiative

The ASEAN Smart Network Initiative is a collaborative effort between ASEAN and the dialogue partner, Japan, with the aim of developing a broadband network covering ASEAN countries. This initiative is expected to solve social issues specific to each ASEAN country and also enhance connectivity among all ASEAN countries. Being at the forefront in the field of ICT, Japan will be providing technical assistance and sharing advanced applications and human resources with ASEAN. This initiative reinforces the vision of the ASEAN ICT Masterplan, as it will promote development of ICT infrastructure, develop human capital, and promote utilization of ICT in improving the welfare of the ASEAN people.

These projects are tailored to solve social issues and they all make use of information dissemination as a solution. For instance, the disaster prevention information system aims to mitigate natural calamities that might adversely affect the ASEAN economy. Information about water levels in rivers, weather, and related proxies is collected and analyzed. It is then transmitted to the public via news broadcast, social media, and other real-time applications. This is useful for conveying important information to the public, such as disaster prevention measures and the need for evacuation.

Lao PDR's medical ICT is another valuable project that incorporates modern ICT to save lives in a rural area where health care facilities are not easily accessible. Scarcity of health care experts is a major challenge for the rural Lao PDR. This project implements a remote health care facility by the introduction of a system that collects vital data such as contractions in pregnant women and fetal heart rates. The system then transmits information to hospitals in urban areas, where physicians will assess health conditions and provide health guidance via a video conference system. Hence patients in rural areas will be able to access health care without going to the hospital. ASEAN is on its way in building smart cities and creating smart people. Projects under the ASEAN Smart Network Initiative interconnect different systems by implementing modern ICT, which results in enhancing social welfare at large.

2.4 SOME NOTES ON DEMOGRAPHIC ISSUES

As of 2015, Singapore and Thailand had the highest percentage of the population over 65 years old (11.7% and 10.5%, respectively). Among other ASEAN countries, the growth of the older population is on the same increasing trend. However, these countries also need to prepare for the inevitable phenomenon. According to projections by the United Nations, the top five ASEAN countries with a high percentage of the population over age 65 in 2050 will be Singapore (33.9%), Thailand (30.1%), Brunei (24%), Vietnam (21%), and Malaysia (16.8%). However, it should be noted that Indonesia, Myanmar, Cambodia, the Philippines, and Lao PDR are not far behind.

With this trend, the governments are trying to cope with the issues brought about by the transition. The demographic dividend, which refers to economic growth owing to the favorable age structure of the population, is declining and may transform into a demographic tax, which can drag the economic performance of the country. There are many economic dimensions associated with this demographic shift. As there is a higher proportion of the aging population, the dependency ratio will rise and workforce pool will shrink. This imposes challenges for current and future governments in minimizing the long-term impact of the changes in the age structure of the population. Other issues pertain to the saving, pension scheme, and other social security systems that will support the lives of the aging population. With regional cooperation and initiatives taken to form a single market and production base, ASEAN countries can work together in solving the issues of an aging society.

2.5 CONCLUDING REMARKS

Despite the advantages in favor of the business sector, this does not necessarily imply a completely smooth road ahead for ASEAN. Firms using labor-intensive techniques of production tend to shift their production base to CLMV, or areas at the borders, to avail a lower wage rate. Otherwise, there will be tougher competition as others will move in a similar direction. Some assisting alternatives that firms may undertake to cope with this competitive pressure include turning to modern techniques of production and investing in research and development (R&D). This entails costs, and therefore not all firms are able to opt for this alternative. Investment in R&D will create distinct features to the products, marking the departure from a labor-intensive industry. An excellent example of such a transition is South Korea, which has succeeded in employing technological innovation in the production of commodities. By transforming into a "creative economy," South Korea could boost exports to a global market. Another example is the Singaporean textile industry. In the past, the textile industry in Singapore was typically mass production of clothing using unskilled labor (Thommasson, 2011). However, firms in this industry transformed themselves by investing in R&D and reinventing their products through modern technology such as nanotechnology and switching to solar energy (Pitsuwan, 2012). Thus, many business firms in ASEAN, especially those producing in mass, are driven to switch from being labor-intensive to knowledge-intensive in order to survive in the market. By innovating their products, firms will be able to compete more effectively. They may be able to establish their own niche market as products have distinct features from the others. Examples are products that blend in cultural patterns and design (such as Thailand's One Tambon (District), One Product programs). Firms need to adapt in response to the new trend of demand and invest more in marketing and innovations. In sum, firms within ASEAN should avail business opportunities and also prepare for competition from outside the region.

Another challenge pertains to intra-ASEAN investment. Business firms within ASEAN can make the most out of the agreements their governments have made, be they liberalization in goods, services, investments, or skilled labor. In fact, ASEAN firms face relatively fewer restrictions on the entry into the foreign market in ASEAN. For the rest of the world, ASEAN has been under a spotlight for quite some time and there are many companies, especially large multinationals, wanting to invest and establish a business empire in this part of the world. Thus ASEAN firms may seek opportunities that come with AEC (low wages, skilled labor, fewer restrictions on investment, low tariffs, larger market, innovations, etc.) and make the most out of the situation. Along with this notion, ASEAN business firms will reinforce the competitiveness and propel the regional economy as a whole.

Further on with digitization, with ASEAN initiatives that prioritize the ICT sector by facilitating movement of goods, investment, and skilled labor in the background, firms in every sector can benefit from the rise of the digital economy. As ASEAN countries are trying to bridge the digital divide in the region by building a strong foundation in terms of infrastructure, expertise, and knowledge, business firms should create linkages among different sectors to realize benefits from interconnectivity and interoperability. Along this line, ASEAN firms will benefit from both enhanced connectivity and interconnection of different systems and sectors. Business potential in some sectors are highlighted next.

2.5.1 Telecommunications and Mobile Applications

The ICT sector can be consider a trendsetter for business firms, as it not only facilitates normal functioning, but also enhances efficiency and quality of products and services. In the coming era where both people and physical things will be more connected through modern ICT, business in telecommunications and mobile applications will be under the spotlight for a long time. With bright prospects, there is need for adjustments in terms of quantity and quality of products and services. The Internet and telecommunications networks should become pervasive and seamless so users can access information at all times. With growing demand for wireless portable devices replacing landline telephones, demand for mobile applications follows. Two major application platforms, Google Play and Apple, already provide software that is interconnected and interoperable. Samsung is also known for its constant innovation that implements the concept of IoT. For instance, consumers can control a Samsung smart TV via their smartphones. Playing a complementary role in all sectors, there are opportunities for the ICT sector in areas of retail trade, transportation, banking, education, and even in agriculture.

2.5.2 Retail e-Commerce

AEC's initiatives have targeted the goods market by liberalizing the sector through removal of tariff and nontariff trade barriers to achieve a free flow of goods within the region. As discussed in a previous section, the ASEAN market is an attractive one, as governments and private firms are working on the improvement of Internet broadband connections and other ICT infrastructure to lessen the digital divide in the region. With a higher Internet penetration rate in the near future combined with the rise of the middle-income population in ASEAN, there are tremendous prospects in retail e-commerce in ASEAN. A recent study estimated the value of the online retail market in the ASEAN 6 (Singapore, Malaysia, Indonesia, the Philippines, Thailand, and Vietnam) to be around USD $7 billion in 2013, which accounts for around 25% of the total retail e-commerce in the region (ATKearney, 2015).

Along the same lines, the Philippines' Department of Trade and Industry, on behalf of the ASEAN Telecommunications and ICT Senior Officials' Meeting, conducted a project to establish a reliable and up-to-date database to assess the readiness of e-commerce in ASEAN countries. The project included a consumer survey, which provided some insights for business firms. It was found that ASEAN buyers hesitate in purchasing products online because of security reasons, which becomes a barrier for e-commerce growth (ASEAN, 2010). This implies that the growth of retail e-commerce depends on the robustness of the financial sector in that economy. For ASEAN's trade liberalization to be boosted, online payment of products must be secured in order to create trust among potential buyers. Besides enhancing Internet connectivity to reach more buyers, financial institutions and public authorities must reinforce regulations to assure online buyers of the security of personal and financial data. In that way, buyers can utilize e-payment instead of placing an order online but paying cash on delivery. This theme revolves around interconnectivity and interoperability to achieve economies of scope.

2.5.3 Banking Sector

In continuation of the previous discussion, financial institutions must be innovative at all times. They should interconnect their functioning with that of business firms. Without interconnectivity, business firms with an online presence cannot grow efficiently. Thus financial institutions must bridge this gap by providing a secure online mode of payment. Fortunately, many banks have already provided Internet banking and other mobile applications where customers can perform financial transactions at home. Moreover, banks can make use of GPS data to track locations of customers, which can be used to provide some insights to anticipate their needs and demands more accurately.

2.5.4 Medical and Health Care

Health care and medication is another area that will benefit from the growth of the ICT sector. In line with the example discussed in an earlier section (Lao PDR's medical ICT), hospitals can work with telecommunications and mobile operators by establishing supportive ICT infrastructure in the rural area to serve as a linkage between the core and periphery. Other innovations include the use of robotics in medication and surgery. Dinsow Mini, an assistive robot developed by Thailand's Computer Telephony Asia Co., Ltd., is an example of an ICT innovation in the health care sector. This product has been created to provide health care solutions for the elderly and the disabled at home. Physicians can communicate with patients through a video conference system. In case of emergency where patients are in immediate need of help, messages can be sent to relatives and nurses via mobile phones. Built-in features in Dinsow Mini have removed the distance between patients and doctors with modern innovations. Implementing ICT in the health care sector under the AEC framework will allow ASEAN to share information about treatments and expand service coverage to less developed areas within the region.

2.5.5 Transportation

The transportation sector is another area where IoT can create new opportunities for business firms. Many cab companies have succeeded in connecting their service with mobile applications. However, they can go beyond that limitation. One interesting example is the All Thai Taxi, which has deployed IoT technology under a joint collaboration with Intel, King Mongkut's Institute of Technology Ladkrabang's Smart City Research Center and ITS Consultancy (Pornwasin, 2015). All Thai Taxi's cars are hybrid with special built-in features such as control units, GPS, Wi-Fi, closed-circuit TV, tablets, and printers. Information about speed, location, and route is sent to the headquarters. Passengers have wider choices of payment, from cash to credit cards, and the receipt can be printed on demand. Hence, All Thai Taxi can collect real-time information, which enables them to monitor and control the quality of their service. Information collected also includes energy consumption and carbon dioxide emission, which can be used for the purpose of business analytics. In addition, this innovation also benefits passengers in terms of convenience and security. This is just one piece of evidence that shows that connection of software and hardware under the concept of IoT opens up more opportunities for business firms. Even though the main objective of Thailand's Traffic Information Collection and Delivery System is to lessen traffic congestion, which is a chronic problem in metropolitan Bangkok, firms in the transportation sector can work jointly with the public authorities and use the information collected to improve the quality of services for customers. As for air transport, many airlines have already implemented modern ICT to facilitate interconnectivity of their services, such as online payment for tickets, self check-in, and in-flight entertainment.

2.5.6 Education

For ASEAN to realize its goals and vision set for E-ASEAN and the ASEAN ICT Masterplan, people should be made aware of how IoT impacts their lives. ASEAN needs to transform into a knowledge-based economy by implementing modern ICT in schools to prepare future generations for the changes to come. Similar to medical ICT, modern technology can reduce disparity in terms of accessibility by connecting rural schools with schools in the city. With a strong infrastructural base, distance learning can be the future of the education sector. In addition, a comprehensive ICT training program to teachers to encourage the use of ICT in education is also a part of the ICT Masterplan to bridge the digital divide. All these require collaborative efforts from schools, concerned government agencies, and telecommunication companies to build a strong foundation for the digital economy in the region.

2.5.7 Other Internet of Things

There are other tremendous opportunities for business enterprises to lay hands on considering product innovation and modern ICT. Some other examples include the use of IoT in the agriculture and energy sector. There are concerns among the global community regarding food security because of limited resources and environmental degradation. One of the policies to mitigate this issue is a move toward a low carbon society. According to Beecham Research, IoT can be implemented to achieve optimal outcomes in terms of quantity, quality, and income. This practice is known as precision agriculture (Hawn, 2015). Advantages to farmers include fleet management of vehicles, livestock monitoring, indoor farming, and storage monitoring. Smart farming makes use of sensors, data analytics, hardware and software, software applications, and telematics to collect information about crop yields, soil nutrition, and rainfall. Nevertheless, smart farming requires a strong ICT infrastructural base, which is an issue for rural areas of ASEAN economies. As for the energy sector, Japan's Toyota City is known for being one of the pioneering cities under the national low carbon society project. The entire city is run by renewable energy and eco-friendly technologies. Smart houses in this project are equipped with telematics and software applications that inform residents of energy use (Toyota Motor Corporation, 2011).

The last issue, but certainly not the least significant, that has been briefly mentioned in this chapter is the transition to an aging society. This is a global phenomenon that will definitely hit ASEAN countries in a few decades. Despite the limitations it imposes on the economies, there are many opportunities for business firms to tap into the new consumer market. Initiatives to achieve a single market and production base of AEC have created more opportunities for firms and facilitated them to expand into a foreign market and raise the standards of their products and services. In addition to the elimination of restrictions surrounding the private sector, ASEAN people are able to travel beyond the borders with more ease. Thus, business related to health care, tourism, and medical tourism can definitely benefit from the growth of the aging population, whose income is likely to be spent majorly on the maintenance of physical and mental well-being. Housing and construction businesses will need to develop innovations with the aim of improving the quality of life of elderly people. With more aging and retired people looking for a peaceful place to settle down, innovative homes and retirement centers equipped with modern technological facilities are some options for firms to capture the market segment. After all, an aging society is inevitable. By overcoming challenges, firms can profit considerably from the transition.

All in all, business potential in AEC, collectively, can be tremendous. One needs thorough consideration of the overview on strengths and weaknesses of each ASEAN country. For instance, CLMV are rich in natural resources, with an abundant supply of unskilled and semiskilled labor at a relatively low wage rate. Thus, these locations are lucrative for multinationals to set up production units. On the other hand, to take advantage of efficient linkages and connectivity, Thailand represents a good candidate as a host country. Thailand is poised to become ASEAN's transport hub, as it is located at the center of the region. With a project on physical infrastructure to connect land, air, and port routes, the Thai logistic business and tourism sector will prosper. Singapore, known to be a global financial hub, is the most attractive destination of FDI. Hence firms need to consider this diversity and adapt to the changing business perspective to survive in the market. For instance, as wages are lower in CLMV countries, the textile industry will certainly reap the advantages. The same applies for other labor-intensive industries. Thus for other countries to maintain their competitiveness, their adjustment in specialization is compulsory. Thailand should maintain its competitiveness in the automobile industry, as the country already possesses highly expert manpower for the production of vehicle parts. However, some other Thai industries such as the textile industry may find it more difficult to compete with others who have moved to CLMV countries. They will need to either move to CLMV economies to avail the low wage rate or innovate their textile products in order to compete in the niche market. Hence, each ASEAN member is able to complement one another depending on their strengths and weaknesses, rather than engaging in cutthroat competition.

REFERENCES

Association of Southeast Asian Nations, 2010. The ASEAN E-Commerce Database Project. The Department of Trade and Industry, The Commission on Information and Communications Technology and Superius Corporation.

Association of Southeast Asian Nations, 2011. ASEAN ICT Masterplan 2015. Association of Southeast Asian Nations, Jakarta. September.

Association of Southeast Asian Nations, 2012. ASEAN Connectivity: Project Information Sheet. ASEAN Secretariat, Jakarta. August.

Association of Southeast Asian Nations, 2014. Investing in ASEAN 2014–2015. Allurentis, London.

Association of Southeast Asian Nations, 2015. ASEAN GDP Grows by 4.6%. ASEAN Secretariat News, Jakarta. August.

ATKearney, 2015. Lifting the Barriers to E-Commerce in ASEAN. CIMB Research Institute, Kuala Lumpur.

Board of Investment, 2015. A Guide to Investment in the Special Economic Development Zones. Office of the Board of Investment, Thailand. August.

Hawn, J., 2015. IoT key to future of farming, civilization. RCR Wireless News. October 25.

Pitsuwan, S., 2012. It Is Better to Know About ASEAN. Amarin, Bangkok. October (In Thai).

Pornwasin, A., 2015. Intel ready to guide partners into a technology minefield. The Nation. September 30.

Thommasson, S.C., 2011. Singapore a textile gateway. Textile World Asia. June.
Toyota Motor Corporation, 2011. Toyota City Low-Carbon Project Model Homes Completed: Trial Operation of Proprietary Energy Management Systems Begins. Toyota Motor Corporation. June.
World Economic Forum, 2014. The Global Competitiveness Report 2014–2015. World Economic Forum, Geneva. 2014.

CHAPTER 3

Investment Promotion and Liberalization in Selected ASEAN Countries

S. Tulayasathien, A. Tejapaibul
Fiscal Policy Office, Ministry of Finance, Bangkok, Thailand

3.1 INTRODUCTION

Foreign direct investment (FDI) is a leading economic growth driver, particularly for small and open developing economies. During the past decades, FDI has been critical to ASEAN[1] growth. Despite brief disruptions as a result of the global financial crisis during 2008 and 2009, FDI inflows to ASEAN grew on average 30.9% per year, significantly higher than the global average of 1.5% per year. As a result, ASEAN has become an important FDI recipient, where its share of FDI inflow has increased from 4.6% during 2005–07, to 10.8% in 2014, as shown in Fig. 3.1.

The rising importance of ASEAN in the global investment arena is not limited to being a mere FDI recipient. In recent years, ASEAN has contributed to increasing FDI outflows, in which the share of outward FDI from ASEAN increased from 2.5% during 2005–07, to 5.9% in 2014, as shown in Fig. 3.2. This corresponds with the fact that the growing outflow from ASEAN surpassed the growth of total global FDI outflows in recent years.

The growing significance of ASEAN in the global investment community is a direct result of investment promotion and liberalization policies, both at regional and individual country levels.

This chapter will explore overall investment trends and the development of investment promotion and liberalization policies in ASEAN in three selected countries, namely Thailand, Vietnam, and Myanmar. The objective is to shed light on the direction of investment development and to

[1] Established in 1967, the Association of Southeast Asian Nations (ASEAN) consists of 10 countries: Brunei Darussalam, Cambodia, Indonesia, Lao People's Democratic Republic (Lao PDR), Malaysia, Myanmar, the Philippines, Singapore, Thailand, and Vietnam.

Internationalization and Managing Networks in the Asia Pacific
http://dx.doi.org/10.1016/B978-0-08-100813-3.00003-1

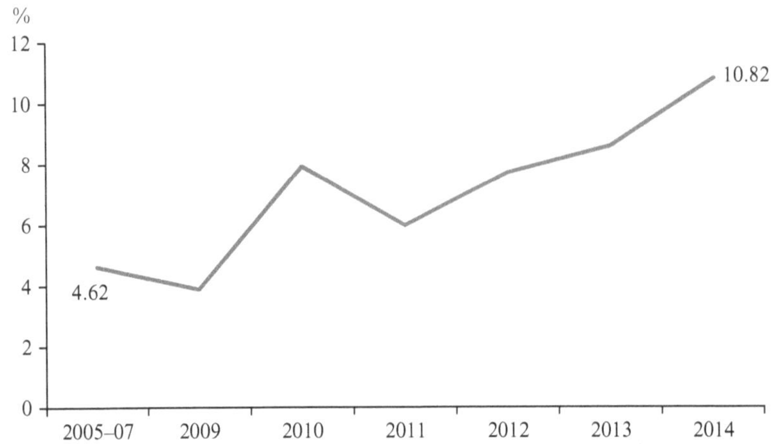

Fig. 3.1 Share of inflow to ASEAN from total global inflow. *(From UNCTAD World Investment Report 2015, calculated by FPO).*

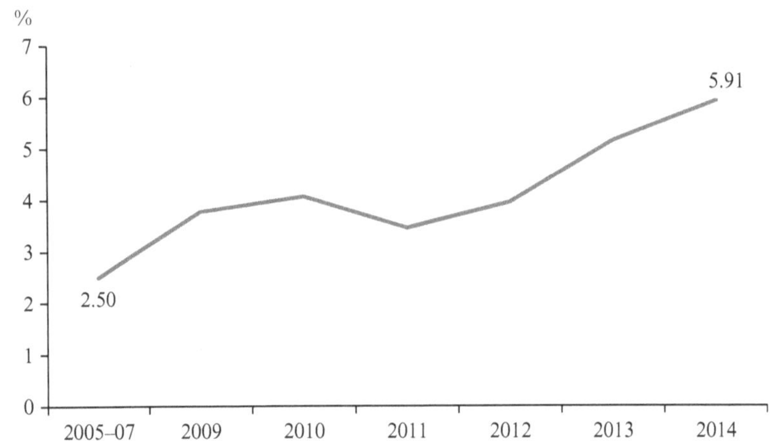

Fig. 3.2 Share of outflow from ASEAN from total global outflow. *(From UNCTAD World Investment Report 2015, calculated by FPO).*

recommend appropriate policies for sustainable development of investment promotion in ASEAN.

3.2 INVESTMENT TRENDS IN ASEAN: FDI INFLOWS

FDI into the ASEAN region has generally experienced a growing trend, climbing an average of 30.9% between 2010 and 2014. Despite several blips during the global financial crise, FDI inflows to ASEAN generally rebounded quickly after each glitch. This was evident in 2011, when FDI inflows to ASEAN were valued at USD 94 billion. This was a 44.9% increase compared to the preglobal financial crisis in 2005–07, where the average was valued at USD 65 billion. Postcrisis, FDI inflows into ASEAN continued to grow at a double-digit rate of 15.6% and 16.6% in 2012 and 2013, respectively, and dropped slightly in 2014 to 5.4%, as shown in Fig. 3.3. Total FDI inflows to ASEAN in 2014 amounted to USD 133 billion, more than double the precrisis annual average. With high FDI inflows, ASEAN became an important FDI recipient. In 2013, ASEAN accounted for 3% of the global GDP, but was able to attract more than 8% of global FDI (The ASEAN Secretariat, United Nations Conference on Trade and Development, 2014). Among the top 20 host economies in the world in 2014, Singapore ranked 5th and Indonesia ranked 4th (United Nations Conference on Trade and Development, 2015).

With high FDI inflows, the share of inward FDI stock to GDP in ASEAN countries increased over time. Presently, the share of inward FDI stock to GDP of Thailand was more than half. This ratio increased from 10.5% in 1997, to 47.1% in 2012, to 46.0% in 2013, and to 53.3% in 2014, with an approximate outstanding amount of USD 2 trillion. This was an

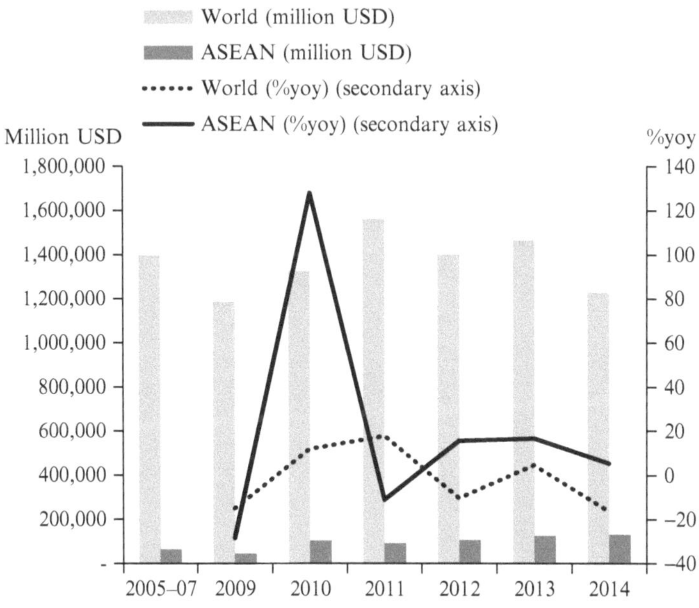

Fig 3.3 World and ASEAN FDI inflow and growth. *(From UNCTAD World Investment Report 2015, calculated by author).*

11-fold expansion compared to the previous decade. The share was slightly lower in Vietnam at 48.9% and 40.9% in Malaysia. In 2014, the share of inward FDI stock to GDP in Singapore was the highest in ASEAN at 296.2% and the lowest in the Philippines at 20.0%, as shown in Table 3.1.

Groups of major investors in ASEAN have not varied considerably over the years. Japan and ASEAN member states as a group have long been on the top list of investors. Together they accounted for 36% of the share for FDI inflows to ASEAN in 2013. Sources of inflow did not change drastically over time, with the exception of China, which has become a new major contributor. In 2013, Chinese investors contributed to over USD 8.6 billion in direct investments into ASEAN. This accounted for 7% of total inflows. The share of China gradually increased from 4% in 2011 to 5% in 2012. Another noteworthy entrance was South Korea, which entered the top 10 list of investors for the first time in 2013, ranking 8th, with an FDI value worth over USD 3.5 billion or 3% of total inflows.

In contrast, major FDI recipient countries changed slightly in recent years. Previously, almost all FDI revolved around ASEAN-5 countries, namely Singapore, Indonesia, Thailand, the Philippines, and Malaysia. Only negligible amounts of FDI went to Cambodia, Lao PDR, Myanmar, Vietnam (CLMV) and Brunei Darussalam. The pattern has changed in recent years, where Singapore has remained the dominant recipient of FDI in ASEAN; however, CLMV countries experienced exceptional growth in performance, investment opportunities, and inward FDI.

Vietnam is a notable case, having received a total of USD 9.2 billion in 2014, a 3.4% growth compared to the previous year. This amount was

Table 3.1 Share of inward FDI stock to GDP of ASEAN countries in 2014

ASEAN member state	Share of inward FDI stock to GDP in 2014 (%)
Thailand	53.3
Indonesia	28.5
Malaysia	40.9
Singapore	296.2
Philippines	20.0
Vietnam	48.9
Cambodia	78.8
Myanmar	28.1
Lao People's Democratic Republic	31.1
Brunei Darussalam	41.2

From UNCTAD World Investment Report 2015, compiled by author.

higher than the Philippines at USD 6.2 billion, and almost as high as Malaysia at USD 10.8 billion. The 15% rise in Vietnam's minimum wages resulted in more FDI flows into other CLM countries, which demonstrated unparalleled labor cost advantages over their neighbor countries. Inflows to other ASEAN economies also grew; in 2014, inflows to Indonesia rose by 20.0% and to Singapore by 4.2%.

Approximately 90% of FDI inflows to ASEAN went into the services and manufacturing sectors (The ASEAN Secretariat, United Nations Conference on Trade and Development, 2014). FDI toward manufacturing rose considerably, from USD 18 billion in 2012 to USD 41 billion in 2013. The main recipient industries were electronics, automobile and automotive parts, finance, real estate, and retail trade. The pattern of the ASEAN FDI recipient sector has been consistent with global trends, in which 63% of inflows went to services and 26% went to manufacturing in 2012 (United Nations Conference on Trade and Development, 2015).

Despite their similar level of development, FDI inflows into CLMV manifested different patterns from one another, depending on their comparative advantages. For Cambodia, the garment and footwear industries were the largest recipients of FDI; for Lao PDR, hydropower generation and electricity trade and transmission were the main recipients of inflows. For Myanmar, extractive and infrastructure sectors were the top recipients of inward FDI, whereas for Vietnam, it was the manufacturing sector that dominated FDI inflows into the country.

3.3 INVESTMENT TREND IN ASEAN: FDI OUTFLOWS

Although the amount of outward FDI flows from ASEAN economies now stand at approximately half the amount of inward FDI flows, the outflow has been growing at an even higher rate than inflows. FDI outflows from ASEAN stood at merely USD 35.6 billion annually on average during 2005–07. The amount magnified to USD 54.9 billion in 2011, equating to a 54.1% expansion. With a high base, the expansion contracted −7.5% in 2012, but then rebounded immediately to a double-digit growth, at 32.4% and 19.2% in 2013 and 2014, respectively, as shown in Fig. 3.4. Total outward FDI from ASEAN in 2014 amounted to USD 80.1 billion, more than double the precrisis annual average. Among the top 20 sources of FDI in the world in 2014, Singapore ranked 10th and Malaysia ranked 17th (United Nations Conference on Trade and Development, 2015).

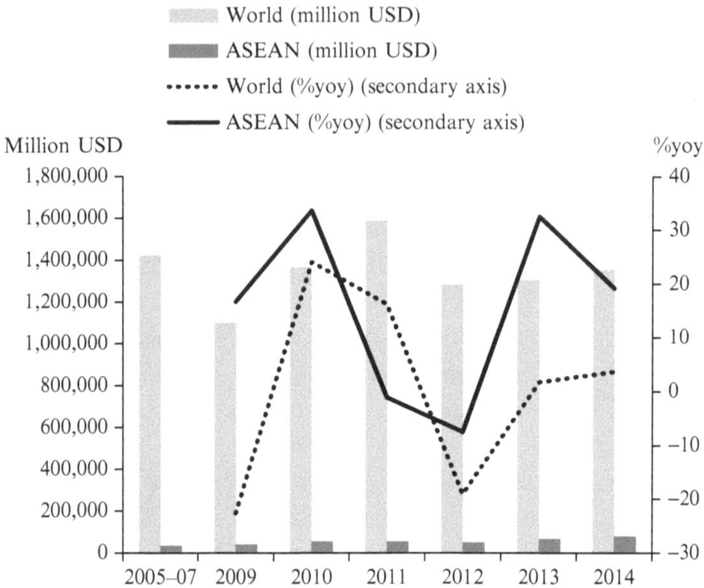

Fig. 3.4 World and ASEAN FDI outflow and growth. *(From UNCTAD World Investment Report 2015, calculated by author).*

Not only did the stock of inward FDI exhibit high growth, the stock of outward FDI showed even higher growth potential. The share of outward FDI stock to GDP in ASEAN countries increased over time. Although the proportion of outward FDI as a percentage of GDP in Thailand remained relatively low at 17.6% in 2014, the stock of outward FDI expanded 29-fold from a mere USD 2.3 billion in 1995 to USD 65.8 billion in 2014. This implies that Thai businesses had become more competitive in the international arena, able to geographically diversify investment. Singapore was the most capable among ASEAN members in terms of ability to generate FDI outflows. Its ratio of outward FDI stock to GDP was as high as 187.1%. This high ratio reflects the fact that many multinational companies use Singapore as their base for their regional investments. Malaysia's ratio was next to highest in ASEAN, where its stock of FDI outflow amounted to USD 1.36 trillion or 41.5% of GDP in 2014, while the amount was at only USD 24.1 billion or 2.7% of GDP in Indonesia, as shown in Table 3.2.

Rapidly rising intraregional investments were one of the main reasons for this upward trend in ASEAN FDI outflows. The share of intraregional investment escalated gradually from 15.1% in 2010 to 17.4% in 2013 (The ASEAN Secretariat, United Nations Conference on Trade and Development, 2014). Indonesia, the Philippines, Thailand, and Vietnam emerged

Table 3.2 Share of outward FDI stock to GDP of ASEAN countries in 2014

ASEAN member state	Share of outward FDI stock to GDP in 2014 (%)
Thailand	17.6
Indonesia	2.7
Malaysia	41.5
Singapore	187.1
Philippines	10.7
Vietnam	4.0
Cambodia	2.9
Myanmar	–
Lao People's Democratic Republic	−0.3
Brunei Darussalam	0.9

From UNCTAD World Investment Report 2015, compiled by FPO.

as new sources of FDI, in addition to the traditional ASEAN investors, Singapore and Malaysia. FDI from Thailand and Vietnam surged to USD 12.1 and 2.0 billion in 2013, up from USD 10.5 and 1.2 billion in 2012, respectively. Most outward FDI from Vietnam concentrated on resource-rich neighboring countries, partly as a result of geographical proximity and cultural affinity. Nearly 50.2% of Vietnamese outward FDI was in ASEAN (The ASEAN Secretariat, United Nations Conference on Trade and Development, 2014).

The materialization of the ASEAN Economic Community (AEC) by the end of 2015 was one reason explaining the significant surge in intraregional investment flows in ASEAN. Countless cross-border investments occurred in order to capture benefits from the enlarged and integrated ASEAN market. This new unified ASEAN market is more than the sum of its parts. Although the combined market size is ~625 million people, almost 25.0% more than the European Union (EU), the opportunities arising from using ASEAN bases as a production or trade springboard to China or India were even larger. Consequently, many companies whose business analysis aligned with this rationale began to expand their presence throughout ASEAN ahead of AEC. This was often carried out in the form of mergers and acquisitions, as well as both vertical and horizontal integration.

Solid regional economic fundamentals were another reason explaining the surge of intraregional investment in ASEAN. Although the recent combined regional economic growth was lower than in previous decades, the average growth of ASEAN-5 member states—namely Indonesia, Malaysia, the Philippines, Singapore, and Thailand—remained higher than the world average. ASEAN-5 economic growth in 2014 was 4.6%, reduced from 5.1% in 2013, and 6.2% in 2012, whereas the world average growth in 2014 was 3.4% and advanced economies' average growth was merely 1.8% (International Monetary Fund, 2014; International Monetary Fund, 2015).

On the financing side, ASEAN+3[2] promoted intraregional investment. The main concept for intraregional investment was that savings accumulated within the region should be assigned for productive use within the region, rather than inexpensively funding growth in other regions. The Asian Bond Markets Initiative (ABMI) of the ASEAN+3 cooperation was created to put a portion of their international reserves into a collective pool and then use it for productive investment in member states. The Credit Guarantee and Investment Facility (CGIF) was established by the ASEAN+3 member states in collaboration with the Asian Development Bank in order to provide credit guarantees for local currency denominated bonds issued by investment grade companies in ASEAN+3 countries. Despite their limited successes, ABMI and CGIF were nonetheless the first milestone toward greater intraregional investment among ASEAN+3 countries.

3.4 REGIONAL INVESTMENT PROMOTION AND LIBERALIZATION POLICY

Unparalleled strategic locations combined with solid economic fundamentals are unarguably a necessity to attract FDI inflows. Nonetheless, these factors are not sufficient enough to secure desirable FDI inflows, both in terms of size and type. For this reason, almost every country in the world has attempted to offer both tax and nontax incentives, aiming to entice valuable FDI from abroad.

Global investment policy frameworks continue to be directed largely toward investment promotion and liberalization. Over 80% of investment policy measures in 2014 geared toward improved entry conditions and reduced restrictions, focusing on investment facilitation and sector-specific liberalization, such as infrastructure and services. More specifically, 37 countries adopted 63 foreign investment related policies. Of these measures, 47 related to liberalization, promotion, and facilitation of investment, while only 9 policies were introduced to add new restrictions on investment. In total, the share of investment liberalization and promotion increased

[2] ASEAN+3 is ASEAN plus China, Japan, and South Korea.

noticeably from 73% in 2013 to 84% in 2014 (United Nations Conference on Trade and Development, 2015).

Ongoing attempts to liberalize FDI policies have been most active in emerging Asian economies, particularly in China, India, and Indonesia. In many cases, these countries loosened limitations on foreign ownership or new business establishments by foreign investors. In some cases, new special economic zones (SEZ) had been set up, or existing rules and regulations on SEZ were revamped. In line with this trend, ASEAN member states continued to introduce favorable measures to improve their investment environment and to attract direct investment from abroad. For example, Indonesia, the largest economy in ASEAN, augmented the foreign investment cap in several industries. The maximum foreign ownership ratio in pharmaceuticals was raised from 75% to 85%, for venture capital operations from 80% to 85%, and for power plant projects in the form of public–private partnership (PPP) from 95% to 100% (United Nations Conference on Trade and Development, 2015).

In a broader scope, ASEAN member states jointly agreed on the ASEAN Comprehensive Investment Agreement (ACIA) aiming to improve the overall regional investment environment. The ACIA was a part of the ASEAN Economic Blueprint 2015. It was a result of a revision and merger of the prior ASEAN Investment Area (AIA) and Investment Guarantee Agreement (IGA) treaties by taking into account main objectives, which were to create a freer investment regime and to achieve economic integration while also accounting for international best practices. The implementation of this particular agreement aimed to bring about an open, transparent, and predictable investment regime whereby covering four main pillars: liberalization, protection, facilitation, and promotion. In terms of liberalization, the ACIA provided a framework for progressive liberalization of existing restrictions in manufacturing, agriculture, fishery, forestry, mining, and services related to these sectors. It also aimed to strengthen investment protection as well as ensure transparency of investment laws, regulations, and administrative guidelines.

In addition to the ACIA, bilateral investment treaties (BITs) with ASEAN's important partners helped facilitate investment at a bilateral level. BITs are purely investment agreements and are to be distinguished from economic cooperation agreements that usually cover both trade and investment aspects. BITs have been widely used to stimulate FDI. The key feature of BITs is that the host country governments accept that private companies operating in their respective countries can take legal actions against the governments, thereby improving confidence among foreign investors. Accumulated annual numbers of BITs have always been on a growing trend. The number of BITs peaked during the 1990s, particularly in 1996. After that the growth rate slowed, but the total number remained on an upward trend. In 2014, a total of 18 BITs were concluded globally. From 1980 to 2014, there were 2926 BITs outstanding (United Nations Conference on Trade and Development, 2015). As for ASEAN, there had also been BITs between ASEAN and China, which were signed in 2009, and BITs between ASEAN and India signed in 2014.

Although this BIT type of agreement was useful in facilitating FDI several decades ago, the situation changed slightly in recent years. As more regional investment agreements and trade and investment agreements emerged while preexisting BITs had not been terminated, the coexistence of the two led to overlaps and inconsistencies. This situation posed a number of legal and policy challenges and exacerbated the spaghetti bowl effect of multilayers of trade and investment treaties.

It was estimated that the cumulative number of BITs that could be terminated or renegotiated at any time would increase from 1325 BITs before 2014 to 1598 BITs by the end of 2018 (United Nations Conference on Trade and Development, 2015). One possible channel through which these BITs can be terminated, and to consolidate the preexisting arrangement of BITs, is through the current megaregional trade and investment negotiations, such as Transatlantic Trade and Investment Partnership (TTIP) and Trans-Pacific Partnership (TPP).

Multinational enterprises (MNEs) operating in ASEAN became major contributors to regional connectivity, especially at the subregional level, through cross-border investments in infrastructure. This type of investment has contributed to the formation of infrastructure and productive capacities in low-income countries. For example, in Myanmar and Vietnam, with improving transport and energy infrastructure, the two countries emerged as an investment destination for labor-intensive manufacturing activities.

For other middle-income countries in the region, further infrastructure expansion is still essential for regional connectivity, which will support other types of productive economic activities, such as trade and tourism. Recognizing this synergetic benefit of FDI in infrastructure, many ASEAN countries have begun to open up infrastructure development to foreign participation through various channels. For example, Indonesia recorded a number of projects in transport infrastructure, especially expressways and railways, in the form of PPP or concessions with total investment value worth over USD 1 billion. Foreign companies are also being allowed to tap into port management services in Indonesia. The opening up of transportation investment to foreign investors could potentially lead to additional intraregional investment flows.

Poor infrastructure development and infrastructure development gaps among ASEAN member states were the main drivers of FDI in infrastructure in this region. According to the World Economic Forum's Global Competitiveness Rankings Report 2015–16, a majority of ASEAN member states were ranked in the bottom half for infrastructure. Only Singapore (ranked 2nd), Malaysia (ranked 24th), Thailand (ranked 44th), and Indonesia (ranked 62nd) were in the upper half of the rankings. Myanmar was ranked 134th out of the total 140 countries for infrastructure.

With a relative lack of infrastructure, ambitious long-term infrastructure investment plans, and infrastructure development gaps among countries in ASEAN, as well as growing interest among major foreign investors, it is certain that FDI in regional infrastructure will continue to grow further.

3.5 INVESTMENT PROMOTION TOOLS

While global investment policy frameworks continue to be directed largely toward investment promotion and liberalization, various tools have been employed by each ASEAN nation to attract FDI and create conducive investment environments.

3.5.1 Tax

Although many innovative investment promotion tools have been devised recently, one tool that will continue to stay in the picture is tax incentives. Countries competing to attract FDI have continued to lower both their corporate income tax (CIT) and personal income tax (PIT).

Singapore is currently the most competitive for CIT. The CIT in Singapore is the lowest in ASEAN, at 17% as of 2014. Thailand lowered the CIT in 2013 to 20% from 30% in 2011, becoming the second lowest rate in ASEAN. CIT in Malaysia, Indonesia, and Myanmar remains at 25%. In the Philippines the CIT is at 30%, which is the highest in ASEAN. It is also interesting to note that Lao PDR has been aggressive in lowering its CIT. The rate was lowered to 24% in 2013, down significantly from 35% in 2011. On the other hand, Cambodia, Indonesia, Malaysia, Myanmar, and the Philippines have not changed their respective CIT over the past 5 years.

Singapore is also the most competitive in terms of PIT. The maximum PIT in Singapore is a mere 20%, while the rate was as high as 35% in Thailand and Vietnam as of 2014. PIT in Malaysia is the second lowest in ASEAN at 26%. The PIT is moderate in Indonesia at 30% and 32% in the Philippines.

Another type of tax rate that most investors take into consideration is the value-added tax (VAT). VAT in ASEAN is generally lower than in other parts of the world, especially those of EU member states. VAT in a majority of ASEAN countries, namely Cambodia, Indonesia, Lao PDR, and Vietnam, is at 10%. The rate is higher at 12% in the Philippines and lower at 7% in Singapore and Thailand. Malaysia set VAT at 6% in 2015, while Brunei and Myanmar do not collect VAT.

Investment promotion policy in terms of tax is usually present in the form of tax reduction or tax exemption. MNEs also consider other types of tax, such us import and export duty as well as withholding tax rates. Therefore countries also offer other types of tax privileges, such as exemption of import duty on machinery, export-oriented raw materials, land proprietary, visas, and work permits for skilled workers.

3.5.2 Special Economic Zones

Some countries offer special privileges in specific areas where investment is highly desirable; examples include border regions, inland industrial clusters, and tourist destinations. These areas are usually referred to as special economic zones (SEZ). FDI in these SEZ are entitled to additional privileges. These privileges can come in various forms, such as additional years of tax exemption or reduction, tax holidays, permission to employ foreign unskilled workers, and favorable conditions for establishment of warehouse and duty-free zones. Moreover, transportation and logistics infrastructure, public utilities, and governmental services are often superior in SEZ in order to create a more conducive environment for businesses to operate and prosper.

3.5.3 Cash Rebate

Another common investment promotion tool is cash rebates. Governments usually offer this benefit to encourage MNEs to carry out certain kinds of activities or practices. In many cases, MNEs are offered cash rebates from research and development (R&D) costs, job training expenses for local employees, and salaries paid to employees with disabilities. For example, Thailand allows MNEs to claim an additional 100% rebate on R&D costs, and an additional 100% deduction for job training expenses and for expenditure on salaries paid to employees with disabilities (Deloitte, 2015).

These are examples of investment promotion tools that are widely used among ASEAN nations. There are many more that can be used to attract FDI, such as enactment of new laws to facilitate investment from abroad. Each country possesses distinct strengths and weaknesses. For this reason, each one designs its own unique investment promotion and liberalization measures that best suit its situation in order to attract businesses and industries that will be particularly beneficial for its economy.

3.5.4 Liberalization of Land Ownership

In general, foreigners are not usually allowed to own land in a country unless it is specifically stated in board of investment (BOI) laws or industrial estate laws. With stringent land ownership restrictions, foreign investors have to lease land from local owners. The restrictions on land leasing vary among countries. For countries using common laws, foreigners are usually allowed to lease land up to 99 years, similar to the United Kingdom and the United States. For countries using civil law, the time limitation is usually shorter. In some cases, the governments relax these limitations on land leases in order to attract FDI. Statutory land leasing limitations in ASEAN countries are depicted in Table 3.3.

The next section will explore the investment promotion and liberalization in three select ASEAN countries, namely Thailand, Vietnam, and Myanmar.

Table 3.3 Land leasing limitations in ASEAN countries

ASEAN member state	Land leasing limitations (Years)
Brunei Darussalam	Up to 99
Malaysia	Up to 99
Cambodia	Up to 99
Vietnam	Up to 70
Myanmar	Up to 70
Singapore	Up to 99
Thailand	Up to 30

From National sources compiled by author.

3.6 INVESTMENT PROMOTION AND LIBERALIZATION IN SELECTED ASEAN COUNTRIES

In addition to regional measures to promote ASEAN as an integrated investment destination, each member state also introduced its own investment promotion and liberalization measures. The measures adopted by each nation differ.

3.6.1 Thailand

During the past decades, FDI became an important determinant of Thai economic growth. Starting with the first national and social economic development plan during 1961–66, the emphasis was placed on domestic production to reduce reliance on import. The BOI was established in 1965 to give incentives for FDI. Later on, the eastern seaboard was established to facilitate international trades, where the focus shifted to FDI in the manufacturing sector for exports. The exports led the growth strategy, with borrowed foreign capital having worked properly, resulting in high average growth at 9.2% during the decade prior to the Asian financial crisis in 1997. Many existing economic growth drivers of the Thai economy emerged during this period, particularly in the automotive and electronics sector.

However, since the 1997 crisis, Thailand underinvested for more than 17 years. Average investment in Thailand after the crisis was around 25%, compared to 50% prior to the crisis. Underinvestment has been an impediment to Thai economic growth. Insufficient investment in logistics has resulted in high cost of transportation, both in terms of money and time. Inadequate mass transit systems resulted in traffic congestion, especially in Bangkok and surrounding areas. Despite construction of the Suvarnabhumi airport in 2006, limited airport and seaport capacity is becoming a significant bottleneck for development, especially in terms of international trade and tourism.

A period of political uncertainty since 2009 and the Great Flood in 2011 further damaged confidence among investors, resulting in delayed and diversion of investment to neighboring countries. Another factor that made FDI in Thailand less attractive compared to other countries in ASEAN in recent years was the increase in the national minimum pay to 300 baht per day in 2012. Furthermore, the effectiveness of the BOI and other tax incentives has diminished, as many other countries have also been offering similar types of investment privileges. In order to secure continuous inflows of FDI, the government needed to improve the investment promotion schemes.

During the past decade, Thailand provided BOI incentives in the form of both tax and nontax measures. Consequently, Thailand became a regional original equipment manufacturer production hub. The old BOI schemes were criticized for the lack of focus in industries that are consistent with national development strategies. Therefore the BOI revamped investment incentives in early 2015, from location-based to activity-based and merit-based incentives. The focus of activity-based incentives centered particularly on knowledge, using technology nonexistent in Thailand that would add to domestic resources or strengthen local supply chains and supporting industries. The focus of merit-based incentives centered mainly on competitiveness enhancement, such as in-house R&D, intellectual property acquisition, training of local employees, industrialization in the 20 poorest provinces, and industrial area development such as SEZ.

Moreover, the government reduced the CIT from 30% to 20% in 2013 in order to compete with peers in ASEAN; this made the CIT in Thailand the second lowest in ASEAN. The government also reduced the customs tariffs of more than 1500 raw materials and intermediate goods to support domestic production.

With its distinctive strategic location, Thailand has attempted to position itself as a regional trade and investment hub. The government announced the International Headquarters (IHQ) and International Trading Center (ITC) to support this ambition. With these schemes, tax and nontax incentives are offered to MNEs setting up their headquarters and regional centers in Thailand, in order to service their regional and global operations. IHQ and ITC will be eligible for BOI privileges as well as CIT exemption for transactions outside Thailand (out-out) and tax reductions for other cross-border transactions (in-out). Personnel working for IHQ or ITC will also be subjected to less stringent migration and work permit processes.

Business activities that have potential to contribute to the new growth engine of the Thai economy have been identified as the "First S-curve" and the "New S-curve" industries, as depicted in Table 3.4. Special tax and nontax privileges are offered to investment in these so-called "Super Clusters."

To provide further funding for high potential businesses, venture capital funds between the government and private sector were established to provide new incentives for R&D and high-value-added production. The Competitiveness Enhancement Fund (CEF) that provides cash rebates and the Thailand Future Fund (TFF) that functions as the investment vehicle in public infrastructure projects, among others, are flagship initiatives that the

Table 3.4 Super clusters

First S-curve	New S-curve
Next-generation automotive	Robotics
Smart electronics	Aviation and logistics
Affluent, medical, and wellness tourism	Biofuels and biochemicals
Agriculture and biotechnology	Digital
Food for the future	Medical hub

From National sources compiled by author.

government pushed forward in order to support investment while simultaneously reducing public fiscal burden.

The new PPP Act and relevant organic laws that cover standardized PPP contracts, project evaluation, and private sector selection procedures will provide a more clear and conducive framework for the private sector to become involved in public infrastructure investment projects. Furthermore, the government recognizes that it is imperative to expedite the long-awaited logistics infrastructure upgrade in order to lower logistics costs as well as provide seamless connectivity in the region. Consequently, the government introduced a PPP fast-track scheme to shorten the PPP process from 2 years to 9 months to facilitate public investment projects.

Another measure to expedite investment is the additional CIT exemption and reduction for up to 8 years, applicable to investment projects submitted for privileges from Jan. 1, 2014, to Jun. 30, 2016, that were able to begin operations or services by 2016. Additionally, expenses on acquiring new assets by Dec. 31, 2016, would be counted twice for tax deduction. These eligible assets included machinery and parts, equipment and other apparatus, computer programs, vehicles, buildings excluding land, and residential properties.

With existing strategic location advantages and a variety of investment promotion measures, the investment environment in Thailand will become even more conducive in the future. As a result, the stock of FDI in Thailand will have a tendency to grow continuously. This freer flow of capital, goods and services, technology, and human resources will promote more vibrant economic activities at the local level, thereby invigorating inclusive economic growth. Moreover, as targeted investment promotion measures focus on the high-tech sector with high growth potential, particularly the New S-curve industries, FDI could raise the overall competitiveness of the Thai economy through knowledge and technological transfer. In addition, the Thai government has recently proposed the establish the Eastern Economic Corridor Development Project to secure its industrial and logistic base in in-land ASEAN.

The Thai government's attempts to stimulate investment have not been limited to only inward FDI. The government has also supported local MNEs to expand business operations beyond national boundaries and to invest abroad in order to utilize resources that may not be widely or readily available in Thailand. The expansion of MNEs abroad can also be beneficial through market enlargement, especially in untapped markets. Outward investments from Thailand, particularly to other nations in the region, have been gaining more momentum, especially during the period characterized by the Thai baht's appreciation.

Among other policies, the Capital Account Liberalization Master Plan was helpful in encouraging Thai companies and investors to diversify their investment portfolios and operate their businesses abroad. It facilitated the creation of environments that support more balanced capital flows and promote financial market development that support regional investment integration. In 2015, the Bank of Thailand (BOT) announced additional measures to relax foreign exchange regulations under this particular master plan. Examples of these measures include permission for Thai residents to invest in securities abroad through onshore banks, allowing qualified investors to directly deposit foreign currencies abroad and invest in foreign securities within a certain limit without passing through local intermediaries, and to raise the limit for purchase of immovable properties including leasehold properties abroad of up to USD 50 million per year, up from USD 10 million (Bank of Thailand, 2015).

3.6.2 Vietnam

The economy of Vietnam has evolved noticeably since the opening of the country. International investment and trade contributed significantly to the formation of the modern Vietnamese economy. This is partly because of the solid fundamentals of its economy. First, the current dynamic economic situation has been characterized by secure socio-political stability. From 1991 to 2010, its average economic growth was as high as 7.5% per year, despite several disruptions from 2011 to 2013. Many reliable international economic analysis organizations anticipated this period of high growth to continue into the near future. Vietnam also currently enjoys a favorable population structure in which ~60% of its population is working age. The labor force size was 46 million people in 2010, with an additional 1.5 million people adding to this statistic each year (KPMG, 2011). This allows Vietnam to stand out from other comparable countries that are typically beginning to experience the problems of an aging society. Furthermore, realizing the benefit of FDI, especially to the current stage of economic development, the Vietnamese government has committed to creating a conducive business environment for foreign investors as well as improving the local legislative and institutional framework.

In recent years, while many competitors such as China and Thailand have passed certain development thresholds, unilateral tariff reductions to these countries by developed countries such as the EU and the United States have gradually reduced or have been eliminated. As a lower-middle-income country, Vietnam can still enjoy these benefits, such as the Generalized System of Preferences (GSP). Many MNEs noticed this opportunity and established their production bases in Vietnam in order to use them as a springboard for export to these advanced countries and to enjoy the GSP benefits.

Vietnam is not complacent about these advantages of being a lower-middle-income country, where it continues to expand the scope of its investment and trade cooperation. Vietnam has been relatively aggressive in investment and trade negotiations. In 2015, Vietnam concluded a free trade agreement with the EU. Vietnam also became one of the 12 founding members of the TPP, which concluded in 2015. There, bilateral and multilateral investment and trade agreements are on top of the existing ASEAN cooperation between Vietnam and nine other neighboring countries within the region.

In addition to investment and trade agreements, Vietnam offers investment incentives to foreign investors, both in the form of tax and nontax incentives. For CIT, it is possible to get tax reduction down to 10%–20% from the regular rate of 25%. Profit remittance tax back to the home country has been exempted in Vietnam since 2004. The import tax of production material for reexport with 270 days has also been exempted. As for PIT for foreign persons residing in Vietnam less than 183 days a year, the tax remains at a flat rate of 20%, compared to a progressive rate for local residents.

Vietnam also provides special privileges for investment in SEZ. The SEZ can be categorized into three main types: export processing zones, industrial zones, and high-tech zones. Foreign investors interested in applying for benefits in these SEZ can apply directly at the provincial management board. The application process takes only 15 days, compared to 60 days for other normal cases.

Despite location advantages and investment privileges offered by the government, economic stability—particularly the Vietnamese VND valuation and inflation rates—is a potential risk for foreign investors in Vietnam. As a small and open economy with the degree of openness at 179.5%,[3] the value of the VND can fluctuate considerably with changes in the balance of payment. Over the past decade, the valuation of VND to USD decreased 41%. This depreciation of VND caused the value of FDI in Vietnam to decrease. Moreover, the inflation rate in Vietnam accelerated at almost 30% during the economic crisis in 2008, and once again at almost 25% in 2012. This accelerated inflation rate is another cause of business cost of FDI in Vietnam.

On the outward FDI side, Vietnam remains at its initial stage of progress. In 2014, FDI outflow from Vietnam amounted to USD 1.2 billion, down from its value of USD 2.0 billion the previous year. The stock of outward FDI equated to 4% of GDP in 2014. Despite small cumulative amounts, outward FDI has also grown, specifically toward neighboring countries in the region, namely Cambodia, Lao PDR, and Myanmar. The main sectors in which Vietnamese MNEs invest in these countries revolves around telecommunications, agriculture, and forestry.

Outward investment from Vietnam is governed by the law on investment promulgated by the National Assembly in 2014. In Article 51, the law states that "investors are encouraged by the State to make outward investment in order to expand the market, improve the export of goods and services, and receipt of foreign currencies, improve access to modern technologies, raise the managerial capability and develop resources for socio-economic development." This law states restrictions on outward FDI from Vietnam, such as projects with investment capital of VND 20,000 billion or above, which must seek approval from the National Assembly, including projects in banking, insurance, securities, journalism, broadcasting, and telecommunications. Projects with investment capital of VND 400 billion or above must seek approval from the prime minister. With clearer rules and regulations on outward investment, coupled with continuous economic development, FDI outflow from Vietnam has a great prospect of continuous growth in the near future.

3.6.3 Myanmar

Similar to Vietnam, Myanmar is another emerging economy with high growth potential in ASEAN. Myanmar opened up its country to international investment and trade since its major political reform in 2011 and

[3] As of 2013, calculated by the author using data from the World Bank

national election in 2015. Although less problematic, political risks stemming from various interest groups with conflicting interests as well as disputes between minority groups still remain.

Myanmar is attractive in the eyes of foreign investors particularly because of its abundant and underexploited resources. At an initial stage of economic development, the lack of facilities and infrastructure provide enormous room for FDI from abroad. Realizing its strength and opportunity, the authorities in Myanmar have made every effort to improve its investment environment to attract inward FDI.

Significant steps have been made to improve regulatory environments surrounding FDI across sectors. The Myanmar Foreign Investment Law was introduced in 2012 to replace an outdated foreign investment law, which was enacted in 1988. A more consolidated new law, the Myanmar Investment Law, is currently being developed in order to substitute the Myanmar Foreign Investment Law of 2012 and Myanmar Citizens Investment Law of 2013. In 2015, the Myanmar Union Tax Law, which reduces the tax rate for nonresidents, and the Competition Law to provide a regulatory framework for competition, monopolies, and mergers and acquisition were enacted. Permanent residence rules to extend the stay of foreign experts were also introduced in 2014 (PWC, 2015).

The Special Economic Zone Law and Dawei Special Economic Zone Law were first promulgated in 2011 in order to set regulations for SEZ. A new version of these laws, called the Myanmar Special Economic Zone Law, was introduced in 2014. Under this new law, a regulatory body called the Central Body for Myanmar Special Economic Zone was established. This law also allowed investors to obtain licenses, permits, and approvals for operations in SEZ more conveniently.

Currently, there are three different SEZ in Myanmar. Thilawa SEZ in Yangon, established in 2013, was the first SEZ. The second was Dawei SEZ located in the Thanintharyi region near Thailand, created to facilitate strategic development projects between the two countries. The third SEZ was Kyaukphyu in Rakhine, which comprises a deep seaport, industrial park, and residences. Special incentives for investment in these SEZ include, for example, CIT holiday up to 7 years; custom duty exemption for up to 5 years for raw materials, machinery, and equipment; and a carry forward of loss for 5 years.

Apart from investment promotion polices in SEZ, MNEs with permits from the Myanmar Investment Commission were eligible for tax incentives and other special privileges. Tax incentives include, for example, CIT relieved for up to 5 years, custom duty exemptions for up to 3 years for raw materials, and a carry forward of loss for up to 3 years.

Another noteworthy step to provide a more conducive investment environment in Myanmar was the establishment of the Yangon Stock Exchange (YSX), which was scheduled to begin operations by the end of 2015. YSX would provide a platform for businesses to gain access to additional capital, while also providing additional investment alternatives for investors. A development of the local financial markets is another factor that can help attract foreign investors.

Along with efforts by the Myanmar government to open its country to foreign investment and trade was the attempt to privatize its state-owned enterprises (SOEs); this endeavor began in 2010. Plans to further privatize SOEs are attractive from the perspective of both local and foreign investors, especially in a resource-rich country like Myanmar. Even so, there are certain economic activities that are reserved only for the government, as outlined in the Economic Enterprises Law. There are 12 prohibited activities, including extraction and sale of teak, air and railway transport services, banking and insurance services, broadcasting and television services, electricity generating services, and manufacturing of products relating to security and defense (PWC, 2015).

At this stage of economic development, Myanmar is still unable to generate outward FDI. Therefore, the focus of investment promotion and liberalization in Myanmar still revolves largely around attracting FDI that can benefit its local economic development.

3.7 CONCLUSION AND POLICY RECOMMENDATIONS

Realizing the benefit of FDI, especially for developing economies like ASEAN, all member states have been quite aggressive in designing and implementing FDI promotion and liberalization policies. The policy tools employed by ASEAN member states have generally been similar, such as CIT, PIT, custom duty reduction, SEZ, cash rebates, liberalization of investment rules and regulations, as well as other types of investment facilitation. Although some tools have positive long-lasting effects in competitiveness building, others such as tax reduction can put strains on each competing member state. This is because FDI competitions are often a zero-sum game. Even though ASEAN has a mutual goal of becoming a single market and production base, the FDI promotion and liberalization policies of each member state are still somewhat uncoordinated. This provides an opportunity for foreign investors to cherry-pick a location for their investments.

Going forward, the key for successful investment promotion and liberalization of ASEAN as a region is a common framework that is flexible enough to address the specific needs of each member, but not too loose that it may spur wasteful competition among member states. For ASEAN to genuinely be attractive in the eyes of foreign investors, investment privileges provided by different member states should be coherent and consistent with other existing regional regimes. There must also be a common scheme to jointly invest or invite third parties to invest in projects that generate benefit and positive externality across the region, such as logistics infrastructure and connectivity investment projects.

As for each member state, investment promotion and liberalization policies should be focused on attracting quality investment rather than quantity, directed toward specific sectors that can contribute positively to their economic development. Member states should identify their own target industries based on their respective competitive advantages and their own niche industries. It is also important to be cautious about certain aspects of investment promotion provisions, such as ensuring technological transfer, closing loopholes for tax avoidance by MNEs, promoting environmentally friendly and responsible investment, as well as regional coordination on investment incentive policies to avoid excessive policy competition among countries in the region. This way the ASEAN member states together can avoid unnecessary territorial competition for FDI, while simultaneously attracting FDI that best suits their own development goals.

REFERENCES

Bank of Thailand, 2015. Press Release No. 23/2015: Capital Flow Relaxation. https://www.bot.or.th/Thai/PressandSpeeches/Press/News2558/n2358e.pdf (Accessed 1 November 2015).

Deloitte, 2015. Taxation and Investment in Thailand 2015: Reach, Relevance and Reliability. http://www2.deloitte.com/content/dam/Deloitte/global/Documents/Tax/dttl-tax-thailandguide-2015.pdf (Accessed 10 November 2015).

International Monetary Fund, 2014. World Economic Outlook: Legacies, Clouds, Uncertainties. https://www.imf.org/external/pubs/ft/weo/2014/02/pdf/text.pdf (Accessed 10 December 2015).

International Monetary Fund, 2015. World Economic Outlook: Adjusting to Lower Commodity Prices. https://www.imf.org/external/pubs/ft/weo/2015/02/pdf/text.pdf (Accessed 1 December 2015).

KPMG, 2011. Investing in Vietnam. https://www.kpmg.com/US/en/IssuesAndInsights/ArticlesPublications/Documents/investing-in-vietnam.pdf (Accessed 12 October 2015).

PWC, 2015. Myanmar Business Guide. https://www.pwc.com/mm/en/publications/assets/myanmar_business_guide.pdf (Accessed 5 October 2015).

The ASEAN Secretariat, United Nations Conference on Trade and Development, 2014. ASEAN Investment Report 2013-2014: FDI Development and Regional Value Chains. http://www.asean.org/storage/images/pdf/2014_upload/AIR%202013-2014%20FINAL.pdf (Accessed 1 October 2015).

United Nations Conference on Trade and Development, 2015. World Investment Report 2015: Reforming International Investment Governance. http://unctad.org/en/PublicationsLibrary/wir2015_en.pdf (Accessed 10 October 2015).

CHAPTER 4

Internationalization Theories: Applications to Asia-Pacific Firms

N. Thirawat
Mahidol University International College, Nakhon Pathom, Thailand

4.1 INTRODUCTION

The evolution of trade agreements and preferential investments between countries is a significant part of globalization. The global economy is taking a definite trend in becoming more international, whereby Asian countries, including Southeast Asian nations, are also a part of this trend. Countries in the Asia Pacific have changed trade and international investment policies by increasing the degree of trade liberalization. To promote foreign investment, various benefits have been given, including both tax benefits and nontax benefits. In addition to this, the Asia-Pacific Economic Cooperation (APEC) is also making efforts to play an important role in the global economy. The main objectives are in developing trade relationships and investing and building economic relationships with neighboring countries, whereby believing that measures to support foreign investment and free trade policies will facilitate trade and investment, also improving the environment for organizations and firms.

In the era of globalization, "going global" is inevitable if firms aim to achieve sustainable growth. Today, the number of overseas business activities integrated into the international production and distribution networks has increased exponentially. As a result, subcontracting, outsourcing, and offshoring have become common aspects of global supply chain management; differences between local and international business activities have gradually diminished because firms internationalize their businesses not only by conducting their operations in foreign markets, but also through cooperation and relationships with foreign suppliers (Ratajczak-Mrozek, 2014; Wong, 2011).

This chapter provides a broad overview of internationalization theories, namely internationalization process theory, network model and institutional theory, and resource-based view theory. This chapter also includes case studies of Asia-Pacific companies' internationalization in relation to each theory.

Internationalization and Managing Networks in the Asia Pacific
http://dx.doi.org/10.1016/B978-0-08-100813-3.00004-3

4.2 INTERNATIONALIZATION PROCESS THEORY

4.2.1 Background

Fonfara (2009) defined internationalization as "a phenomenon occurring when a firm enters a relationship with a party outside the country of origin in which the firm's operations at the local level are different from its activities in foreign markets." The aforementioned definition conforms to the definition of internationalization provided by Pierscionek (2003) in which "internationalization of a company is the business relationship with foreign markets, regardless of form or scope." However, Gorynia (2007) proposed that if at least one product or service of a firm relates to activities in foreign markets, this circumstance should be considered internationalization.

On the other hand, internationalization can be defined as a process. According to Nowakowski (1999), internationalization is the development of a company with a process-oriented nature. Pietrasienski (2005) clarified this statement by elaborating the fact that internationalization is a process based on the increase of product exports and transfer of production to foreign countries. Johanson and Vahlne (1997) also stated that "internationalization is a result of gradual adaptation to the changes in external and/or internal business environment."

The process-based perspective is a major traditional way of analyzing internationalization. This traditional approach explores the entry process and firms' activities in particular overseas markets, including forms of expansion, internationalization motives, and stages and levels of internationalization (Ratajczak-Mrozek, 2014). Over the last few decades, varying definitions of internationalization as a "process" have been developed by numerous thinkers. According to studies written by Johanson and Vahlne, internationalization also refers to the process in which the enterprise gradually increases its international engagement, particularly to build required resources and engage in global competition (Johanson and Vahlne, 1990; Johanson and Vahlne, 1997). Similarly, Mathews (2006) suggested that internationalization is considered a process when firms begin integrating themselves into global markets and thereby change the dynamics of international competition. He also affirmed that accelerated internationalization is achieved through organizational innovations that are well adapted to international economic activities. These statements align to the definition of internationalization coined by Calof and Beamish (1995), which states that "internationalization is a process of adapting enterprises' operations, strategies, structures, and resources and so on, to international circumstances."

One of the most commonly cited models in literature related to internationalization is the Uppsala model developed by Johanson and Vahlne (as cited by Carneiro et al., 2008). The model demonstrates two main stages of internationalization, which include (1) enterprises' selection of new overseas destinations for expansions based on their physical proximity to the host country, moving to more psychically remote countries once they have gained experience and knowledge from prior international business activities; and (2) gradual escalation of resource commitments in each chosen market once the enterprises gain experience in each host country (Carneiro et al., 2008).

Based on the concept of the Uppsala model, internationalization can be henceforth characterized by the following facts:

1. The internationalized firms have been successful at the local level (the internal market).
2. The internationalized firms start to move to geographically nearby markets and later expand farther to more distant markets. This is because there are fewer factors obstructing bilateral cooperation between countries in the same region or within reach, such as language, culture, politics, and so on.
3. These firms begin penetrating foreign markets through export operations, and then begin to engage in more ambitious activities (Wojtkiewicz, 2015).

Hollensen et al. (2011) argued that the increase in both geographic diversification and market presence led to increased levels of internationalization through different ways of operation (sporadic export, independent intermediaries, foreign trading branches, and foreign trading and production branches). This coincides with the Uppsala model.

The Uppsala model also illustrates how international expansion is based on a bank of cumulative decisions that stimulate greater commitments derived from knowledge acquisition about the global market (Sim and Pandian, 2003). This emphasizes the importance of knowledge accumulation regarding foreign markets and psychic distance (factors disturbing or preventing the flow of information between a firm and host countries such as diversities in language, education level, business practice, culture, and industrialization level) (Meyer and Thaijongrak, 2013). In other words, firms tend to initiate their overseas operations in other developing countries, most commonly their neighboring countries, as a result of less psychic distance (Wells, 1983; Khan, 1986). According to Dunning (1986), the process of internationalization can be explained by the investment development path (IDP) model. He insisted that internationalization activities of firms are linked to the economic development of a country and suggested that the competitive advantages of internationalization are key determinants of the state's economic development process and firms' internationalization strategies. Similarly, Meyer and Thaijongrak's (2013) "stages model" portrays how firms generally go through specific stages of entering markets and operating their businesses overseas. At the beginning, firms have no interest in international expansion and have no knowledge about foreign markets. However, they gradually increase their business operations abroad and undertake higher commitments progressively.

It can therefore be concluded that firms initiate internationalization processes by entering a country nearby, and later move to other foreign economies with respectively greater psychic distance, along with an increase in commitment. When firms begin to expand their market commitment, they initially form low commitments (e.g., establish a small joint venture) and progress to higher levels of commitment (e.g., set up a larger joint venture or wholly owned subsidiary). In other words, commitment gained from the extent of ownership in various economies closely correlates with psychic distance (Sim and Pandian, 2003). According to Johanson and Vahlne (1990), higher commitments across borders support an enterprise to acquire knowledge and experience about foreign business circumstances, such as information about customers, competitors, and regulatory institutions. This knowledge enables a firm to assess its current status in the global markets, the level of its market commitment, and the opportunities to put forward the investment. Correspondingly, firms will develop competitive capabilities and market knowledge sufficient for becoming successful players at the international level. In addition, the process of foreign investment decision-making constitutes the commitment to a position in a business network in a foreign economy. The concept of commitment here refers to (1) the amount of resources committed, which should be equal to the size of investment; and (2) the intensity of commitment because it would be difficult to source alternative resources (Meyer and Thaijongrak, 2013).

Another theoretical model that has been highly recognized in the field of international business is the eclectic paradigm. This model was developed to explain the motives and reasons why international operations are carried out, including the locations and means of internationalization (as cited by Ferreira et al., 2013). Since the beginning, Dunning considered internationalization a progressive process of investment development influenced by the globalized economy. Dunning (1993) proposed a taxonomy of three factors that lead to enterprises engaging in internationalization, known as the "eclectic paradigm": ownership, location, and internalization (OLI).

Ownership advantages are the competitive advantages that firms currently own and can be transferred to other operational destinations, especially overseas. These advantages can be a specific resource, skill, or asset that enhances product and/or service value. Ownership advantages may derive from superior technology, better management, or even more efficient manufacturing process. On the other hand, location advantages apply to certain locations such as particular regions or countries, which usually only benefit enterprises that are located there because they cannot be provided in remote areas. This means it is necessary to have operations on site in order to gain advantages such as lower costs of production, better accessibility, knowledge availability, favorable policies, and the like. Lastly, internalization advantages result from the exploitation of internal firm advantages. In other words, companies tend to gain more profit and advantages through their own production rather than manufacturing through a partnership arrangement like licensing or a joint venture.

Dunning (1993) categorized the motives of international expansion into four types, as described next.

Type 1: Resource Seeking

Firms tend to seek access to natural resources, raw materials, and/or other manufacturing factors in more fortunate conditions, such as lower labor costs.

Type 2: Market Seeking

Firms usually enter new markets to expand their customer base.

Type 3: Efficiency Seeking

Firms commonly seek to improve efficiency by increasing their productivity. There are multiple ways to achieve this, such as specialization of resources.

Type 4: Strategic Asset Seeking

A majority of firms aim to develop their skills, resources, and personnel capabilities to enhance competitiveness. In this scenario, location becomes less important in exchange for increased ownership and internationalization advantages.

In the same manner, Yeung (1994) concluded that other motives of international business expansion derived from a set of *push* and *pull* factors, listed here:

1. sluggish domestic markets
2. exploitation of local market knowledge
3. exploitation of relative firm-specific advantage
4. protection of or access to foreign economies

5. diversification of risks
6. establishment of cultural and ethnic networks

In the context of emerging economies, especially in the Asia-Pacific region, Dunning et al. (1998) argued that internationalization of newly industrialized countries (NICs) is influenced by globalization and regionalization of markets as well as the need for value-adding activities. Based on Dunning's investment development path model, the escalation of these firms' internationalization activities correlates to economic development in their countries. Between 1977 and 1985, the internationalization trend typically focused on countries that were less developed than the home countries, where there were lower wage rates and relaxed regulatory institutions. Companies from China, Japan, and other NICs tended to locate production operations and facilities in neighboring countries in their own region as a result of inadequate experience and technological capability for successfully investing in developed economies (Vernon-Wortzel and Wortzel, 1988; Dunning, 1986; Khan, 1986; Lecraw, 1977). In other words, it is safer to expand international activities in other developing countries or neighboring countries where firms can fully take advantage of existing capabilities, skills, and resources with minimized adaptation. Subsequently, when their international skills and experience develop, companies tend to expand their operations to more remote countries (Johanson and Vahlne, 1997). For example, after business expansion into lesser developed countries within the same region and gaining knowledge and experience necessary for internationalization, multinationals from South Korea and Taiwan began to enlarge their international activities in the Triad countries, including the United States, Western Europe, and Japan, to a greater extent (Dunning et al., 1998).

4.2.2 Case Studies of BANPU, Creative Technology, Daewoo Motor Company, and Constellation New Zealand Ltd.

According to Meyer and Thaijongrak (2013), the internationalization process theory explains modern strategic operations of multinationals from Asian emerging economies. Furthermore, the fundamental process of experience acquisition accelerating stages of increasing commitment justifies the evolution of these firms over time. In this study, they illustrate the internationalization processes of six Thai companies, including BANPU. For BANPU Public Limited Company (BANPU), a leader in the Thai mining industry, its process of internationalization proceeded through a number of stages. First, its strategies conformed to the Uppsala model, whereby BANPU's international expansion started with product exports, followed by the establishment of overseas sales offices. In 2001, the company began investing abroad toward foreign direct investment into Indonesia, Vietnam, and China, respectively. Along the aforementioned operations, the firm steadily adapted itself to the host governments, customers, and partners, supporting their investment in the host countries. In the mining industry, local knowledge about regulatory institutions and systems is essential for successful overseas investment. In other words, it can be predicted that BANPU's internationalization was stimulated by a good understanding of business practices and cultures in Asia. Therefore, when BANPU decided to expand its business operations to Australia, it indicated that BANPU had reached the upper stages of the internationalization process where there is a wider psychic distance between the firm and the host country, as well as increased geographic diversification and market presence. In the company's annual report for 2010, the CEO of BANPU revealed that the purchase of Centennial Company in Australia was a colossal step for BANPU in terms of breaking out of its comfort zone.

Another interesting case study for internationalization of Asia-Pacific multinational enterprises is found in the research done by Sim and Pandian (2003). Their empirical research studies the internationalization processes, strategies, and operations of Asia-Pacific firms, including Creative Technology. Creative Technology is a successful multinational enterprise (MNE) in the field of electronics and multimedia that has expanded its operations globally, not only within the Asia-Pacific region, but also in more than 80 countries, including the United States, Africa, and Europe. In the early stages, the majority of the case firms from Singapore tended to concentrate in the Asia region before moving to developed states. Just like other MNEs from emerging markets, the decision to internationalize was affected by the geographical and resource limitations of firms; companies thus initially extended products and technologies to nearby countries with identical economic and cultural circumstances. This initial stage of internationalization conforms to the internationalization process theory developed by the Uppsala School. However, the difference between Creative Technology and other Singaporean case firms is that Creative Technology (as well as some other Singaporean electronic companies) expanded operations directly to developed markets in the 1990s, when the government adopted the regionalization program supporting overseas manufacturing to enhance the country's overall economic competitiveness, while other manufacturing enterprises focused their business activities in Asia. This shows that unlike common MNEs from emerging markets, Creative Technology's competitive advantages are its niche technology advancement, especially its research and development (R&D) and product development, or the "knowledge" necessary for promoting the firm itself along the stages of internationalization. Furthermore, Creative Technology generally used wholly owned subsidiaries (WOSs) in North American and European regions, while primarily utilizing joint ventures (JVs) in Asia. This reflects the necessarily greater control to maximize production flexibility and technological advantages in more remote regions where psychic distance factors are highly evident. Therefore, this case study also demonstrates the skepticism toward Johanson and Vahlne (1997) internationalization process theory because Creative Technology decided to use WOSs in high psychic distance destinations rather than follow low-equity entry modes for more culturally distant states like the United States or Europe, signified by the theory.

The globalization of Daewoo Motor Company (DMC) of Oh et al. (1998) suggested the evolution process of firms' internationalization. At the beginning, Daewoo Motor Company adopted a state-of-the-art philosophy in order to succeed in international markets; it had to become a niche in leading automobile markets like the United States and Western Europe by increasing its investments in marketing, R&D, and design while seeking opportunities in emerging markets such as China, Southeast Asian countries, Eastern Europe, and so on in order to establish strong brand recognition and gain some location advantages in the early stages of market development. Similar to other Korean multinationals, DMC acquired advantages from entering emerging markets or nearby countries because it was also an emerging MNE, which proficiently comprehends the company's business systems and practices. The company operated in numerous emerging economies such as the Czech Republic, Romania, India, the Philippines, Vietnam, Indonesia, and Iran, planning to further invest in Russia and China. The benefit of its international expansion to these countries was presented by the fact that the company could import competitively priced production components and reduce its losses due to increasing exports. Simultaneously, DMC had sent off its R&D units around the world, for example, Worthing Technical Center in the United Kingdom or Daewoo Motor Engineering in Germany. These R&D units specialized in the fields in which the host countries are highly competent. Therefore it can be concluded that DMC expanded in local markets and developed technological capabilities at the same time in order to compete in a notably competitive global economy. In other words, the processes of internationalization can be integrated into a single but lengthy stage.

Lastly, Alonso (2010) discussed internationalization strategies of New Zealand wineries, which included internationalization processes of small- and medium-sized enterprises. According to the "Internationalization and the Wine Sector" section in the study, numerous wine entrepreneurs in New Zealand decided to internationalize their business due to recent revisions to laws and regulations in which lower tariffs, reductions in logistical costs, and fewer barriers to international trade allowed the wine producers to export their products overseas. Hence many wineries engaged in international trade, and their steady development led to the restructuration or takeover of New Zealand's wineries by large MNEs; this includes the case of Constellation New Zealand Ltd. Constellation Brands, a US-based international corporation that bought New Zealand's leading wineries and put them together under the name of Constellation New Zealand Ltd. The author argued that before the rebranding process, firms had to go through the process of tradition and image building, especially to deal with increasingly demanding consumers around the globe. Moreover, there was need of production and technological development to aid its internationalization process to improve and maximize its exporting strategies. Nevertheless, in the global arena, being a larger winery was advantageous compared to smaller entrepreneurs, as it allowed for the enjoyment of a larger consumer base.

4.3 NETWORK MODEL AND INSTITUTIONAL THEORY

4.3.1 Background

The network model theory takes a competitive advantage-based perspective on internationalization, which demonstrates the internationalization process of firms guided by their network capabilities. Johanson and Vahlne (2009) suggested the broadening of the internationalization concept by considering not only foreign business contexts, but also network positions in general. According to Johanson and Mattsson (1988), the network model of internationalization is the analysis of a firm's internationalization process in which it establishes and develops positions and inward connections in foreign networks through utilization of international extension, penetration, and integration. International extension in this case is defined as the building up of relationships with new foreign counterparts, while international penetration refers to the state in which the firm already exists in a particular foreign network and then develops its position. The integration process is defined as the coordination between positions in diverse national networks (Johanson and Mattsson, 1988).

Moreover, the internationalization of business networks can be analyzed from two main perspectives, which are spatial embeddedness and vertical embeddedness. The term "embeddedness" is used for showing a firm's diversified dependencies on various kinds of relationship networks. Spatial embeddedness is defined as the proximity between network partners affecting a company's performance, while vertical embeddedness, with its more comprehensive definition, refers to all the relationships between various levels in a network, such as geographical levels (international, regional, national, and local), supply chain (producer, supplier, distributor, and consumer), and within a specific business setting (industry, company, and individual) (Halinen and Törnroos, 1998).

In terms of companies from developing countries, especially Asian firms, network-based business strategies are clearly highlighted. Unlike firms from developed economies that are equipped with advanced technological expertise and skills, firms from developing economies tend to rely greatly on network capabilities (Pananond, 2004). This statement agrees with studies on third-world multinational enterprises (MNEs) stating that "the competitive advantages of MNEs from developed countries are derived from advanced technology or superior resources; therefore, MNEs from developing countries which lack these advantages are obliged to search for competitive advantages from other sources, including foreign networks" (Yeung, 1994). These network relationships can lead to a number of crucial competitive advantages such as cost reductions and, in turn, revenue increases, complementary resources from various foreign partners, and so on (Pananond and Zeithaml, 1998). In the same manner, according to Jarillo (1988) and Johanson and Mattsson (1988), the benefits of network ties are composed of (1) specialization in core businesses of the value chain because "division of labor" increases productivity and encourages economies of scale; (2) flexibility to share risks and outsource, so firms are no longer bound with activities not essential to them and are able to act quicker than rivals; (3) decrease in transaction costs due to the mutual awareness and trust between partners in the networks; and (4) better access to key resources from their partners' environment (Wong, 2011).

The main sources of these network relationships are close ties with financial sources, connections with foreign technology partners, and political connections, which can contribute to firms' domestic growth and international expansion effectively (Pananond, 2004). More specifically, Pananond (2004) analyzed the main factors leading to Asian firms' internationalization based on the network model theory, as follows. First, business networks commonly result from cultural traits in Asian societies, especially among the Chinese. When firms from the same home countries or ethnicities expand in the region, their personal relationships can serve as competitive advantages because their common cultural background can encourage trust and reduce transaction costs. Second, it is clear that Asian enterprises tend to rely on their network relationship because of their underdeveloped institutional context and weak market mechanisms. In brief, competitive advantages taken by developing economies, particularly Asian firms, are not usually firm-specific ownership advantages (e.g., large capital base, superior management skills, expertise, and technology), but network relationships, organizational structures, and cultural resemblance.

However, advantages dependent upon network capabilities can restrict firms' potential in improving technology, skills, and operational experiences abroad as well as limit their options to locate their businesses to only countries with similar institutional and/or cultural environments (Pananond, 2004). Moreover, in terms of Asian context specifically, the informal networks can worsen the lack of transparency in developing economies and, hence, negatively affect the financial system enormously. To illustrate, after the 1997 Asian economic crisis, the term "cronyism" was coined by numerous scholars. It refers to corruption and profit-making behavior based on personal ties in informal networks among the elites (Wade, 1998). Additionally, tremendous dependence on network relationships can expose the firms to additional transaction costs stemmed from inefficiencies and political instability (Scott-Kennal and Enderwick, 2005).

Therefore, if firms begin to focus more on creating capabilities and market-supporting institutions are simultaneously developed, there will be the transition from a network-based dimension to market-centered strategy (Peng, 2003). In other words, networks will eventually transform from strong ties to weak ties due to the changes in institutional environments (Peng and Zhou, 2005). These two types of ties benefit firms in different ways. For instance, the advantages of strong ties are the sharing of technology and knowledge, higher quality information, informal alternatives to formal contracts, and increased business opportunities. On the other hand, advantages of weak ties are less costs to maintain, less time consumption, and distant connections with other partners who may offer genuine and unique information (Powell, 1990; Granovetter, 1985). Both strong and weak ties are valuable for enterprises, but under different circumstances.

The institutional theory or institution-based view conceptualizes a country's institutions as the rules of the game that comprise both informal constraints (business customs, traditions, and codes of conduct) and formal rules (laws and property rights), which enable and constrain different strategic choices (Peng and Delios, 2006). According to Peng and Zhou (2005), networks can transform from strong to weak ties when market institutions become more rule-based and have less government control and interference in which new sets of ties become more wide-ranging. This change in institutional environment in either home or host country or both leads to changes in costs and benefits associated with the enterprises' product and geographic diversification strategies.

The characteristics of institutional transitions can be evaluated by the level of network strength and dimensions of the network content standpoint (Peng and Zhou, 2005). First, networks can be categorized into *strong ties* and *weak ties*. During the network-intensive stage, strategic strong personal ties enriched over a long period of intensive interaction with a smaller group of people, especially government officials, managers, and entrepreneurs, tend to dominate the firm's decision-making because formal rules supporting market systems are not well established. Moreover, since the early stages of institutional transitions, ties may be transformed into weak ties instead of being completely faded out. To clarify, institutional transitions unavoidably progress when there is the necessity to compete with market-based capabilities and the resources needed for the firm growth are insufficient (Peng and Zhou, 2005).

Second, there are two main dimensions of institutional transitions, which are *political* and *legal* dimensions (Peng and Zhou, 2005). In terms of transitions of political institutions, network ties could be downsized when there are changes in the level of limited resources controlled by governments, the level of government intervention in the private sector, and the level of unpredictability for regulatory policies. First, it is clear that accessing scarce resources like land and licensing for business entry is a significant advantage of network relationships in developing economies. Thus the level of resources under government control affects the extensiveness of enterprises' dependence on the government (Child and Lu, 1996). Second, the level of government involvement in business decisions and operations such as pricing, investment, and wage rates also impacts the weight of network ties between firms and governments (Child and Lu, 1996; Hellman and Schankerman, 2000). Third, it is important for firms to maintain in-depth relationships with governments, as accessing policy information on a timely basis is required for keeping firms' activities from regulatory risk. Nonetheless, due to the increase in economic liberalization, privatization, gradual development of commercial banking systems and securities markets, and stable and transparent regulatory policies, governments gradually have less control over the resources, along with a decrease in firms' dependence on the governments (Child and Lu, 1996).

Simultaneously, the transitions of legal institutions are stimulated by the extent of legal frameworks managing business transactions and the effectiveness of such frameworks, particularly business law enforcement (Peng and Zhou, 2005). Before, the inadequacy of formal legal and regulatory frameworks brought about the far-reaching utilization of network relationships in order to reduce transaction costs and regulatory uncertainty. However, such weak legal systems favoring personal ties also limit business opportunities (e.g., potential relationships with other firms) and simultaneously undermine competition in the market. Therefore the growth of legal frameworks is likely to transform strong network ties to weak ties, which can provide more heterogeneous information and competitive opportunities (Peng and Zhou, 2005). Nevertheless, it should be noted that as long as the institutions are still imperfect, business networks will continue to remain important. This is especially true for the Asia-Pacific region, where there are not only immature capital markets, but also governments that still greatly influence resource allocation and business decision-making and operations (Peng and Delios, 2006).

4.3.2 Case Studies of Charoen Pokphand Group, Siam Cement Group, Lion Group, Toyota Group, and Sri Lankan Small Business Entrepreneurs

Pananond (2004) examined how network ties and institutional transitions play a significant role in business for multinationals from many Asian developing economies, especially the Charoen Pokphand (CP) Group and Siam Cement Group (SCG). In general, it can be concluded from the study that the internationalization process of Thai multinational enterprises (MNEs) was rarely influenced by their acquired technology and expertise, but rather relied more on networking capabilities derived from close relationships with financial sources, links with foreign partners, and political connections in order to facilitate their domestic and international expansion. Historically, from 1989 to 1997, Thai MNEs expanded and seized opportunities in nearby countries primarily using their competitive advantages based on their network ties from mid to high levels due to their deficient technological expertise. These Thai firms exploited these capabilities to effortlessly invest in other Asian developing economies where market institutions were typically weak. However, they were eventually deadlocked with technological insufficiency in return

(Pananond, 2004). As an illustration, CP Group's activities in China were clearly by-products of its connection with the Chinese authorities and interested investors. Even after the Asian economic crisis, CP Group continued its precrisis behavior that entirely depended on its network capabilities, ignoring the obligation to improve its technological skills and expertise. Still, it should be noted that some Thai MNEs started to benefit from their exceptional competitive advantage and collected experience after the postcrisis years. For example, Siam Cement Group decided to invest in the fields in which they were technologically confident, such as ceramic tiles and sanitary wares in the Philippines. This means, in SCG's case, the group not only concentrated on the areas in which it was strongly capable of increasing its production capacity, but it also internationalized its business using spatial embeddedness by directing most of its overseas operations to neighboring countries in Southeast Asia, such as Indonesia, Malaysia, Vietnam, and the Philippines, in efforts to escalate competitiveness (Pananond, 2001; Pananond, 2004). Another key factor facilitating Thai MNEs to business expansion to the international arena was the financial liberalization policies adopted by the Thai government in the early 1990s. These new frameworks contributed to capital liberalization together with better access to international financial markets and more favorable regional investment environments, up until the Asian economic crisis in 1997 (Pananond, 2004).

To extend her analysis, Pananond (2007) explored the changing dynamics of international expansion by Thai multinational companies after the Asian economic crisis with case studies of the Charoen Pokphand Group and Siam Cement Group once again. The study confirmed that the internationalization of both CP Group and SCG was driven by their networking capabilities. During the precrisis period, CP Group exploited its political connections and links with other foreign business partners and financial institutions, including ethnic ties with common cultural backgrounds and languages with the Chinese, to expand its overseas activities. Similarly, during the same period, SCG established alliances with leading regional enterprises and also took advantage of its strong connections with financial institutions. The research also suggested that after the crisis, there was a slight change in their international expansion trend. For CP Group, there was a higher amount of transparent partnerships with foreign technological partners, but the connections with host country governments still remained highly significant. In contrast, SCG tended to focus solely on technological partnerships. Furthermore, institutional changes like the adoption of China's Open Door Policy also influenced CP Group's commitment to the country.

Another case study of Asia-Pacific MNEs' internationalization aided by ethnic networks can be found in the research entitled "Internationalization Strategies of Emerging Asian MNEs—Case Study Evidence on Singaporean and Malaysian Firms" written by Sim (2006), in which Lion Group was used as a case firm. According to the survey, all of the case study firms, including Lion Group, admitted that they used their ethnicity and networks to support overseas operations. The collected data showed that Lion Group, a Malaysian conglomerate in the fields of steel, motor vehicles, retailing, foods, property, and plantations, had operated its businesses in various countries such as Indonesia, Taiwan, China, the United States, and Germany. The key motives of the firm's internationalization were market expansion and diversification. More importantly, it is clear that one of its strategic advantages was network localization, in which its ties with Chinese networks accommodated the joint venture arrangement. Ethnic networks were eminently emphasized in the company's foreign operations because the enterprise, especially its CEO, had fostered extensive connections and political networks in China and other countries in the region for decades; without a doubt, this was successful because the company was Chinese controlled and considered "(Malaysian) Chinese investors." In other words, the cooperative activities in such networks were based on Chinese personal relationships called "guanxi," generally ethnically related. The development of this kind of entrustment and collaborative behavior was influenced by their common dialects and resembling cultural attitudes and backgrounds. The benefits of these ethnic networks to Lion Group included the acquisition of local knowledge, access to local markets, distribution systems, connections with local bureaucrats and businesspeople, potential business partners and associates, financing, and many more.

Hatani (2009) also analyzed the internationalization of Japanese firms using network-based and institutional-based views, using Toyota Group's expansion in China as the case study. In this study, the term "preclusterization" was coined as a new pattern of internationalization by Japanese multinationals. It is an enhanced form of network-based internationalization in which supplier companies of a business group enter into a host country and then cluster in the location targeted for the full entry of the parent company. The progress of Toyota's entry into China was affected by the institutional changes in the host country. Though the group had declared its intention to invest in China, Toyota was not originally allowed to produce cars there due to the Chinese government's 1994 Auto Industry Policy. In 2000, Toyota finally received the government's permission to produce cars, but only with a 50/50 joint venture with Tianjin Auto Company; the venture later started manufacturing their cars in China in 2002. Nonetheless, Toyota suppliers' initial settlements in China were facilitated by favorable incentives provided by special economic zones in China. In terms of developing a network and cluster, after the group's equity engagement with Tianjin Auto, an increasing number of Toyota suppliers began to settle around the location upon the prediction that Toyota would build its assembly plant over there sooner or later. In addition to key suppliers' active anticipation, Toyota Group had prepared its preclusterization by establishing the commitment between the core firm and the locality by setting up technical schools, training centers, and regulated service stations in the host country since 1980. In brief, the entry of Toyota Group to China can be discussed by applying both network and institutional theories.

According to Hewapathirana (2014), relationships between Sri Lankan small business entrepreneurs and Sri Lankan emigrants in other countries are critical factors supporting their international expansion. The author affirmed that global marketing had acknowledged the values and contributions of international diaspora and ethnic networks. Sri Lankan emigrant communities in other countries played a significant role in linking potential entrepreneurs to the business partners from their home country. In other words, these emigrants were the entrepreneurial agents who brought economic prosperity to both their host and home countries through bridging (networking with relatives, friends, and acquaintances) and linking (networking with professionals, business experts, and anticipated customers). The findings of the study suggested that the close ties between 10 Sri Lankan small business entrepreneurs in the country and Sri Lankan emigrant entrepreneurial agents in other countries had created the following values: "relationship in business is like a family," "money is not the prime concern," "do the best, give the best, tell the truth," and "continued friendship means continued business." These practices and values brought about the acquisition of knowledge, exchange of resources and opportunities, facilitation of international market entry, cross-border socioeconomic ties, and so on. Ultimately, they contributed to these 10 Sri Lankan small business entrepreneurs' international business growth and expansion.

4.4 RESOURCE-BASED VIEW THEORY

4.4.1 Background

The resource-based view theory emphasizes the importance of the enterprise's internal resources that stimulate the enterprise's performance and growth, which are difficult to imitate. Originally, the resource-based view theory was developed from the internationalization process theory in which the acquisition of knowledge is highlighted and static advantages become insignificant. Compared to the internationalization process theory, the motivation of the two theories is resembled, which is to gain extra returns and sustainable wealth by utilizing distinctive inputs or resources as well as the ability to obtain such resources more effectively than competitors in the market. Therefore the development and application of capabilities are required to overcome imperfect knowledge and subjective limitations; in other words, it deals with the resource management to maximize productive performance and administrative organization (Connell, 2008; Penrose, 1985).

According to Penrose's *The Theory of the Growth of the Firm* (1959), an enterprise is the organizer of resources in order to create unique and creative products and services that are competitive in the market. She also conceptualized the basic elements of the resource-based view theory as follows.

1. *Firm*: an accumulation of valuable resources acquired and dismissed by the determination of administrators for different uses and time consumption
2. *Resources*: physical and human resources that can be independently used due to their potentials
3. *Firm governance*: an administrative framework in which resources are combined together by administrative decisions or authoritative communication through term contracts, leases, and patent license agreements

The history of the resource-based view theory began when Werferfelt's (1984) *A Resource-based View of the Firm* coined the term "resource-based view" and emphasized the importance of resources and their implications for each company's operations. A few years later, Barney (1991) presented a comprehensive definition of resources as "a potential source of competitive advantage," which subsequently became the foundation of the theory's theoretical framework. In 1993, Amit and Shoemaker expanded the concept of resources into "resources and capabilities that can be the source of sustained competitive advantage." This follows Barney's (1991) suggestion that sustained competitive advantage derives from a company's resources and capabilities, including management skills, organizational processes, and knowledge gained from the accumulation of information and technology. Above all, the evolution of the resource-based view theory was extended by the categorization of two types of resources as well as the extensive description of capabilities as explained next (Tabares et al., 2015).

Tangible resources are defined as fixed and current assets of a firm that have a permanent capacity, such as factories, equipment and machinery, natural resources, raw materials, manufacturing techniques, stocks, and so on (Werferfelt, 1984).

Intangible resources are defined as abstract assets resistant to imitation efforts by competitors, thanks to the innate complexity and particularity of their aggregation process, which prevents the possibility of duplication and alternatives in the short or medium term (Fahy, 2000). This kind of resource is also known as "intellectual capital," which includes human, structural, and relational capital (as cited by Tabares et al., 2015).

Human capital refers to a workforce's skills and attitude required for problem-solving and innovation development, as well as know-how, experience, and expertise.

Structural capital refers to organizational and technological capital such as organizational culture, values, internal structures, management, learning instructions and procedures, research and development, manufacturing techniques, intellectual protection (copyrights and trademarks), patents, technological supervision, and so on.

Relational capital refers to existing deep-rooted stakeholders' internal and external relationships of the firm. These include the relationships between the enterprise and its customers, shareholders, workers, suppliers, distributors, business partners, competitors, private and public sectors, social networks, and media.

On the other hand, capabilities are the by-products of different intellectual capital asset combinations toward miscellaneous interactions of human activities that involve an enterprise's resources (Amit and Shoemaker, 1993). In addition, Makadok (2001) broadened the concept by defining a capability as an inherent, nontransferable, firm-specific advantage that can enhance the productivity of other resources owned by the company. Hence, resources are a collection of usable factors possessed or regulated by the firm, while capabilities are the firm's capacities to utilize such resources. Amit and Shoemaker (1993) suggested that enterprises with higher intellectual capital assets (human, structural, and relational) also have higher potential to develop beneficial organizational capabilities, and that enterprises with these higher organizational capabilities have higher capacity to enter international markets sooner than expected. Specifically speaking, even if they are in the same industry, different companies may have different sets of resources and capabilities; hence, when comparing them by an assumed business activity, some companies may be more capable of succeeding in this activity than others. Moreover, these resources and capability differences among enterprises may be enduring because it would be too costly to develop or obtain them (Reddy and Rao, 2014).

Additionally, there are four key characteristics that a resource must contain in order to produce a sustainable competitive advantage, as listed here (Barney, 1991):

1. A resource must be valuable
2. A resource must be rare or unique
3. A resource must be immobile, which means it cannot be facilely sold or traded
4. A resource must be nonsubstitutable, which means it is not easily copied

In terms of internationalization, the sources of these resources are not only internal, but also external; therefore, the internationalization of a multinational company is the process in which the firm progressively increases its international engagement in order to develop overseas relationships and access resources, markets, information, and technologies, ultimately creating value through a combination of these resources toward their operations, allowing the company to share risks and outsource value-chain activities (Wong, 2011). The benefits of internationalization based on the resource-based view theory are listed here (Jarillo, 1988; Johanson and Mattsson, 1988):

1. specialization in core businesses of the value chain that improve the efficiency and economies of scale through the division of labor
2. flexibility (due to fewer commitments to nonessential activities) and rapidity to become the pacesetter of the market
3. transaction cost reductions on account of mutual trust between network members as a result of their durable cooperation
4. access to key resources from the host countries or foreign environment

In conclusion, the resource-based view theory argues that firms that possess rare, valuable, nonalternative, difficult-to-duplicate resources and capabilities tend to accomplish more sustainability and competitiveness. These advantages enable firms to succeed in foreign markets and also further enable them to accumulate resources from the internationalization process. In terms of Asia-Pacific multinational enterprises, based on the resource-based view perspective, firms generally did not internationalize for financial diversification but rather to establish new business ventures across industries rapidly and at low costs. Hence their internationalization is based on resources and coordination skills that could be accumulated if political-economic circumstances allow them to gain and sustain the capability of integrating their resources from both domestic and international sources (Guillen, 2000).

4.4.2 Case Studies of Li & Fung Group, Pohang-Yeongil Port, Boost Juice, and an Indian Pharma Multinational

According to Wong (2011), Li & Fung Group, a multinational with a wide-ranging network of more than 15,000 suppliers around the globe and more than 200 offices and distribution centers in more than 40 countries, was used as a case study to evaluate how the company cultivated its performance and enlarged its resource utilization to acquire market opportunities and shape its products' value along the internationalization process based on the resource-based view theory. First of all, like other multinationals such as Nike, Dell, and Wal-Mart, Li & Fung Group is an excellent example of possessing effective global supply chain management and productive outsourcing due to the activities overseas. For instance, Li & Fung Group did not have its own plant but the "network resources integrator," which efficiently organized myriad activities in value chains and developed mass, time-sensitive products like fashion accessories, gifts, handicrafts, entertainment articles, and sporting goods; this could be considered the combination of human capital and structural capital. Second, Li & Fung Group developed itself from a small trading company to a pioneer in the international market by enhancing its key competencies despite environmental revolutions and widening its relational networks all over the world. To illustrate, its global networks and advanced information systems facilitated Li & Fung's ability to apprehend the trend of clients' needs, select skillful designers, trustworthy suppliers, and locate its factories in the right place to provide customers with satisfactory goods at a reasonable price. This can be perceived as the combination of human capital, structural capital, and relational capital altogether. In other words, the main factors influencing the group's success were its (1) specialization in core competencies such as market knowledge and advanced information system technology, (2) capacity and flexibility to quickly react to changes in the global market, (3) global supply chain management that serves customers worldwide with value-added products, and (4) strategic relational networks. In brief, Li & Fung's resources were effectively integrated by its dynamic supply chain management to make use of its resources in the global value chain and create sustainable competitive advantages.

Cho and Ha (2009) also demonstrated how Pohang-Yeongil Port, as an active Korean business player in the global arena, developed its unique resources such as free trade zone, industry cluster, and information and communications technology (ICT) infrastructure to attract multinationals' foreign direct investments, which led to ameliorated performance. The authors argued that there was generally a direct relationship between the execution of the resource-based view and better performance due to the fact that resources are key to sustainable competitive advantages. According to the resource-based view theory, physical capital can be easily imitated or gained by their business rivals, but human and organizational capital cannot. Therefore, sustainable competitive advantages derive from long-lasting intangible resources like human, structural, and relational capital. In fact, the location advantages of Pohang-Yeongil port were not adequately attractive for the customers compared with its competitors. For example, Korea's maritime industry was not competitive in the international market and the port itself was just a regional port. However, Pohang-Yeongil port had developed its resources that were rare, valuable, immobile, and nonsubstitutable to solve the aforementioned problems. First, it provided accessible free trade zones of port hinterland complex and other incentives for cargo and ship owners. Second, with the availability of free trade zones, it formed industry clusters that allowed the port to build up competitive advantages and improve its performance through globalized supply chain management. Third, its well-developed ICT infrastructure had become an important organizational resource for combining global production and global distribution together. Advanced communication technologies like groupware systems also played a significant role in the port's global supply chain management.

Menzies and Orr (2014) show the significance of strategic resources of Boost Juice Company, an Australian multinational enterprise, which supported its successful internationalization to Malaysia. The first main resources of Boost Juice's internationalization, as confirmed by the authors, were human capital and relational capital. The CEO of Boost Juice, Janine Allis, had successfully expanded Boost Juice to many other international destinations beforehand, such as Hong Kong; thus she had accumulated knowledge and experiences required for the establishment of Malaysian operations. Apart from the company's executives, franchisees in Malaysia also played a vast role in Boost Juice's internationalization. These franchisees were individuals and organizations that had valuable understanding of Malaysian culture and informal institutions, which was crucial for the prosperous management and development of the Malaysian market. The company also gave importance to the selection of potential employees and their training, particularly in the area of customer service, motivation, and enthusiasm in order to provide a fun and positive environment for the customers with the potential to swap to other alternative juices or products anytime. Furthermore, Boost Juice's products were the result of research and development efforts in terms of being a nutritious alternative to fast food (structural capital). For example, Boost Juice's products were 98% fat free and did not contain any artificial flavoring or colors. The company focused on innovation and product development because it was one of the best ways to sustain its market position ahead of its competitors. Moreover, Boost Juice's marketing and branding via social media was also crucial, particularly in appealing to younger customers. There was also the introduction of new innovative products such as unique flavors or new smoothie lines to differentiate its products from competitors.

Other research done by Reddy and Rao (2014) discussed how firm-specific resources enriched the sustainable growth of a leading Indian pharmaceutical multinational in the global arena. Due to privacy concerns, the authors kept the identity of the case firm confidential, but explained the company with the following characteristics: (1) the company's annual revenues were over USD 2 billion; and (2) the company had three main business divisions: generics, active pharmaceutical ingredients, and proprietary products. Based on the resource-based view theory, the authors emphasized the quantity of human capital embedded in the company as evidence of the company's productive resources as follows. First, the company had a healthy research and development team in the field of synthetic organic chemistry, consisting of 30% PhD graduates and 70% postgraduates. It also had an analytical chemistry team for testing chemical reactions, consisting of 25% PhD graduates and 75% postgraduates, as well as a production and chemical engineering team that had helped enhance the whole operation, consisting of 10% PhD graduates, 60% postgraduates, and 30% graduates in the field of chemistry and chemical engineering. Furthermore, the majority (90%) of its project management team members were certified by the Project Management Institute of the United States. Lastly, all the business managers in its marketing and business development team had a master's degree in business management. The authors defined the capabilities of the company in three main areas: processes related to the presales exercise, practical implementation of the very project and applicable control mechanisms, and activities related to postdelivery customer involvement. To sum up, the competitive advantages of this company based on the resource-based view theory were shaped by a consistent series of resources and capabilities that could not be easily copied by competitors.

4.5 CONCLUSION

This chapter discusses the literature on the main internationalization theories, which are internationalization process theory, network and institutional theories, and the resource-based view theory, along with case studies of Asia-Pacific companies' internationalization related to each theory. Companies discussed as case studies in this chapter included BANPU, Creative Technology, Daewoo Motor Company, Constellation New Zealand Ltd, Charoen Pokphand Group, Siam Cement Group, Lion Group, Toyota Group, Sri Lankan Small Business Entrepreneurs, Li & Fung Group, Pohang-Yeongil Port, Boost Juice, and an Indian Pharmaceutical Multinational. The literature illustrates that the pioneer researchers on multinational enterprises' international expansion, such as the Uppsala model and Dunning's internationalization motives, contributed greatly to the development of the internationalization process theory. The resource-based view theory is also an evolution of the internationalization process theory, while network and institutional theories cover the implications that the internationalization process theory cannot explain or inadequately explains. This chapter provides insightful information on internationalization of Asia-Pacific multinational enterprises, which can be further used as the foundation of conceptualizing an integrated internationalization model of firms in the Asia-Pacific region.

REFERENCES

Alonso, A.D., 2010. Internationalization of small and medium New Zealand wineries: an exploratory study. Small Enterprise Res. 17 (1), 58–73.

Amit, R., Shoemaker, P.J.H., 1993. Strategic assets and organizational rent. Strateg. Manag. J. 14 (1), 33–46.

Barney, J., 1991. Firm resources and sustained competitive advantage. J. Manag. 17, 99–120.

Calof, J.L., Beamish, P.W., 1995. Adapting to foreign markets: explaining internationalization. Int. Bus. Rev. 4 (2), 115–131.

Carneiro, J., Da Rocha, A., Ferreira da Silva, J., 2008. Challenging the Uppsala internationalization model: a contingent approach to the internationalization of services. Asia Pac. Bus. Rev. 5 (2), 85–103.

Child, J., Lu, Y. (Eds.), 1996. Management Issues in China: International Enterprises. Routledge, London.

Cho, H., Ha, Y., 2009. Determinants of FDI inflow in regional port with resource-based view and institutional theory: a case of Pohang-Yeongil Port. Asian J. Shipping Logistics 25 (2), 305–331.

Connell, C.M., 2008. Firm and Government as actors in Penrose's process theory of international growth: implications for the resource-based view and ownership-location-internationalization paradigm. Aust. Econ. Hist. Rev. 48 (2), 170–194.

Dunning, J.H., 1986. The investment development cycle and third world multinationals. In: Khan, K.M. (Ed.), Multinationals of the South. Francis Porter, London.
Dunning, J., 1993. The Globalization of Business. Routledge, London.
Dunning, J., van Hoesel, R., Narula, R., 1998. Third World multinationals revisited: new developments and theoretical implications. In: Dunning, J.H. (Ed.), Globalization, Trade and Foreign Direct Investment. Elsevier, Amsterdam, pp. 255–286.
Fahy, J., 2000. The resource-based view of the firm: some stumbling-blocks on the road to understanding sustainable competitive advantage. J. Eur. Ind. Training 24 (2–4), 94–104.
Ferreira, M.A.S.P.V., Pinto, C.S.F., Serra, F.A.R., Santos, J.C., 2013. A bibliometric study of John Dunning's contribution to international business research. Rev. Bus. Manag. 15 (46), 56–75.
Fonfara, K., 2009. Zachowanie przedsiebiorstwa w procesie internacjonalizacji. Polskie Wydawnictwo Ekonomiczne, Warszawa.
Gorynia, M., 2007. Strategie zagranicznej ekspansji przedsiebiorstw. Polskie Wydawnictwo Ekonomiczne, Warszawa.
Granovetter, M., 1985. Economic action and social structure: the problem of embeddedness. Am. J. Sociol. 91 (3), 481–510.
Guillen, M.F., 2000. Business groups in emerging economies: a resource-based view. Acad. Manag. J. 43 (3), 362–380.
Halinen, A., Törnroos, J.A., 1998. The role of embeddedness in the evolution of business networks. Scand. J. Manag. 14 (3), 187–205.
Hatani, F., 2009. Pre-clusterization in emerging markets: the Toyota group's entry process in China. Asia Pac. Bus. Rev. 15 (3), 369–387.
Hellman, J., Schankerman, M., 2000. Intervention, corruption and capture: the nexus between enterprises and state. Econ. Transit. 8 (2), 325–368.
Hewapathirana, G.I., 2014. Bridging, bonding and linking global entrepreneurs: the case of Sri Lanka. Hum. Resour. Dev. Int. 17 (2), 164–182.
Hollensen, S., Boyd, B., Dyhr Ulrich, A.M., 2011. The choice of foreign entry mode in a control perspective. IUP J. Bus. Strategy 8 (4), 7–31.
Jarillo, J.C., 1988. On strategic networks. Strateg. Manag. J. 9 (1), 31–41.
Johanson, J., Mattsson, L.G., 1988. Internationalisation in industrial systems—a network approach. In: Hood, N., Vahlne, J.E. (Eds.), Strategies in Global Competition. Croom Helm, London, pp. 287–314.
Johanson, J., Vahlne, J.E., 1990. The mechanism of internationalization. Int. Mark. Rev. 7 (4), 11–24.
Johanson, J., Vahlne, J.E., 1997. The internationalization process of the firm: a model of knowledge development and increasing foreign market commitments. J. Int. Bus. Stud. 8 (1), 23–32.
Johanson, J., Vahlne, J.E., 2009. The Uppsala internationalization process model revisited: from liability of foreignness to liability of outsidership. J. Int. Bus. Stud. 40 (9), 1411–1431.
Khan, K.M. (Ed.), 1986. Multinationals of the South: New Actors in the International Economy. Frances Pinter Publishers, London.
Lecraw, D., 1977. Direct Investment by Firms from Less Developed Countries. Oxf. Econ. Pap. 29 (3), 442–457.
Makadok, R., 2001. Toward a synthesis of the resource-based and dynamic-capability views of rent creation. Strateg. Manag. J. 22 (5), 387–401.
Mathews, J.A., 2006. Dragon multinationals: new players in 21st century globalization. Asia Pac. J. Manag. 23 (1), 5–27.
Menzies, J.L., Orr, S.C., 2014. Internationalization of boost juice to Malaysia. Asian Case Res. J. 18 (1), 175–197.

Meyer, K.E., Thaijongrak, O., 2013. The dynamics of emerging economy MNEs: how the internationalization process model can guide future research. Asia Pac. J. Manag. 30 (4), 1125–1153.
Nowakowski, M.K., 1999. Wprowadzenie do zarzadzania miedzynarodowego. Difin, Warszawa.
Oh, D., Choi, C.J., Choi, E., 1998. The globalization strategy of Daewoo Motor Company. Asia Pac. J. Manag. 15 (2), 185–203.
Pananond, P., 2001. The Making of Thai Multinationals: The Internationalization Process of Thai Firms. University of Reading, Reading, UK.
Pananond, P., 2004. Thai multinationals after the crisis trends and prospects. ASEAN Econ. Bull. 21 (1), 106–126.
Pananond, P., 2007. The changing dynamics of Thai multinationals after the Asian economic crisis. J. Int. Manag. 13, 356–375.
Pananond, P., Zeithaml, C.P., 1998. The international expansion process of MNEs from developing countries: a case study of Thailand's CP Group. Asia Pac. J. Manag. 15, 163–184.
Peng, M.W., 2003. Institutional transitions and strategic choices. Acad. Manag. Rev. 28, 275–296.
Peng, M.W., Delios, A., 2006. What determines the scope of the firm over time and around the world? An Asia Pacific perspective. Asia Pac. J. Manag. 23 (4), 385–405.
Peng, M.W., Zhou, J.Q., 2005. How network strategies and institutional transitions evolve in Asia. Asia Pac. J. Manag. 22 (4), 321–336.
Penrose, E., 1959. The Theory of the Growth of the Firm. Blackwell, Oxford.
Penrose, E., 1985. The Theory of the Growth of the Firm: Twenty-Five Years Later. Acta Universitatis Upsaliensis, Uppsala.
Pierscionek, Z., 2003. Strategie konkurencji i rozwoju przedsiebiorstwa. Wydawnictwo Naukowe, Warszawa.
Pietrasienski, P., 2005. Miedzynarodowe strategie marketingowe. Polskie Wydawnictwo Ekonomiczne, Warszawa.
Powell, W., 1990. Neither market nor hierarchy: network forms of organization. Res. Organ. Behav. 12, 295–336.
Ratajczak-Mrozek, M., 2014. Companies' simultaneous embeddedness in local, international and global networks—a conceptualisation from the perspective of local enterprises and their degree of internationalisation. Poznań Univ. Econ. Rev. 14 (1), 31–47.
Reddy, M.R.S., Rao, V.P., 2014. Application of the resource-based view: a case of an Indian pharma multinational. IUP J. Bus. Strategy 11 (1), 54–67.
Scott-Kennal, J., Enderwick, P., 2005. FDI and inter-firm linkages: exploring the black box of the investment development path. Transl. Corp. 14 (1), 105–137.
Sim, A.B., 2006. Internationalization strategies of emerging Asian MNEs—case study evidence on Singaporean and Malaysian firms. Asia Pac. Bus. Rev. 12 (4), 487–505.
Sim, A.B., Pandian, J.R., 2003. Emerging Asian MNEs and their internationalization strategies—case study evidence on Taiwanese and Singaporean firms. Asia Pac. J. Manag. 20 (1), 27–50.
Tabares, A., Alvarez, C., Urbano, D., 2015. Born globals from the resource-based theory: a case study in Colombia. J. Technol. Manag. Innov. 10 (2), 155–165.
Vernon-Wortzel, H., Wortzel, L.H., 1988. Globalizing strategies for multinationals from developing countries. Columbia J. World Bus. 23 (1), 27–35.
Wade, R., 1998. The Asian debt and development crisis of 1997: causes and consequence. World Dev. 26 (8), 1535–1553.
Wells, L.T., 1983. Third world multinationals: the rise of foreign investment from developing countries. The MIT Press, Cambridge, MA.

Werferfelt, B., 1984. A resource-based view of the firm. Strateg. Manag. J. 5 (2), 171–180.
Wojtkiewicz, A., 2015. Internationalization and internalization theories as tools for assessing the effects of companies' internationalization. Actual Problems Econ. 167 (5), 32–38.
Wong, J., 2011. A relational view of resources-based theory: the case of internationalization of Li & Fung group. J. Hum. Resource Adult Learn. 7 (2), 34–39.
Yeung, H.W.C., 1994. Transnational corporations from Asian developing countries: their characteristics and competitive edge. J. Asian Bus. 10 (4), 17–58.

CHAPTER 5

Internationalization Strategies of ASEAN Firms

N. Thirawat
Mahidol University International College, Nakhon Pathom, Thailand

5.1 INTRODUCTION

For decades, the internationalization of multinational enterprises (MNEs) has become a key issue in the field of international business studies. Internationalization has generally been defined as the process of a firm "increasing engagement in international operations overseas" and "adaptation and development in terms of operations and organizational principles (including, strategies, structure, and resources) to new environments" (Welch and Luostarinen, 1988; Calof and Beamish, 1995; Cavusgil, 1984). Beginning with pioneer researchers in the 1950s and 1960s, early academic work focused on environmental factors and institutions that influenced an organization's internationalization process and organizational management at the macro level, rather than the microeconomic industrial organization (such as a firm's unique assets) or managerial and strategic issues as proposed in more recent studies (Pisoni et al., 2014).

Internationalization is the process of cross-border business expansion, which requires changes in perspective and business positioning. As a result, internationalization strategies center on changing perspectives and/or organizational positions (Melin, 1992). In this research, internationalization strategies are divided into two types: international strategies and global strategies.

According to Twarowska and Kąkol (2013), international strategies and global strategies are different. Based on their study, an international strategy is defined as "the growth of subsidiaries acting and operating independently as if they are local companies, with minimum engagement of the parent company." On the other hand, "global strategy" refers to a wide variety of business strategies and adaptations to the local business environment that can be flexibly applied throughout the globe. Therefore, a global strategy not only covers strategies for subsidiaries, but also the whole network of

Internationalization and Managing Networks in the Asia Pacific
http://dx.doi.org/10.1016/B978-0-08-100813-3.00005-5

subsidiaries and partners worldwide. More specifically, global strategies require higher degrees of engagement and coordination from headquarters compared to international strategies because a firm's strategic activities in different locations must be planned and conducted interdependently at the global level. In terms of product standardization, an international strategy is designed to respond to local business needs; therefore, modifications of products, services, and production processes are necessary. Global strategic plans, on the other hand, are generally a framework for standardizing operations and products in every country. With regard to strategy integration and competitive actions, international strategies allow subsidiaries to independently plan and execute competitive plans in accordance with the analysis of local rivals or on a "stand-alone basis," while global strategies emphasize competition at the global level (Yip, 2002). This chapter regards both types of strategies as internationalization strategies.

This chapter explores major contemporary concepts in the area of international business studies in the 21st century, which is "internationalization strategies," coupled with case studies of MNEs within the Association of Southeast Asian Nations (ASEAN) region.

5.2 THEORIES INFLUENCING INTERNATIONALIZATION STRATEGIES

In terms of theories driving international business expansion strategies, there are three theoretical models commonly cited by academics and thinkers: Vernon's (1966) product life cycle model, Johanson and Vahlne's Internationalization Process Model (1977), and Dunning (1988).

Vernon's (1966) product life cycle model is a combination of the country-based perspective and an individual firm's perspective on international trade and investment through emphasis of product innovation, economies of scale, and uncertainty in international trade patterns. According to Vernon, the product life cycle has several stages that influence internationalization of MNEs and the product itself. The first stage, known as the introduction stage, is where the product is developed domestically. From there, it suggests that exports of the product allow better economies of scale in terms of manufacturing. As export activities grow and foreign direct investments in overseas production bases are established in host countries with increasing product demand, the cycle enters into the growth stage of the model. The next level, or maturity stage, is where main markets are fully prospered and the product is standardized. Here, production is relocated to other host countries with lower labor costs, higher demand, or better technology. Ultimately, when the manufacture (as well as demand, in some cases) departs the country where the product was originally invented, the project hits the decline stage, the last portion of the model.

Johanson and Vahlne's Internationalization Process Model (1977) or Uppsala model illustrates two major stages of internationalization that are important components of a company's strategic planning. The first stage comprises the selection of new foreign markets for international expansion, based on geographical proximity. It suggests that firms initially tend to favor host countries close by, and then move to more physically remote countries at a later stage, after gaining sufficient experience and knowledge from previous overseas business activities. The resource commitments in each selected host country eventually increase when firms progressively obtain valuable experience in each location. It can therefore be inferred that the internationalization process of firms starts with successes in domestic markets, and then commences to progress into the neighboring countries. From there, businesses tend to extend their operations to more destinations farther away, as there are fewer obstacles in terms of bilateral collaboration between neighboring countries or countries that have similar culture or institutions. Generally, these MNEs enter new markets through exports, and eventually take on progressively challenging activities (Wojtkiewicz, 2015).

The eclectic paradigm, as coined by Dunning (1988), was created to display motives as well as the location and internationalization channels of a firm's international expansion efforts (Ferreira et al., 2013). According to his latter research in 1993, Dunning summarized the three aspects of internationalization and four motives for internationalization that influence strategic planning.

The three elements that form the eclectic paradigm are ownership advantages, location advantages, and internationalization advantages. Ownership advantages, which are the first type of competitive advantage, refers to those that companies own and that can be transferred to host countries. These usually consist of particular resources, skills, or assets that can constitute value to their goods and/or services as a result of advanced technology, effective management, and efficient production processes. Location advantages are specifically gained from certain locations, especially in nearby countries; examples include low production costs, better market access, and know-how. The last aspect is internalization advantages, which refer to profits and advantages gained from a company's internal production rather than through partnership agreements such as licensing or joint ventures.

Internationalization further consists of four motives, categorized by Dunning (1993) as resource seeking, market seeking, efficiency seeking, and strategic asset seeking. He said firms generally attempt to invest or operate overseas in order to access natural resources, raw materials, and other production necessities in more favorable environments, known as resource seeking. Furthermore, a considerable number of companies seek to operate in foreign countries in order to expand customer bases (market seeking) or to improve efficiency by escalating productivity through increasing plants (efficiency seeking). Lastly, new operational environments can also offer skills, resources, and personnel capabilities necessary for heightening business competitiveness (strategic asset seeking). These motives are embedded in each international strategy, respectively discussed in Section 5.3.

Another approach for analyzing internationalization strategies of MNEs is to study the strategies of different kinds of firms and their strategic options. Tsai and Eisingerich (2010) categorized internationalization strategies in accordance with various types of firms in their research entitled "Internationalization Strategies of Emerging Markets Firms."

The first kind of international firms is "regional exporters and/or importers." These geographically focused firms gain competitive advantages by responding to customers' demands in specific regions (usually geographically nearby) through application of cheap resources. Regional exporters/importers tend to limit themselves to markets in developing countries because these companies do not have adequate firm-specific knowledge and marketing capability to compete at the international level. Furthermore, it requires lower costs and less risk to enter developing markets due to lower levels of competition compared to countries where the economy is well developed or in faraway countries.

The second type of international firms is "global exporters and importers." Firms in this category concentrate on import and export activities worldwide in order to exploit new market opportunities so they have more competitive advantages than regional exporters/importers. Global exporters/importers usually have adequate marketing competencies, but do not engage in high-value-adding activities, for example, developing research and development (R&D) in order to receive their own patents because they still have insufficient firm-specific knowledge. Furthermore, they differ from multinational challengers as they are limited to inbound and outbound logistics.

Third, "multinational challengers" refer to firms from emerging markets that have extra resources and capabilities to compete with MNEs from developed countries by serving a group of markets with the products manufactured, processed, and/or distributed by their internal potential. These enterprises are attentively operative in foreign markets and predominantly involved in high-value-adding activities like R&D and branding because they possess high levels of expertise and marketing competence.

The last type of international enterprises mentioned in Tsai and Eisingerich's (2010) study is original equipment/design manufacturing. Companies in high-tech industries from emerging markets like India or Taiwan are called "born-global firms," owing to their advances in informational and communication technologies that allow rapid internationalization at a very early stage. Compared to other types of international firms, original equipment or design manufacturing companies tend to be more knowledge intensive and specialized in contractual production activities due to their limited capital.

Even though implementing a fundamental strategy is crucial to the MNEs' achievement, top executives should consider strategic options in case they need to cope with an unpredictable future. To create strategic options, it is necessary to:

1. *Recognize long-term growth.* Firms in general must consider and implement strategies with the future in mind. For example, in order to achieve sustainable long-term growth, pharmaceutical enterprises or medical device enterprises need to execute sustainable strategies that require the newest creations of applicable drugs and devices for future use.
2. *Conduct risk and crisis management.* Predicting future emergencies is highly important for each enterprise. CEOs must realize industry/market changes or consumer tendencies on a consistent basis in order to mitigate the potential crises and survive at the international level.
3. *Build up socially responsible investments.* Socially responsible investments have become critical for MNEs that desire to gain more recognition in markets. Nowadays, consumers have become well informed and concerned about the goods they buy due to advanced social networking and wider reaching communication channels. To create branding and expand social capital, many MNEs decide to invest in public projects for social benefit as well as the benefit of the company's customers and stakeholders. Some examples of public projects include religious campaigns and expression of freedom, human rights, environmental responsibility, labor rights, and product safety.
4. *Preserve a healthy company culture.* A strong company culture can help MNEs augment productivity and unity within organizations. It can also

encourage good morale and an overall sense of community. Common characteristics of good company culture are diversity, fairness, respect in ideas, pride in roles, and equal opportunities. To sustain a healthy internal culture, companies may provide stock benefits to the employees, give them evident recognition, or invest in employee training.

These aforementioned elements demonstrate the need to distinguish personal bias from objective data (Fung, 2014).

5.3 CONTEMPORARY INTERNATIONALIZATION STRATEGIES

This section presents internationalization strategies of modern firms from different dimensions, using case studies of ASEAN firms that applied these strategies to their global business expansion.

5.3.1 Internationalization Strategies in Entry Dimension

Based on the study entitled "International Business Strategy: Reasons and Forms of Expansion into Foreign Markets" written by Twarowska and Kąkol (2013), there are a number of foreign market entry strategies, which can result in a different degree of risk and require different commitment levels from MNEs. More specifically, the two main entry modes for international expansion include a nonequity mode that covers export and contractual agreements like licensing and franchising, and an equity mode that involves joint ventures and wholly owned subsidiaries. Implementing an international development strategy in general involves a process of several steps, starting from indirect exports to more committing agreements.

One of the most common internationalization strategies in the nonequity mode is import and export of products and services. Exporting refers to the process of trading goods or services manufactured in a country to other destinations, which can further be classified into direct and indirect types. Direct export refers to MNEs directly involving themselves in marketing goods and services in oversea markets, whereas indirect exports refer to the process in which products are transported across borders by other agents and firms, without any special activities adapted to the international market; this is because the foreign sale is handled in the same way as in the domestic market. An example of this is Charoen Pokphand Foods PCL (CPF), a leader in the Thai agro-industrial and food business for both domestic consumption and exports. At present, the enterprise's international activities cover 13 countries via subsidiaries in China, Vietnam, Turkey,

India, Malaysia, the United Kingdom, Laos, Russia, the Philippines, Taiwan, Belgium, and Tanzania. The company also set up an associated company in Cambodia. Financial transactions carried out by CPF circulated in both domestic and foreign currencies; these foreign currencies were derived from exports and profits retrieved from overseas investments. In the same manner, the group spent foreign currencies to import raw materials, machines, equipment, and new investments across borders (Charoen Pokphand Foods, 2014).

Licensing is also a nonequity-mode strategy in which firms enter a foreign market at a low risk level. An international licensing agreement requires the firm to grant and/or transfer patent rights, trademark rights, copyrights, and know-how on merchandise and production processes to the licensee. In exchange for those grants, the licensee will manufacture the licensor's goods, market them in the assigned area, and pay the licensor fees and royalties concerning the sales volume of the goods. This kind of contractual agreement is usually appreciated by the host country's authorities as it contributes to the host country's development, especially in technology. There remain few cases of ASEAN firms as licensors, compared with the quantity of licensees in the market. An example of an ASEAN firm as a licensee is provided in the report written by Askew (2015). The news stated that Singapore-based Frase and Neave Company had secured a licensing deal with Nestle, a major multinational food and beverage enterprise from Switzerland, to produce and distribute the Carnation, Bear Brand, Bear Brand Gold, Ideal Milk, and Milkmaid products among ASEAN member countries. This license was agreed effective for 11 years and 7 months, by which the company would be able to extend a term of 10 years up until the end of Jan. 2037. As cited in the same report, Dato Ng Jui Sia, the CEO of Frase and Neave's nonalcoholic beverages division, remarked that Nestle's Carnation and Bear brands currently had a solid customer base in ASEAN, so she believed that the company still had massive regional potential. In addition to this, Frase and Neave Company planned to invest USD 9.2 million in a new filling and packaging line at its production base in Thailand to manufacture Carnation evaporated milk in 2015.

Another nonequity-mode internationalization strategy is franchising. This type of strategy resembles licensing except for the fact that the franchising organization is usually directly engaged in the development and supervision of the marketing activities. Similar to licensing, this system is operated in the way that semiindependent business owners (franchisees) pay fees and royalties to the parent company (franchisor) in exchange for the right to trademark, copyright, and sell goods or services, including the right to use the business format and operational system. Franchising agreements often last longer than licensing agreements, and franchisors generally provide a wider compilation of rights and resources needed for operating business like the franchisor, such as equipment, managerial systems, operation manuals, training guidelines, site approvals, and so on. Another difference between licensing and franchising is that licensing includes intellectual property and trade secrets, while franchising is restricted to trademarks and operational know-how. International franchising offers a number of advantages such as low political risk, low cost, simultaneous expansion into various parts of the world, higher potential of financial investment, and managerial capabilities. Nonetheless, this strategy also poses weaknesses, which are paving the way for future competitors (former franchisees), lower demand of capable franchisees or engaging into agreements with incapable candidates with potential to ruin the company's name and reputation, and higher capital costs for investment (in comparison with other modes like exporting and licensing). For instance, the Pho24 is one of the main divisions of the Nam An Group, an authentic Vietnamese food company and a Vietnamese MNE. The company consists of a variety of brands regulated under its administration, such as Maxim's and Terrace Café. In 2011, there were 52 Pho24 stores in Vietnam and 21 stores outside the country, including those in South Korea, Cambodia, the Philippines, Hong Kong, Macau, Australia, and Indonesia. About 34% of stores in Vietnam were franchised, compared with entire international operations (toward the use of master franchising agreements). Sales value from the whole franchise system was USD 12 million in 2010, so the company planned to increase the quantity of stores in Japan, China, and the United States during 2011–12 (Frazer and Merrilees, 2012).

On the other hand, equity-mode strategies like foreign joint ventures are common forms of internationalization. Different from licensing, MNEs in joint ventures have an equity position and management authority in the foreign host company. With this strategy, a partnership between the parent company and host country firm is established, often giving rise to the formation of a third company. Joint ventures allow MNEs to have better control over operations and deeper access to local market information. As a result, there is a lower exposure of risk expropriation owing to close relationships with local firms and avoidance of control problems, unlike other forms of foreign market entry strategies. Host country firms also play a significant role in supporting integration of MNEs in a foreign environment.

To illustrate, Krungsiam Beverage Company Limited incorporated its energy drink line, Commando, to India via joint venture with Poorav Group, which became the sole importer of Commando energy drinks from Thailand. This strategic move aimed to compete with Red Bull, which dominates the present market and fulfills demand for the growing energy drink market in India. The market has seen a 15%–20% growth rate annually due to increased popularity among the younger generation, particularly as a drink mixer with alcohol bases, like how Red Bull pulled out in the market (Thai Energy Drink Commando, 2014).

Another major equity mode is strategic alliances. This refers to an array of cooperative agreements between enterprises, which include collaborative research, formal joint ventures, and minority equity participation. Contemporary strategic alliances have three main characteristics: they are formed by companies from highly industrialized countries, they have a purpose to formulate new products and technologies rather than distributing current ones, and they are usually initiated for temporary periods. A main goal of strategic alliances is technology exchange because innovations are created by interdisciplinary development; it is challenging for a single enterprise to have adequate resources and capabilities to accomplish research and development targets effectively. However, strategic alliances can bring about the risk of competitive cooperation, as one or both partners may attempt to utilize the alliance to take advantage of the other. As an illustration, according to the research entitled "Alliance Formation, Partner Diversity, and Performance of Singapore Startups" conducted by Pangarkar and Wu (2013), the majority of the case firms (57.9% out of 76), which were Singaporean Internet companies, had formulated 80% or higher of strategic alliances with either Singapore-based or international organizations, primarily owing to more demand for management, time, and expertise posed by international alliances. Moreover, the case firms in the same study affirmed that strategic alliances benefited them in the form of enhanced credibility and reputation, enhanced marketing, and wider access to technology and know-how. It should be noted that such skills are not easy acquired and are often shared through firm alliances only. The case companies suggested that strategic alliances were least advantageous in terms of managerial skills and capital; still, the majority confirmed that strategic alliances had considerable influence on performance.

Finally, international enterprises generally form direct investment, which is an equity-mode internationalization strategy in a production unit overseas; this requires the largest amount of commitment, as there is 100%

ownership. Direct investments can be classified into two main types: direct acquisition in the host market and green field investment. The first type, direct acquisition, is attractive as it allows quick access to foreign markets and has lower risks than green field investment because it is easier to precisely estimate the results of an acquisition. A green field investment, on the other hand, refers to the founding of a new wholly owned subsidiary. Though complicated and requiring large investment (in other words, the costs of setting up a new business in a foreign country also pose a high risk), green field investment grants full control to the company and provides above-average returns. Furthermore, this strategy is time-consuming, as the firm has to install new operations, distribute networks, and implement suitable marketing strategies to gain competitiveness in the new market. In the Southeast Asian region, with regard to forms of outward foreign direct investments from Malaysia, it is generally suggested that the quantity of Malaysian MNEs has increased compared to the total number of global outflows of foreign direct investments, particularly to neighboring ASEAN member countries. Malaysia's share of the total outward foreign direct investments in Southeast Asia rose by 11% (from 8% to 18%) between 1990 and 2013 (Yean et al., 2015). An example of a Malaysian MNE highly active in foreign direct investments is PETRONAS. PETRONAS (Petroliam Nasional Berhad), a Malaysian national oil and gas company founded in 1974, has invested abroad since the 1990s, having established hundreds of affiliates and associated companies in more than 30 countries. The company's foreign investments in 2010 were reported to value USD 7.34 billion. Such vast investment facilitated the company to engage in a greater array of international activities, further increasing and maintaining Malaysia's oil and gas reserves (Yean et al., 2015).

5.3.2 Internationalization Strategies in R&D and Technology Transfer Dimension

Research and development (R&D) strategies are a basic element for lifelong development of MNEs. As stated in the study conducted by Belderbos et al. (2012), MNEs that had R&D across borders tended to have a productivity advantage over domestic firms. This conformed to the idea that companies generally become multinational in order to exploit greater intangible assets such as management skills and technological know-how. However, firms have to deal with additional costs of international establishment and the possible opportunity costs derived from foreignness.

There are four fundamental internationalization strategies in terms of research and development (Le Bas, 2007). The first strategy is foreign direct investments in R&D. This type of strategy aims to reduce disadvantages gained from a specific kind of technology in the home country by selecting a host country with acknowledged capabilities in selected technologies. The second strategy is how firms use their domestic strengths to invest in R&D in order to make use of corporative specifics in foreign environments, mainly in countries where there is inadequacy of the specific technology. Furthermore, firms internationalize their R&D efforts by focusing on technologies that hold advantages in both home and host countries. This means firms will get into the dynamic learning process and eventually build their own technological capital. The last strategy is referred to as the market-oriented technology strategy, which concentrates on foreign direct investments in the field of research and development. Firms tend to use this strategy in response to situations where they decide to invest in technologies overseas when neither the home or host country can offer technological advantages. Thus, this strategy is not technologically oriented, but usually results from mergers and acquisitions.

Recent studies have supported the success of R&D and technology strategies for internationalization. According to Belderbos et al. (2012), if corporate headquarters are able to utilize and integrate foreign knowledge and R&D into operations, overall performances will improve. In their study, an example of successful R&D is cited from Iwasa and Odagiri (2004). It found that R&D in US branches of Japanese companies had positive impacts on parent companies due to the availability of specific technological strengths in the United States. According to the research conducted by Merdzanovska (2015), approximately 98% of 700 case firms that were leading companies in the field of R&D were MNEs. Based on the same study, these firms had 69% share in the total R&D business; this included major MNEs like Ford and Siemens that even invested in R&D in amounts more than the total costs of some developed states such as Spain, Switzerland, and Israel. Clearly, innovative development activities were operated not only in home countries, but also in other parts of the world. In other words, technology transfer plays an important role in internationalization because it is one of the main reasons MNEs globalize through licensing, joint ventures, production cooperation, franchising, direct investments, and so on. Because technology transfer can provide know-how, experience, and even equipment under various circumstances, MNEs seek not only home, but also foreign sources of technology to gain competitiveness.

In the study entitled "Technology Transfers and Knowledge Management in Developing Economies: Case Study of an Indonesian Manufacturer" written by Wibowo (2013), Trias Sentosa Tbk PT (TRST) Company, an average Indonesian polypropylene and polyester films producer, is presented as evidence of the impact of international technology transfers on the development of local technological capabilities of the local enterprise. The study ratified international technology transfers as a method to enhance and facilitate technical license support, capital merchandise import, technical consultancy, foreign direct investment, and involvement in foreign markets. This logically supported the motivation of internationalization using R&D and technology transfer strategies. Nonetheless, to maximize development of technological capabilities, it suggested that local firms should expend more on in-house research and development activities as well as upgrade knowledge management systems.

5.3.3 Internationalization Strategies in Diversification Dimension

Presently, diversification strategies are perceived as highly crucial for internationalization. It is not a trend but a logical move for increasing profitability, risk reduction, enlarging market share, maximizing debt capacity, boosting growth, extending business life cycles, and accessing human and financial resources (Elabdin Ahmed, 2015). According to Merdzanovska (2015), MNEs tend to apply diversification strategies to international expansion, including when there is a possibility of decreased business growth, when companies want to expand into industries with advanced technologies and when companies are reputable enough to expand into alternative businesses.

To design a diversification strategy, one must consider the location of production, technology, manufacturing (for new technology lines), and multinational diversification (Li and Yue, 2008). Specifically speaking, firms tend to diversify manufacturing locations in order to internationalize their production, for example, by locating manufacturing operations in different states. Firms may also diversify similar merchandise by production with different technologies. Then, in order to diversify the manufacturing process, firms usually produce goods with new technology lines, but using the same technologies. Finally, multinational diversification is a strategy that combines all other strategies; it enables the production of new goods with new technologies, at new locations.

Diversification strategies are more common among developing countries. The reason behind this is that firms performing in developed economies incur higher costs of diversification compared to benefits (as cited by Yigit and Behram, 2013). Similarly, effective markets in developed countries discover and find diversification costs more than less effective markets in institutionally developing countries, as this requires more costs on firm restructuration in agreement to open market institutions. On one hand, firms from developed countries can use the strategy effectively if they seek to gain particular resources rather than generic resources, due to the fact that they can exploit benefits from economies of scope. Still, some researchers argued that firms from developed economies gained sustainable competitive advantages from firm-specific resources only, suggesting that they should focus on one industry or at least on a restricted number of related businesses (Yigit and Behram, 2013).

The study done by Chen and Ho (2000) illustrated Singaporean enterprises benefiting from the establishment of capital markets through diversification. Based on the study, Singapore-based companies needed to diversify by establishing internal capital markets due to the country's small-sized and open national economy. However, it also found that diversified companies were valued less than single-segment companies; multisegment companies are valued less only in the case of low insider ownership. This is because if managers have lower ownership stakes in their companies, they are likely to pursue value-reducing diversification comparative to those with a higher number of stakes; thus private interests may overshadow value loss from diversification.

5.3.4 Internationalization Strategies in the Product-Pricing Dimension

Brouthers et al. (2005) cited Day's (1990) hypothesis that there are three major generic product strategies: economy, value, and premium strategies. When a firm's product is considered to have higher prices with higher quality in comparison with other competitors' products, it can be implied that the firm is using the premium strategy. The economy strategy, on the other hand, refers to the application of lower-relative-price quality products, and the value strategy results from low-price/high-quality (superior value) or high-price/low-quality (inferior value) combination products.

Their study applied the three generic product strategies to formulate a global product strategy. They advocated that regional differences in costs, business environment, competitive structures, and the like brought about the development of different perceptions of typical home-country product strategies between countries. For instance, they concluded that Japanese firms widely used the superior value strategy, the United States commonly utilized the economy strategy, and the European Union widely adopted the premium strategy. According to the previous literature cited in the same study, the MNEs that followed these three regional stereotypes (superior value, economy, and premium strategy) performed better than domestic firms and had higher levels of profits that other multinationals that utilized other product strategies.

In the ASEAN context, the economy strategy is emphasized, as ASEAN products are considered to have relatively low technical capacity and often poor quality and low price, similar to most emerging markets. The common strategic plan of ASEAN MNEs is to maximize the market share, which leads to higher sales volume and lower unit costs, resulting in long-term profits (Kotler et al., 2010). According to Rajiani and Buyong (2013), successfully exported Malaysian articles are usually positioned in the low-price section in the markets. Case studies of Air Asia and Proton were used for illustrating successful application of the economy strategy and value strategy, respectively. It found that these enterprises had a cost advantage compared to other foreign companies, due to lower R&D and product development rates, lower capital costs, and lower costs of restructuration. In other words, these kinds of MNEs focused on particular driving factors such as seeking advantages overseas, gaining governmental support, and subsidization, increasing sales volume, and enhancing cost efficiency in production. In the case of Air Asia, a Malaysian airline awarded the best global low-cost airline prizes, the study certified that a vast quantity of Malaysian exporters were inspired by Air Asia's success and were thus motivated to apply the economy strategy due to the mentioned driving factors, believing that a low-price strategy was a key competitive advantage. In contrast, Proton, a Malaysian national car producer, focused more on acquiring managerial skills and human resources, accomplishing international reputation, and brand recognition and enhancing products and technologies in order to achieve high-price/low-volume products. To illustrate, in 2012, Proton Prevé, under the design of Italian Lamborghini, was released. It became the premier Malaysian car, awarded the full five-star safety judged by the Australasian New Car Assessment Program of Australia and New Zealand. In summary, Malaysian enterprises are likely to reposition from "high-volume production focusing on cost efficiency and low price" to "high-price segment focusing on innovation and technology selective niches" due to the fact that they will eventually lose labor cost advantages (compared with other ASEAN countries) and would face more intense domestic competition. Therefore in the long run, Malaysian firms may need to redesign strategies to narrow down their core industries within a worldwide scope.

5.3.5 Internationalization Strategies in the Subsidiaries Dimension

This subsection reviews the roles of subsidiaries in the overall strategy of MNEs. Stopford and Wells (1972) stated that most MNEs tend to develop a resemblance in organizational structures if they have similar strategies, even though they are in different industries. Based on their study, after early stages of international structure development with autonomous subsidiaries, firms usually set up an international business division in order to heighten control and coordination of their expanding overseas operations. This division administers all international activities and later becomes the essence of international expertise. Subsequently, when the division grows and the total sales increase, MNEs need to "go global" with a global perspective. Once firms have decided to expand their business operations on an international scale, new structures of their international divisions are constructed into two forms: worldwide product division and geographic area division. Worldwide product division refers to high diversification of products in which each domestic product division is responsible for the worldwide activities of each particular line of products. On the other hand, area divisions focus on geographic diversity in which each of them is responsible for a particular geographic region of the world.

According to the research by Pisoni et al. (2014), three major types of subsidiaries should be taken into account in terms of international business expansion. These kinds of subsidiaries are characterized by different geographic scopes, range of value-adding activities, and level of autonomy. The first type of subsidiary that plays a role in MNE internationalization is called the local implementer (or "miniature replica," as coined by White and Poynter (1984)). It is a subsidiary, principally operating in the host country to manage the whole range of value-adding activities of the headquarters. The local implementer generally adjusts a company's global products to local market demands; this can be called a multidomestic strategy. Second, the specialized contributor is a subsidiary regulating firm's particular specialization activities. In other words, this kind of subsidiary is specialized in a particular set of value-adding activities that are firmly united with the activities operated by other subsidiaries under the firm's international network. This strategic subsidiary is also referred to as a product specialist, owing to a series of value-adding activities. The last type of strategic subsidiary mentioned in the research is the world mandate. This is a subsidiary cooperating with the headquarters to advance and implement strategies. Strictly speaking, this subsidiary's activities are unified on the global scale, but individually administered by the subsidiary itself; hence, this kind of subsidiary is featured by worldwide integration and local receptivity.

On the other hand, Bartlett (1986) offered another approach to internationalization through subsidiaries. His work also highlights the coordination among subsidiaries like Porter (1986), but takes more consideration on the degree of adaptation to local context. In other words, a company can carry out various strategies in each subsidiary that best fits the parent company's overall strategy. This conforms to Jarillo and Martinez's (1990) study in which the geographical localization of activities such as R&D, manufacturing, and marketing, as well as the degree of integration of these activities operated at international level, influence the organization's decision. In reference to the research, firms may decide to follow an autonomous strategy (which means it independently regulates most of the operations in the value chain), receptive strategy (which means it operates only a few value chain activities in the host country), or active strategy (which means it acts as the center of the unified network of subsidiaries that perform diverse activities within the group). According to Bartlett (1986), there are three types of organizations influencing these strategies: global organizations, multinational organizations, and transnational organizations.

An example of an ASEAN subsidiary is Thoresen Thai Agencies Public Company Limited. One of the purposes for this firm setting up subsidiaries was to expand fleet size to assist accumulative revenue growth. Thoresen Thai Agencies' management team had serious intentions to enlarge the size of the company's fleet of rigs and vessels in order to promote long-range offshore services. The evidence of this strategic plan is in the addition of new shipping vessels made by the company's subsidiary in Singapore (Thoresen Shipping Singapore) in 2014, which raised the total number of the company's owned vessels to 24. This planned expansion of fleet size provided the firm opportunities to meet the rising demand of shipping services effectively (Thoresen Thai Agencies, 2015).

5.3.6 Internationalization Strategies in Branding Dimension

According to Lee et al. (2016), branding strategy refers to "the utilization of branded ingredient or component on merchandise by a brand." This strategy supported MNEs to achieve higher promotion efficiency, better access to distribution, higher quality, and higher profit margins. In general, MNEs are able to use the same brands to perform in all markets, modify them more or less, or develop whole new brands in order to respond to the different demands of each market. Based on another study conducted by Grębosz and Otto (2013), there are four main methods for launching a brand in a foreign market:

- project an existing brand
- develop and launch a new local brand by the enterprise itself
- purchase a local brand or get hands on a strong brand
- license a brand

The branding strategy is considered effective when it can facilitate consumers' decision-making process and reduce the image of risks from the products. Moreover, having a brand can secure the level of standardization of the firms' products/services (De Chernatony and McDonald, 1994). Another recent branding strategy is called cobranding. The cobranding of two brands can be accomplished when brand A is a relatively well-recognized brand in market X, but not in market Y; hence, brand A decides to collaborate with brand B, which is renowned in market Y. Therefore this strategy is highly useful for introducing a new brand internationally and significantly benefits both sides (Grębosz and Otto, 2013).

As an illustration, the cobranding marketing partnership between Thai Smile Airways, a subsidiary airline of Thai Airways International, the national airline of Thailand, and Cartoon Network Amazone, the world's first Cartoon Network themed waterpark located in Thailand, was a powerful strategic move for promoting Thailand's tourism industry in 2014; the move also partially helped the country reach its targets in terms of visitor arrivals and expenditure in 2015. According to the report published by the Tourism Authority of Thailand (2014), Mrs. Somrak Kumputch, Deputy Governor for Administration, Tourism Authority of Thailand believed that this partnership would appeal to more family travel and increase the average length of stay and daily expenditure of visitors to Thailand.

5.4 CONCLUSION

This chapter has reviewed the literature on contemporary internationalization strategies in many aspects, including the definition of internationalization strategies, related theories, internationalization strategies in various dimensions (entry, R&D and technology transfer, diversification, product pricing, subsidiaries/branding), international strategies classified by types of firms (regional exporter and importer, global exporter, and importer, multinational challenger, original equipment/design manufacturing), strategic options, and further criticism on how MNEs' structure follows their internationalization strategies. In this chapter, the examples used for illustrating each internationalization strategy are case studies of MNEs mainly from the Southeast Asian region, such as CPF, Frase and Neave Company, Krungsiam Beverage Company Limited, PETRONAS, TRST, Air Asia, Proton, Thoresen Thai Agencies, Pho24, and Thai Smile Airways. For successful implementation of internationalization strategies, strategic options that should be complied with the strategies include recognition of long-term growth, risk and crisis management, socially responsible investments, and strong company culture. Internationalization strategies of ASEAN MNEs discussed in this chapter provide insights on how these firms have evolved through time and caught up with multinationals from developed countries.

REFERENCES

Askew, K., 2015. F&N secures Nestle dairy licensing deal in ASEAN. Global News. 13.

Bartlett, C.A., 1986. Building and managing the transnational: the new organizational challenge. In: Porter, M.E. (Ed.), Competition in Global Industries. Harvard Business School Press, Boston, MA, pp. 367–401.

Belderbos, R., Gilsing, V., Lokshin, B., 2012. Persistence of, and interrelation between horizontal and vertical technology alliances. J. Manage. 38 (6), 1788–1811.

Brouthers, L.E., O'Donnell, E., Hadjimarcou, J., 2005. Generic product strategies for emerging market exports into triad nation markets: a mimetic isomorphism approach. J. Manag. Stud. 42 (1), 225–245.

Calof, J.L., Beamish, P.W., 1995. Adapting to foreign markets: explaining internationalization. Int. Bus. Rev. 4 (2), 115–131.

Cavusgil, S.T., 1984. Organizational characteristics associated with export activity. J. Manag. Stud. 21 (1), 1–22.

Charoen Pokphand Foods Public Company Limited SWOT Analysis, 2014. Charoen Pokphand Foods Public Company Limited SWOT Analysis, pp. 1–7.

Chen, S., Ho, K.W., 2000. Corporate diversification, ownership structure, and firm value: the Singapore evidence. Int. Rev. Financ. Anal. 9, 315–326.

Day, G.S., 1990. Market Driven Strategy. Free Press, New York.

De Chernatony, L., McDonald, M.H.B., 1994. Creating Powerful Brands. Butterworth-Heinemann, Oxford.

Dunning, J.H., 1988. The eclectic paradigm of international production: a restatement and some possible extensions. J. Int. Bus. Stud. 19, 1–31.

Dunning, J., 1993. The Globalization of Business. Routledge, London.

Elabdin Ahmed, A.Z., 2015. The role of diversification strategies in the economic development for oil-depended countries: the case of UAE. Int. J. Bus. Econ. Dev. 3 (1), 47–57.

Ferreira, M.A.S.P.V., Pinto, C.S.F., Serra, F.A.R., Santos, J.C., 2013. A bibliometric study of John Dunning's contribution to international business research. Rev. Bus. Manag. 15 (46), 56–75.

Frazer, L., Merrilees, B., 2012. Pioneering Asian Franchise brands: Pho24 in Vietnam. J. Mark. Channels 19 (4), 295–309.
Fung, A., 2014. International business strategies: a review and extension of theories. Chin. Econ. 47 (5/6), 116–130.
Grębosz, M., Otto, J., 2013. International expansion of brands by realization of co-branding strategy. J. Econ. Manage. 14, 77–87.
Iwasa, T., Odagiri, H., 2004. Overseas R&D, knowledge sourcing, and patenting: an empirical study of Japanese R&D investment in the US. Res. Policy 33, 807–828.
Jarillo, J.C., Martínez, J.I., 1990. Different roles for subsidiaries: the case of multinational corporations in Spain. Strategic Manage. J. 11 (7), 501–512.
Johanson, J., Vahlne, J., 1977. The internationalization process of the firm: a model of knowledge development on increasing foreign commitments. J. Int. Bus. Stud. 8, 23–32.
Kotler, P., Ang, S.H., Leong, S.M., Tan, C.T., 2010. Marketing Management: An Asian Perspective, Fifth ed. Prentice Hall, Singapore.
Le Bas, C., 2007. The determinants of home-based augmenting and home-base-exploiting R&D activities: some new results on multinationals' location strategies. In: DIME Workshop Juan-les-Pins, May 10th and 11th, Jan. 2007-01-23.
Lee, C.-H., Tseng, C.-L., Chu, K.-K., 2016. Exploring strategy fit of competition on foreign enterprise and brand strategy. Int. J. Organ. Innovation. 8 (3), 99–111.
Li, J., Yue, D.R., 2008. Market size, legal institutions, and international diversification strategies: implications for the performance of multinational firms. Manag. Int. Rev. 48 (6), 667–688.
Melin, L., 1992. Internationalization as a strategy process. Strateg. Manag. J. 13, 99–118.
Merdzanovska, M., 2015. The technology strategy of transnational companies. Econ. Dev. 17 (1/2), 361.
Pangarkar, N.B., Wu, J.J., 2013. Alliance formation, partner diversity, and performance of Singapore startups. Asia Pac. J. Manag. 30 (3), 791–807.
Pisoni, A., Cortili, M., Onetti, A., 2014. The internationalization strategies of Italian MNCs in India. Int. J. Transp. Manag. 19 (3), 227–243.
Porter, M.E., 1986. Competition in Global Industries. Harvard Business School Press, Boston, MA.
Rajiani, I., Buyong, E., 2013. Repositioning strategy for Malaysian companies internationalization. SE Asian J. Manag. 7 (1), 1–15.
Stopford, J.M., Wells Jr., L.T., 1972. Managing the Multinational Enterprise: Organization of the Firm and Ownership of the Subsidiary. Basic Books, NY.
Thai energy drink Commando now in India via JV with Poorav Group, pitted against Red Bull, targets sale of 1.2 L cans per day, 2014. FRPT- Retail Snapshot, p. 21.
Thoresen Thai Agencies Public Company Limited, 2015. Thoresen Thai Agencies PCL SWOT Analysis, pp. 1–8.
Tourism Authority of Thailand, 2014. TAT hails co-branding partnership between Thai Smile Airways and Cartoon Network Amazone. Accessed 20 February 2016. http://www.tatnews.org/tat-hails-co-branding-partnership-between-thai-smile-airways-and-cartoon-network-amazone/.
Tsai, H.-T., Eisingerich, A.B., 2010. Internationalization strategies of emerging markets firms. California Manage. Rev. 53 (1), 114–135.
Twarowska, K., Kąkol, M., 2013. International business strategy - reasons and forms of expansion into foreign markets. Active citizenship by knowledge management & innovation. In: Proceedings of the Management, Knowledge and Learning International Conference 2013, pp. 1005–1011.
Vernon, R., 1966. International investment and international trade in the product cycle. Q. J. Econ. 80 (May), 190–207.
Welch, L.S., Luostarinen, R., 1988. Internationalization: evolution of a concept. J. Gen. Manag. 14 (2), 34–55.

White, R.E., Poynter, T.A., 1984. Strategies for foreign-owned subsidiaries in Canada. Bus. Q. 49 (2), 59–69.

Wibowo, W., 2013. Technology transfers and knowledge management in developing economies: case study of an Indonesian manufacturer. J. Entrep. Manag. Innov. 9 (4), 5–27.

Wojtkiewicz, A., 2015. Internationalization and internalization theories as tools for assessing the effects of companies' internationalization. Actual Probl. Econ. 167 (5), 32–38.

Yean, T.S., Nee, T.Y., Yi, A.K.J., 2015. Outward foreign direct investment from Malaysia. J. SE Asian Econ. 32 (3), 358–374.

Yigit, I., Behram, N.K., 2013. The relationship between diversification strategy and organizational performance in developed and emerging economy contexts: evidence from Turkey and Netherlands. Eur. Bus. Rev. 3 (2), 121–136.

Yip, G., 2002. Total Global Strategy. Prentice-Hall, London.

CHAPTER 6

Global Supply Chain in Asia

O. Sivarak
Mahidol University International College, Nakhon Pathom, Thailand

6.1 INTRODUCTION

As the old saying goes, "A chain is only as strong as its weakest link." Business competition no longer exists between companies, but now presents itself between supply chains. Since the 1980s, foreseeing benefits of collaborative relationships, firms began to concentrate on supply chain management in order to compete effectively in the global environment (Lummus and Vokurka, 1999). For companies to be viable in supply chains, they must compete in terms of cost, quality, flexibility, agility, and customer responsiveness (Ibrahim et al., 2015).

Over time, the Internet, email, and other technologies have become universal, which has resulted in the expectations of consumers growing disparately. While the world becomes smaller and more connected, supply chains become longer and more complex. Companies expanding globally expect to take advantage of various opportunities offered by global supply chains. Simultaneously, companies are challenged with much diversity, especially in Asia. Balan et al. (2006) found that culture was the most critical factor impacting global supply chain management, while technology was the second-most critical factor. Foreseeing future trends in Asia will help companies adjust quickly to their global supply chain operations in order to perform at their full potential. This will benefit companies, supply chains, and the world as a whole.

6.2 DEFINITIONS

Definitions of supply chain have been proposed in literature and in practice by many scholars. Some researchers provide historical perspectives of supply chains, while others attempt to gather, report, and define supply chains.

La londe and Masters (1994) describe a supply chain as "the set of firms that pass materials forward."

Lummus and Alber (1997) define a supply chain as "the network of entities through which material flows." These entities may comprise suppliers, carriers, manufacturers, distribution centers, retailers, and customers.

Internationalization and Managing Networks in the Asia Pacific
http://dx.doi.org/10.1016/B978-0-08-100813-3.00006-7

Lummus and Vokurka (1999) provide a historical perspective of supply chains in "Defining supply chain management: a historical perspective and practical guidelines."

Mentzer et al. (2001) define a supply chain as "a set of three or more entities (organizations or individuals) directly involved in the upstream and downstream flows of products, services, finances, and/or information from a source to a customer."

Stock and Boyer (2009) gather and report several definitions of supply chain in "Developing a consensus definition of supply chain management: a qualitative study."

Verma and Boyer (2010) define a supply chain as a network of organizations that works together to convert and move goods from raw materials to the end customer.

Jacobs and Chase (2011) define a supply chain as "a process that moves information and material to and from the manufacturing and service processes of the firm."

Collier and Evans (2012) define a supply chain as "the portion of the value chain that focuses primarily on the physical movement of goods and materials, supporting the flow of information and financial transactions through the supply, production, and distribution processes."

Reid and Sanders (2013) define a supply chain as "the network of activities that delivers a finished product or service to the customer."

The Council of Supply Chain Management Professionals (2013) explains that a supply chain starts with unprocessed raw materials and ends with finished goods used by customers. The supply chain links many companies together. The materials and information are interchanged through the logistical process, from acquisition of raw materials to delivery of finished products. Venders, service providers, and customers are linked in the supply chain.

Heizer and Render (2014) define supply chains as suppliers, manufacturers, service providers, distributors, wholesalers, and retailers who deliver products and/or services to the final customers.

In general, the basic supply chain comprises suppliers, manufacturers, distributors, retailers, and customers. However, the parties involved and the complexity in chains vary between industries. It may be more accurate to refer to supply chains as a supply chain network. A "network" is a complex structure of cross-linked organizations with two-way exchanges between them; a "chain" is a simpler and sequential set of links (Harland et al., 2001).

Levels of supply chain complexity

Level 1: A direct supply chain

A direct supply chain comprises a company, supplier, and a customer involved in the upstream and/or downstream flows.

Level 2: An extended supply chain

An extended supply chain consists of suppliers of the immediate supplier and customers of the immediate customer. All are involved in the upstream and/or downstream flows.

Level 3: An ultimate supply chain

An ultimate supply chain includes all parties involved in the upstream and downstream flows, from the ultimate supplier to the ultimate customer.

In the ultimate supply chain, a third-party logistics (3PL) company, a financial provider, and a market research company may take part in supporting the ultimate supply chain.

Fig. 6.1 Levels of supply chain complexity (Mentzer et al., 2001).

Mentzer et al. (2001) proposed three degrees of supply chain complexity, including a direct supply chain, an extended supply chain, and an ultimate supply chain, presented in Fig. 6.1.

The flow of the supply chain embroils the physical flow of products and services, the information flow, and the financial flow. From suppliers to customers, the physical product flow includes the movement of goods and services, as well as customer returns or service needs in the reverse direction. The information flow involves order transmission and delivery status, whereas the financial flow consists of payment schedules, credit terms, and consignment arrangements.

The direction of the flow can be categorized as upstream and downstream. The upstream is the direction toward suppliers, while the downstream is directed toward customers.

All final products or services delivered into the hands of customers are the end results of every part of the supply chain. As products or services move from the origin to the destination, their value increases. The quality of products relies not only on any specific part, but also on all parts of the supply chain. The supply chain of palm oil is an example of how each party contributes to the value-added process of palm oil. From palm seeds, suppliers cultivate palm oil, refine it, and crush it through a palm processor. The raw palm oil is then passed on to the manufacturer to be processed and packaged as palm oil for final product delivery. The palm oil package will then be sent to wholesalers or put on shelves of retailers within or outside of the country. In the final stage, customers can then purchase palm oil for their meal preparation or other purposes.

6.3 SUPPLY CHAIN COLLABORATION

Apart from suppliers, manufacturers, distributors, and retailers, other stakeholders are also involved in the supply chain to facilitate the movement of the products, services, information, and money. These stakeholders are industry organizations, government agencies, and other players who have an interest or stake in the business and supply chain. Therefore the coordination and collaboration among every party of the supply chain is essential to success in bringing about customer satisfaction. Collaboration in the supply chain strengthens relationships and teamwork between members. Anthony (2000) states that supply chain collaboration occurs with the share of responsibility among two or more companies by exchanging common planning, management, execution, and performance measurement information.

Supply chain collaboration can be categorized into two main categories: vertical and horizontal collaboration (Barratt, 2004). Vertical collaboration includes customers and suppliers, while horizontal collaboration includes competitors and noncompetitors.

Many researchers have proposed frameworks for supply chain collaboration (Matopoulos et al., 2007; Simatupang and Sridharan, 2005; Gilmore, 2005). Simatupang and Sridharan (2005) proposed an integrative framework for supply chain collaboration, including five connecting features: collaborative performance systems, decision synchronization, information sharing, incentive alignment, and integrated supply chain processes.

Gilmore (2005) developed a simple framework for supply chain collaboration showing three levels of collaboration, as displayed in Fig. 6.2.

The benefits of collaboration can be seen in lower inventory levels, lower transportation and warehousing costs, fewer defective items or waste, lower stock-outs, shorter lead times, higher inventory turns, better customer service, and quicker decision-making.

On the other hand, important issues such as barriers around trust, real reengineering of processes between trading partners, and the allocation of benefits from true collaboration may arise with true collaboration (Gilmore, 2005). How these issues are addressed is vital to the success of the supply chain.

Framework for supply chain collaboration

Level 1: Transaction integration

The collaboration in level 1 involves basic business processes and transactions using the Internet, electronic data interchange (EDI), or proprietary tools. This is the execution level in which transactional data is exchanged between partners. The transactional data includes work orders, purchase orders, point-of-sale information, invoices, and payments.

Level 2: Information sharing

The same Internet, (EDI), or proprietary tools, as well as other tools, are used in level 2 to support better managerial decision-making. The information sharing includes component and product forecasting, capacity and transportation plans, orders, product descriptions, inventory, prices, and promotions.

Level 3: True collaboration or strategic collaboration

The collaboration in level 3 is true collaboration, in which trading partners plan and redesign processes together, and share risk and rewards. The collaboration in this level will help improve supply chain plans and forecasting accuracy, and resolve critical issues.

Fig. 6.2 Framework for supply chain collaboration (Gilmore, 2005).

6.4 INFORMATION AND COMMUNICATIONS TECHNOLOGY AND SUPPLY CHAINS

On top of stakeholders' collaboration, the flow of physical products and services, information, and finance has to be synchronized and orchestrated along the supply chain. The advancement of information and communications technology (ICT) is an enabler of speed and efficiency along the supply chain. Visibility and integration from true collaboration and information sharing through advanced ICT can help all parts of the supply chain have a better view and better ability to cope with demand and supply variations. Supply chain managers can be accountable and ensure tight control to stay ahead of the game. Significant investments have been made in enterprise software and systems, such as enterprise resource planning (ERP), material requirements planning (MRP), customer relationship management (CRM), and supply chain management (SCM) (Razmi et al., 2009).

MRP is an information system that converts the finished product requirements from the master schedule into time-phased requirements for subassemblies, component parts, and raw materials, and works backward from the due date using lead times and other information to determine when and how much to order (Stevenson and Sum, 2007). MRP supports companies with net requirements as well as time of the requirement.

ERP systems integrate all business functions into a single information system to provide storage, retrieval, analysis, and reporting ability in a timely manner. ERP allows the company to see a holistic view of business operations based on unified information, allowing the supply chain to respond promptly based on updated information.

CRM is a software solution that enables firms to collect specific data on customers (Reid and Sanders, 2013). CRM software allows companies to learn more about the needs and wants of customers. Behaviors of customers are also studied in order to build relationships and loyalty.

ICT gives supply chains the ability to understand business requirements and situations to be able to respond more timely and efficiently, and to remain competitive.

6.5 SIGNIFICANCE OF GLOBAL SUPPLY CHAINS

Globalization is changing the way companies and countries strive to be more efficient and to succeed in the world market. Globalization is defined as "a set of beliefs that fosters a sense of connectivity, interdependence, and integration in the world community" (Ali, 2001).

Globalization is also defined as the production and distribution of a homogeneous type and quality of products and services on a worldwide basis (Hodgetts and Luthans, 1994).

Business dictionary defines globalization as "the opening of local and nationalistic perspectives to a broader outlook of an interconnected and interdependent world with free transfer of capital, goods, and services across national frontiers."

Prasad and Sounderpandian (2003) define a global supply chain as "a series of firms networking and outsourcing throughout the globe."

The difference between global and local supply chains are that different parts of the supply chain are spread worldwide. Alternatives suppliers of raw materials, products, services, and labor can be found around the world, whereas customers located in different parts of the world have diverse requirements.

The advances in distribution systems and ICT allow companies to take advantage of a globally connected world. Potential benefits gained from globalization are gigantic and abundant. Companies will have opportunities to lower their operating costs, to enter larger and newer markets, to have access to resources, and to utilize knowledge and skills from anywhere in the world.

6.5.1 Lower Operating Costs

Large and small companies reduce their production costs by sourcing from low-cost countries and expand their revenue growth by selling internationally (Ruiz-Torres and Mahmoodi, 2008). Globalization also provides opportunities for companies to lower labor costs by moving parts of their operations overseas. For several years, many companies have moved their manufacturing facilities to China to acquire lower labor cost. As the cost of labor in China has increased over the past two years, growing by approximately 10% annually, companies are now searching for alternate sources. For example, in August 2011, Panasonic Corporation announced the closing of its lithium-ion battery factory in Beijing to cut 1300 jobs.

6.5.2 Larger or New Market Entry

Companies expand abroad to access larger or newer markets. They can benefit from shared infrastructure, research and development, services, and operations. Economies of scale can also be achieved. For example, Aditya Birla Group, a USD 41 billion multinational corporation based in India, employs 120,000 workers of 42 nationalities and operates in 36 countries, earning more than half of its revenue outside India.

6.5.3 Resource Accessibility

Globalization involves access to new and more resources. Each part of the world is rich in different natural resources. For example, Iran shares the richest reserves of gas fields with Qatar. The total amount of natural resources is worth almost USD 27.3 trillion. As Iranian companies plan construction of an Iran-Oman undersea gas pipeline in two years, seven foreign companies have declared interest to join them (Haghighati, 2016).

6.5.4 Knowledge and Skills Acquisition

Companies can locate their facilities in another country to be connected to knowledge and skills. For example, although the labor cost is high in Switzerland, Germany, and Japan, foreign companies establish their facilities to get access to highly skilled workers in financial services, technology, and engineering (Verma and Boyer, 2010).

6.5.5 Tax and Financial Incentives

To attract foreign investments, many countries have set up a free-trade zone or a tax-free area in their borders. The production within the area will be exempt from certain taxes or be entitled to a discount from taxes. For example, Thailand established several free-trade zones that allow companies operating within the country to be exempted from duties and tariffs on goods entering or leaving the country. Decision-making in supply chains related to types of operation and location are important in terms of tax and financial incentives toward company success.

6.5.6 Political Instability, Economic Crisis, Disasters, and Tragedies

Political instability, economic crisis, disasters, and tragedies that occur on one side of the world could affect the whole supply chain on the other side. Thailand is recognized as a global automobile production hub, especially for automakers in Japan. Due to the Thailand's flood crisis in 2011, Japanese automakers, namely Toyota, Honda, and Nissan, lost 240,000, 150,000, and 33,000 cars, respectively. Nissan took less time to recover compared to other automakers due to its diversified source of supply and globalized procurement system. The decrease in production also impacted the sales for trade partners importing cars from Thailand. The reduction in Thailand's automobile production influenced consumption of automobiles in Malaysia and Indonesia. Malaysia's automobile sales decreased by −25% until April 2012, and Indonesia's consumption also became negative in November 2011. Moreover, the import of transportation equipment from Thailand to the Philippines declined by 21.5% in 2011. The other assembly plants in Southeast Asia relying on parts from Thailand also faced shortages. This illustrates that the damages experienced by one party in the supply chain, such as suppliers, assembly plants, and warehouses, translate into damages across the supply networks. (Haraguchi and Lall, 2015). After Thailand's floods in 2011, many companies revised their operations. The lesson learned from the disasters relative to supply chains was not to put all eggs into one basket. Toshiba Thailand implemented dual or triple sourcing policies, including alternative modes and routes of delivery as risk management alternatives for potential future supply chain breaks from natural disasters.

6.6 SUPPLY CHAIN IN ASIA

Asia is the world's largest and most populous continent; a factor that most Asian countries have in common is rapid growth rate. Since the late

1970s, Asian economies have dramatically outperformed the rest of the world on growth in gross domestic product (GDP) per capita. Many global companies thus seek to exploit growth in Asia's markets by expanding their physical presence and organizing themselves regionally.

However, much diversity exists in Asian economies. Asian countries are a bewildering mixture of market sizes and maturity in development stages. Customers' tastes and preferences also evolve constantly. Several literatures have discussed the diversity in Asia. Ling (2014) categorized Asian countries into two groups by nature of the diversity. The first group was categorized by its rapid growth in cities that attract people from rural areas, while the second group gathered rapidly industrialized economies that attracted an international workforce. Countries' diversity in this continent, including ethnicity or race, religion, languages, purchasing power, infrastructure, and trade policy, creates more challenges for the supply chain. Guild (2009) pointed out that even the most sophisticated multinational companies must change significantly to realize potential growth in Asia.

6.6.1 Diverse Ethnicity or Race

A continent as immense as Asia, having the largest population of all continents, is bound to have vast variations in race and ethnicity. According to Rashidvash and Mirak (2015), almost every race in the world can be found in Asia. Skin colors vary from white to yellow and brown to black, and every shade between. Physique and facial appearance are also greatly dissimilar. Such physical dissimilarities can affect how companies offer products or services. The size, length, and width of products may not be standardized, or many stock keeping units may be coped in order to better respond to customers' requirements in the region. This leads to more complex product design and stock management systems along the supply chain.

6.6.2 Disparity of Religions

The Pew Research Center (2014) produced an index of religious diversity that ranked 232 countries on the Religious Diversity Index (RDI), using a 10-point scale in which the highest score indicated wider variety. The study was based on eight commonly recognized world religions: Buddhism, Christianity, Islam, Hinduism, Judaism, unaffiliated, folk religions, and other minorities. Asian countries, which were the majority of countries, had an RDI score of 7.0 and above. These countries were also grouped into six regions, where the Asia Pacific (RDI: 9.2) was the region with the highest religious diversity level, followed by Sub-Saharan Africa (RDI: 5.8), Europe

(RDI: 4.6), North America (RDI: 4.2), Latin America-Caribbean (RDI: 2.1), and Middle East-North Africa (RDI: 1.5). Customers' customs in Asia believe that disparity in religions could interrupt the normal supply chain routine. Adjustments in business and supply chain are required, as shown in the example of Muslims' holy month of Ramadan and Hindus' Diwali festival.

During the month of Ramadan, the ninth month in the Islamic calendar, Muslims cannot eat, drink, smoke, sex, tell lies, or even chew gum during the day (Mirsane and Shafagh, 2016). The fast begins before dawn and ends after dusk. Muslims stay up late to break their fast and get up early to finish breakfast. In some countries, the fast could last up to 20 hours. Restaurants and businesses may have to amend opening hours to suit prayer times. As people buy more food while breaking their fast in the evening, the demand for consumer goods, especially food, increases throughout the holy day. At the same time, workers' productivity may decline as a result of behavioral changes during Ramadan (Campante and Yanagizawa-Drott, 2015).

Hindus celebrate their ancient Diwali festival in autumn (northern hemisphere) or spring (southern hemisphere) every year. Diwali is also known as a festival of light. Many businesses can boost their demands with major sales promotions during this holiday. According to Khanna and Sampat (2015), Amazon's business in India grew manifoldly over the past few years during Diwali as online shopping gathered momentum throughout the country. With warehouse services and supply chain performance, India has become one of the fastest growing markets for the online retail industry.

6.6.3 Language Differences

Apart from English, Chinese, and Arabic, people in Asian countries converse in many other primary languages. English-speaking countries in Asia comprise Brunei, Darussalam, India, Pakistan, the Philippines, Singapore, and Sri Lanka, while Hong Kong, Macau, Tibet (Tibet Autonomous Region within the People's Republic of China), Singapore, and Taiwan (Republic of China) are predominantly Chinese-speaking countries. Many countries in the Middle East, including Bahrain, Iraq, Israel, Jordan, Kuwait, Lebanon, Oman, Palestinian territories, Qatar, Saudi Arabia, Syria, United Arab Emirates, and Yemen are Arab-speaking countries. Because there is no one common language in Asia, companies are forced to customize products' labeling and promotions to meet customers' language preferences. The communication among supply chain parties and directions relayed to line staff can be misunderstood or lost in translation. Different language preferences could also contribute to errors or mistakes.

6.6.4 Purchasing Power Incongruence

The gross national income per capita 2015 reported by the World Bank shows that Qatar's purchasing power parity is USD 140,720, while Cambodia's is a mere USD 3290. The GDP per capita for countries in Asia are also widely dispersed. According to the International Monetary Fund report in October 2015, the GDP per capita in Singapore (53,224) is about 30 times higher than in Lao People's Democratic Republic (PDR) (1785), about 40 times higher than in Myanmar (1269), and about 50 times higher than in Cambodia (1140). The wide diversity of purchasing power among Asian countries also affects the way companies customize their products and increases complexity in companies' supply chain management. Guild (2009) provided several instances, such as Procter & Gamble (P&G), Levi Strauss, and LG Electronics. P&G reengineered its premium products to focus on features and attributes valued most by Asian customers. By reducing the cost of packaging, which is less important to consumers than a wide choice of flavors, P&G was able to cut the price of Crest toothpaste in China by more than 50%. Levi Strauss was able to reach less affluent young consumers in China by allowing three-monthly installment payments for jeans priced over USD 33. LG cut the duration of order-fulfillment cycles in Asia from months to weeks to ensure freshness of the products and a quick response to trends.

6.6.5 Infrastructure Variation

In Asia, some countries such as Japan and Singapore have well-planned infrastructure, while others such as India and Indonesia are less planned. The movement of goods cannot be guaranteed in terms of delivery time and cost, as products traveling between provinces can be stopped unexpectedly at internal borders for inspection. The uncertainty may cause higher buffers in inventory or an attempt to increase productivity to lower initial costs. With no control over road construction, some companies relocate their manufacturing plants to serve their customers in megacities, treating them as separate markets, while other companies send their products to a single logistics platform, instead of many retailers, to transport their products together. With diverse infrastructure, exchange of information between supply chain parties is also challenging. Even though companies have systems in place for internal operations, many do not have similar structures to integrate or monitor data of their immediate and extended supplier network. Without quality infrastructure, transportation will incur higher costs, longer lead time, and lower agility and flexibility.

6.6.6 Dissimilarity of Trade Policies

Though there are many attempts to integrate Asian countries and their trade policies, there is still no unified custom process for countries in Asia. For example, the Association of Southeast Asian Nations (ASEAN) Economic Community was established in 2015 to create a unified market across ASEAN countries by harmonizing economic regulations, including trade procedures, financial capital flows, and labor migration. The ASEAN Economic Community (AEC) has 10 participating countries, including Brunei, Cambodia, Indonesia, Lao PDR, Malaysia, Myanmar, the Philippines, Singapore, Thailand, and Vietnam. DHL Trend Research (2016) found low participation in AEC by small and medium enterprises (SMEs) due to procedural complexity in applying for tariff preferences. The long transportation of goods between Malaysia and Thailand is also an example of trade policy dissimilarity. In spite of great connectivity between Malaysia and Thailand, there remains no agreement to allow seamless movement of vehicles. Long delays for onward shipment and the need for manual loading of goods also exist.

6.7 FUTURE TRENDS IN ASIA

Because of a fast-growing and continuously changing environment, Asia has been evolving rapidly and will continue to grow in the future. Companies are now looking into innovations, automation, robotics, and new technologies to manage their end-to-end supply chain. The future trends in Asia that affect the global supply chain will be discussed next.

6.7.1 E-commerce

E-commerce is defined as "the ability of businesses to buy and sell goods and services over the Internet" (Harsono, 2014). In the past few years, e-commerce has become more prominent. More and more people prefer to shop online, which causes more and more businesses to open their e-commerce channels. Briggs (2016) reported that e-commerce in Asia grew 32% in 2015. The Asia 500 web sales from about USD 411 billion were conducted through the seven largest online marketplaces. Rakuten and Alibaba accounted for an approximate 75% share of USD 835 billion in the Asia-Pacific e-commerce market. The total of 500 online sales was up to USD 220 billion, or 54% from 2014 to 2015. With USD 562.66 billion in sales projected for 2015, China became the biggest e-commerce market in the world. Chan et al. (2001) defines e-commerce as "the sale and purchase of goods or services by electronic means." E-commerce allows companies to extend their business, operating hours, and geographical area from limited industry, opening times, and locations in comparison to traditional commerce. For example, Amazon.com originated as an online bookstore, but quickly expanded to new markets and products such as music, videos, electronics, home and kitchen, clothing, and so on. Online customers can shop at any time and from anywhere. Transactions are completed via electronic means such as website, email, electronic data interchange, or electronic fund transfer instead of face-to-face operations between customers and sellers, and the processing time is tremendously reduced. The e-commerce trend will affect retailers and will alter overall supply chain management. E-commerce will affect how supply chains operate and how each component interacts. Supply chain challenges from the rise of e-commerce are also tense; the ability to access remote areas is one of them. Supply chain infrastructure needs to be broadly established in order to reach customers in rural areas. Furthermore, higher logistical cost will present itself from a large number of orders and return quantities. More importantly, security issues will also affect the willingness to shop online by many customers. E-commerce also opens the floor for SMEs to compete with multinational firms in the global economy. As exporters, tens of millions of SMEs worldwide have joined the e-commerce market, such as Amazon, eBay, Rakuten, Alibaba, and Flipkart (Manyika et al., 2016).

6.7.2 Automation and Robotics

Based on the Markets and Markets Report (2016), the market of automated material handling equipment is expected to grow at a compound annual growth rate of 7.9% between 2016 and 2022 and is expected to reach USD 44.68 billion by 2022, with the Asia Pacific as the leading and fastest growing market. Automation will provide flexibility and agility for an overstretched supply chain and support companies to gain opportunities from fast-growing Asian economies. Automated companies can reduce their operation time, maximize their productivity, and increase their process accuracy. Automation will allow companies to efficiently utilize their limited capacities and resources toward achieving their main objectives. Automation will also permit companies to allocate their labor for better skilled jobs. On the other hand, companies with scarce labor can be automated and operate at their full potential. For example, in 2015, about 40% of employers in Singapore reported talent shortage and various companies were faced with land scarcity and rising real estate costs. Many experienced third-party logistics (3PL) companies also offer automation technology to provide support in automated distribution centers and allow companies to use the same warehouse spaces to store more products and to achieve better inventory visibility.

In addition, companies are taking automation to a more advanced level by utilizing robotics. Amazon showed its commitment to robotics technology by acquiring Kiva Systems, which is worth USD 775 million, and opened Amazon robotics in 2012. While Amazon and many large corporations use advanced and luxurious automation and robots in their operations, many SMEs also adopt affordable robots to reduce their workforce size and increase their operations efficiency. With the USD 25,000 cost, Baxter robots can work for thousands of hours without stopping. O'Neil (2016) pointed out that Baxter robots can work more than 2000 hours continuously, at a rate that would not be possible with a human workforce. The same rate would require four 24-hour shifts that would cost, at a rate of USD 9 per hour, about 80% more than the entire cost of the robot. Robotics and automation are also used in the seafood industry to reduce production costs and increase product quality (Buljo and Gjerstad, 2013).

6.7.3 Augmented Reality

Augmented reality (AR) is a technology providing a seamless interface that bridges the gap between the virtual and real worlds (Behzadan et al., 2008). It superimposes digital information with the user's environment of the real world, such as image, sound, video, or GPS data generated on the user's view in real time. Since 1990, AR has been used in many industries, such as e-commerce, automotive, and architecture. Augmented reality has been used in retail and e-commerce to facilitate the purchasing process by helping customers virtually try on products quickly and easily. The design and construction can also be virtually viewed throughout the process. Together with a car's camera, radar, and GPS, drivers can be supported with augmented visual power for navigation, road features, points of interest, and possible dangers. Examples include Shiseido's makeup mirror, IKEA's AR catalog, Converse's shoe sampler, Ray-Ban's virtual fitting room, Burberry's beauty box, Autodesk's AutoCAD, Visidraft, IBM's augmented reality glass, and Hyundai's new virtual manual. In 2016, Pokémon Go went viral and became the most downloaded mobile application in the history of the App Store in the first week of its release. Using augmented reality, Pokémon Go fills the world with animated characters, attracting more than 20 million active users to chase after them and causing a worldwide obsession.

The common use of AR in different industries will alter the normal supply chain and its operations. Augmented reality is also used to benefit the supply chain itself. The prospective applications of AR in the supply chain are profuse. It will add more value to supply chain operations by reducing error rate and decision-making time (Cirulis and Ginters, 2013). For example, visual picking and smart glass can expedite warehouse operations. Pickup time of products can be decreased in human-operated warehouses. Companies are now investing more and more in projects related to AR in the supply chain, including load optimization of trucks, equipment repairs, safety, quality control, and projection of route optimization and delivery address. BMW, GM, and Volkswagen are investing in Google Glass, hoping to enhance factory workers' productivity and efficiency in the area of quality inspection and hands-free barcode scanning. The AR market is expected to grow, and Asia is the fastest growing region in the AR market.

6.8 CASE STUDIES OF SUPPLY CHAINS IN ASIA

As diversities in Asian countries reveal many opportunities, companies are stretching their supply chain and working harder than ever. Diversities provide not only opportunities, but also challenges to companies and supply chain management. The opportunities and challenges still leave room for companies to discover new business models with the assistance and initiatives of their supply chain.

CASE STUDY 1 The Big Bad Wolf Book Sale

Have you ever imagined yourself shopping for books in a warehouse-sized store that is open the entire day and features millions of discounted books? Since 2009, thousands of people have been traveling to the Big Bad Wolf, the world biggest book sale, held annually in Malaysia. With the vision of "Read More for Less," the Big Bad Wolf Book Sale is now offering millions of books and nonbook items at a huge discount of 50%–95% to readers in both Malaysia and overseas.

In 2006, Andrew Yap and wife Jacqueline Ng, founders of the Big Bad Wolf Book Sale, started their BookXcess business by selling magazines and were later introduced to remainder and overprinted books by their suppliers. BookXcess set two objectives: to increase book readership and to increase customer relationship. The founders believed that making books more

Continued

CASE STUDY 1 The Big Bad Wolf Book Sale—cont'd

affordable would help cultivate reading habits for more people in society and would eventually increase book readership. The couple also perceived that better customer service is a must in the book retail business; therefore they emphasize basic courtesy and friendliness. For this reason, BookXcess gives precedence to customer needs and immediately changes for the better.

In the book industry, publishers from time to time overprint books and cannot sell all of them to regular bookstores. Leftover books are new and unread books that publishers normally dump, shred, pulp, or sell off in bulk to reduce excess inventory. BookXcess purchases these books in bulk at a discount. As publishers are trying to clear their stock, the bulk buy of these books allows BookXcess to offer an immense discount to readers, even though the margin is very thin.

BookXcess's first 500-square-foot store, located on the second floor of Amcorp Mall, offered only 500 titles and relied on only one supplier. In less than two years, the couple managed to double the store size to 12,000 square feet and moved to the third floor of the same mall, providing thousands of titles from many suppliers within and outside of the country.

In 2009, BookXcess launched the Big Bad Wolf Book Sale, a gigantic annual book sale in Malaysia. By request from fans, BookXcess has continued the Big Bad Wolf Book Sale on the road to several cities in Malaysia over the years. In 2016, the Big Bad Wolf Book Sale expanded globally to neighboring countries, including Indonesia and Thailand. It plans to visit China, Vietnam, and other countries around the region in the near future.

The Big Bad Wolf Sale offers a wide range of fiction, nonfiction, and children's books. In addition to this, nonbook items were added to the book sale, including posters, tin signs, pop art, car replicas, box sets, and collector's items. The company also provides free gift-wrapping services to encourage customers to buy books as gifts.

After BookXcess had held the Big Bad Wolf Book Sale for five years, the company came up with the 24-hour book sale to attract young crowds. At the Malaysia International Exhibition & Convention Center book sale in 2014, the Big Bad Wolf Book Sale was advertised as 278 hours of nonstop book sales. Around midnight, people were queuing up to get the exclusive limited edition anthology Malam specially published for the Big Bad Wolf by Buku Fixi, one of the most respected publishers in Malaysia. Within 4 hours, 2500 out of 3000 copies of Malam books were sold. The following day, the Malam books were put up for sale at an opening bid of MYR 50, about five times the original price at the book sale.

As early as 11 months prior to the Big Bad Wolf Book Sale, the founders began sourcing for remainder and overprinted books from publishers in Australia, Europe, and the United States. The main publishers included

CASE STUDY 1 The Big Bad Wolf Book Sale—cont'd

Harper Collins, Penguin Random House, and Alfred A. Knopf. The husband was responsible for nonfiction titles, while the wife took care of fiction and children's books. Both founders also spent two weeks at six major trade book fairs to procure books for their big event. Having a short time frame for the event and believing in a hands-on approach, the founders used the red-eye flight technique to maintain their efficiency in book procurement. They slept on flights in order to arrive at the destination in the morning, on time to meet with their publishers.

After sourcing books, the couple arranged the books to be delivered to the warehouse, where their full-time employees were ready to sort, prepare, and categorize books for the big sale. The company started off with only 25 full-time employees. To be able to handle about 3.5 million books every year, the company has acquired more employees, especially part-timers. Preparing for the big sale, the company employs 700 part-time employees to run every aspect before and after the sale, including applying price tags, setting up locations, restocking displays, running security, unloading books, packing up books, and tearing down decorations. BookXcess only looks for employees who work for passion and love of books. The company keeps a small number of full-timers because of its belief in small-team dynamics and efficiency. All part-timers are divided into teams and report to the full-timers. Each team is responsible for different aspects of the event. Team members rotate for the leadership roles.

The Big Bad Wolf Book Sale arranges a clear walk-through for book shoppers. Books are categorized and put on tables, and then payments can be made at an abundance of cashiers. Security is handled well and an appropriate number of staff members are placed to ensure the event runs smoothly.

In 2014, the company decided to purchase its own warehouse after having difficulty getting books to the event space from three different rented warehouse locations. The warehouse cost MYR 50 million. The company finally received loan approval from CIMB after rejection from nine banks. Apart from the high warehouse investment cost, the company has to bear about MYR 500,000 overhead cost, including utilities, salaries, and loan repayment. In addition, the company spent over MYR 1.3 million on hall rental fees, MYR 1.8 million on shipping costs of the books, and MYR 1.6 million on hiring part-timers.

Originated in 2009 in Kuala Lumpur, Malaysia, with 150,000 books, the Big Bad Wolf Book Sale now offers as many as 3.5 million books and has 500,000 visitors. For several years of success in bringing quality books to a large audience, BookXcess had not forgotten the children who may have been forgotten by society. A "Red Readerhood" project has been initiated for

Continued

CASE STUDY 1 The Big Bad Wolf Book Sale—cont'd

book donations. Customers can purchase books from the event or bring brand new books to the Red Readerhood corner to donate them to underprivileged readers. Additionally, BookXcess introduced a new channel to sell bargain books online at http://www.bookxcessonline.com. BookXcess fans can now order discounted books online at any time and have them delivered to their home.

Sources: Hafizi (2014), Kong (2015), and Nair (2013).

CASE STUDY 2 Dabbawala, the Lunch Box Delivery Service

Since 1890, dabbawalas have been delivering freshly homemade lunch boxes from homes to offices of Mumbai's workers. The first dabbawala, Mahadeo Bhavaji Bachche, started a lunch box delivery business in Bombay, also known as Mumbai, with only 100 dabbawalas. These original workers emigrated from the hills of Maharashtra. The first attempt to unionized dabbawalas in 1930 was not successful, and in 1956, "Nutan Mumbai Tiffin Box Suppliers Trust" was registered as a charitable trust. The trust was converted to a commercial entity called "Mumbai Tiffin Box Carriers Association" in 1968. Raghunath Megde serves as the current president of the association.

Mumbai is the capital city of the state of Maharashtra in India. In 2016, Mumbai had a metro population of about 20.7 million and urban population of over 22 million. Mumbai is a densely populated city and one of the largest cities in India in terms of population, trade activity, and business. Because land is costly, Mumbai's populaces commonly live in low-cost constrained housing far from work, resulting in long commutes by the city's busy mass transit system. Because of high expenses from buying lunch and the preference for home-cooked food, Mumbai's workers do not prefer to eat out. It is also not possible for workers to carry their lunch to work with them on the crowded urban transit. The dabbawala business helps fulfill these workers' needs.

Every morning, homemade lunches are freshly cooked and prepared in metal lunch boxes called dabbas or tiffins. These lunch boxes are picked up from homes and delivered to the offices by lunch time. The empty lunch boxes are also returned home in the afternoon. How poorly educated dabbawalas efficiently manage the complex deliveries with high volume, time, and traffic constraints is a lesson to be learned by global companies expanding their business in Asia.

CASE STUDY 2 Dabbawala, the Lunch Box Delivery Service—cont'd

After the lunch boxes are picked up from homes, dabbawalas carry them by foot or bike to the nearest train station. At the station, lunch boxes are labeled, indicating names and addresses, and sorted into wooden crates according to their destination. The crates are forwarded by train to the closest station heading to the final destination. Each dabbawala will handle the lunch boxes, which will be individually hand delivered to the office before lunch time. In the afternoon, the empty lunch boxes are returned on the reverse route back to their homes.

The standards set by the dabbawala supply chain came long before the concept was introduced in the Western world. Every weekday, approximately 200,000 meals, or about 400,000 transactions, are hand delivered by 5000 dabbawalas at a low cost of USD 0.33, and in an eco-friendly way. Only bare feet, bicycles, and trains are used in the lunch transport. Providing the Six-Sigma standard, the accuracy rate of dabbawalas' famous supply chain is only one mistake out of six million deliveries.

Dabbawalas' success relies on their process and execution. Known for its reliability and accuracy, the integrated supply chain concentrates on the entire system, the flow of products and information, the process, and efficient execution. A simple coding system of letters, numbers, and colors is implemented to identify handlers as well as origin and destination locations. Other information such as the name of the receiver will be included as necessary. The minimum code used is just enough for the right delivery. Each dabbawala is assigned to 200 self-managed teams, having the most experienced person acting as a supervisor in each team. Each supervisor has local autonomy, managing 25 dabbawalas and other related decisions. Based on demand and performance, the team members will also have authority on the acceptance and rejection of newcomers. All dabbawalas will maintain good relationships with their customers while working on getting new customers. The pace of the delivery is determined by Mumbai's train system driving dabbawalas to work efficiently on a tight schedule. The supply chain is visible in that a late delivery at one point will be revealed to everyone. The problem will be addressed immediately by the next train as a backup transport to guarantee on-time delivery. Additional dabbawalas are allocated to fill in when needed. Therefore, each dabbawala is cross-trained to be able to handle all tasks.

Working as a family by supporting each other, dabbawalas create a bonding community work environment. The uniformity of the lunch container in terms of size makes it easy to manage, and the same clothing style makes it easily recognizable. The efficient management systems, together with collaboration and synchronization on all parties in the supply

Continued

CASE STUDY 2 Dabbawala, the Lunch Box Delivery Service—cont'd

chain, are the key for success of dabbawalas. The system with minimum use of technology becomes a lesson learned in supply chain management.

Universities and many multinational companies are interested in the success of dabbawalas. Radio Mirchi asked for assistants from dabbawalas to promote its morning show for four days. Tech giants such as Microsoft attempted to distribute flyers and advertisement materials throughout the network of the dabbawalas. However, the plan was discontinued after the trial run because it required extra time and created interruptions for dabbawalas' tight supply chain system.

After more than 100 years of success, dabbawalas adopted some technology in their supply chain operations, aiming to increase volume and expand their services. With the use of a short message service (SMS) ordering system, dabbawalas have gained about 15 new orders every day. The website www.mydabbawala.com has also been created for customer orders. Looking to the future, dabbawalas plan to offer groceries and other daily necessities to their customers as new services.

Sources: Baindur and Macario (2013), Maes and Vanelslander (2012), Patel and Vedula (2006), and Pathak (2010).

6.9 CONCLUSION

Global dynamics and unpredictable environments provide tremendous opportunities, but they also present challenges to companies. In order to compete successfully in the global market, companies turn their focus to building a strong collaborative chain of supplies. Effective collaboration with supply chain partners requires organizations to share valuable information in real time. Today's ICT advancement makes it possible for a visible, collaborative, and effective supply chain to work collaboratively and prepare all members for global diversities, especially in Asia. Diversities also allow some room for new business models. Understanding Asian diversities and future trends will push companies to be ahead of the game.

REFERENCES

Ali, A.J., 2001. Globalization: the great transformation. Adv. Compet. Res. 9 (1), 1.

Anthony, T., 2000. Supply chain collaboration: success in the new internet economy. Achieving Supply Chain Excellence through Technology. Montgomery Research, San Francisco, CA, pp. 241–244.

Baindur, D., Macario, R.M., 2013. Mumbai lunch box delivery system: a transferable benchmark in urban logistics? Res. Transp. Econ. 38, 110–121.

Balan, S., Vrat, P., Kumar, P., 2006. Assessing the challenges and opportunities of global supply chain management. Int. J. Value Chain Manag. 1 (2), 105–116.

Barratt, M., 2004. Understanding the meaning of collaboration in the supply chain. Supply Chain Manag. Int. J. 9 (1), 30–42.

Behzadan, A.H., Timm, B.W., Kamat, V.R., 2008. General-purpose modular hardware and software framework for mobile outdoor augmented reality applications in engineering. Adv. Eng. Inform. 22 (1), 90–105.

Briggs, B., 2016. E-commerce in Asia grows to 32%. Internet Retailer. Available from: https://www.internetretailer.com/2016/02/02/e-commerce-asia-grows-32&gt.

Buljo, J.O., Gjerstad, T.B., 2013. Robotics and Automation in Seafood Processing. Woodhead Publishing Limited, Norway.

Business Dictionary.com. Available from: http://www.businessdictionary.com/definition/globalization.html&gt.

Campante, F., Yanagizawa-Drott, D., 2015. Does religion affect economic growth and happiness? evidence from Ramadan. Q. J. Econ. 130 (2), 615–658.

Chan, H., Lee, R., Chang, E., Dillon, T., 2001. E-Commerce: Fundamentals and Application, first ed. Wiley & Sons; Chichester, p. 21. Available from:https://archive.org/stream/2001ECommerceFundamentalsAndApplicationsHenryChan/2001%20-%20E-Commerce%20Fundamentals%20and%20Applications%20(Henry%20Chan)_djvu.txt.

Cirulis, A., Ginters, E., 2013. Augmented reality in logistics. Procedia Comput. Sci. 26, 14–20.

Collier, D.A., Evans, J.R., 2012. OM, student ed. South-Western, Cengage Learning; Ohio, p. 23 (Chapter 2).

Council of Supply Chain Management Professional, 2013. Supply Chain Management Terms and Glossary. Available from: https://cscmp.org/sites/default/files/user_uploads/resources/downloads/glossary-2013.pdf?utm_source=cscmpsite&utm_medium=clicklinks&utm_content=glossary&utm_campaign=GlossaryPDF.

DHL Trend Research, 2016. Demystifying Asia Pacific trade trends. Asia Pacific Insights. DHL Trend Research, Troisdorf.

Gilmore, D., 2005. Just what is supply chain collaboration? Supply Chain Digest.Available from: http://www.scdigest.com/assets/FirstThoughts/05-07-07.cfm?cid=253.

Guild, T., 2009. Think Regionally, Act Locally: Four Steps to Reaching the Asian Consumer. McKinsey Quarterly; Tokyo.

Hafizi, A., 2014. The Big Bad Wolf Now has Backup. The Malaysian Reserve. Available from: http://themalaysianreserve.com/new/story/big-bad-wolf-now-has-backup&gt.

Haghighati, N., 2016. Several Foreign Firms Interested to Join Iran-Oman Gas Pipeline. Petro Energy Information Network. Available from:http://www.shana.ir/en/newsagency/262758/Several-Foreign-Firms-Interested-to-Join-Iran-Oman-Gas-Pipeline&gt.

Haraguchi, M., Lall, U., 2015. Flood risks and impacts: a case study of Thailand's floods in 2011 and research questions for supply chain decision making. Int. J. Disaster Risk Reduct. 14 (3), 256–272.

Harland, C.M., Lamming, R.C., Zheng, J., Johnsen, T.E., 2001. A taxonomy of supply network. J. Supply Chain Manag. 37 (3), 21–27.

Harsono, A., 2014. The impact of E-Commerce in supply chain management at Dell Inc. Int. J. Disaster Risk Reduct. 1 (3), 11–18.

Heizer, J., Render, B., 2014. Operations Management: Sustainability and Supply Chain Management, eleventh ed. Pearson Education; Boston, p. 468 (Chapter 11).

Hodgetts, R., Luthans, F., 1994. International Management. McGraw-Hill, New York, NY.

Ibrahim, H.W., Zailani, S., Tan, K.C., 2015. A content analysis of global supply chain research. Benchmarking Int. J. 22 (7), 1429–1462.

Jacobs, F.R., Chase, R.B., 2011. Operations and Supply Chain Management, Global ed. McGraw-Hill/Irwin, New York, NY.

Khanna, P., Sampat, B., 2015. Factors influencing online shopping during Diwali festival 2014: case study of Flipkart and Amazon.In. J. Int. Technol. Inf. Manag. 24 (2), 65–86.

Kong, X., 2015. A day with the big bad wolf. Kinibiz. Available from: http://www.kinibiz.com/story/issues/149903/1-day-the-the-big-bad-wolf.html&gt.

La Londe, B.J., Masters, J.M., 1994. Emerging logistics strategies: blueprints for the next century. Int. J. Phys. Distrib. Logist. Manag. 24 (7), 35–47.

Ling, O.G., 2014. Diversity and the Challenges Facing Asian Cities Today. In: The Management of Diversity in the Asian City, Senior Research Fellow. Institute of Policy Studies, Singapore https://www.dss.gov.au/our-responsibilities/settlement-and-multicultural-affairs/programs-policy/a-multicultural-australia/programs-and-publications/1995-global-cultural-diversity-conference-proceedings-sydney/public-policy-and-diversity/diversity-and-the-challenges-facing.

Lummus, R.R., Alber, K.L., 1997. Supply Chain Management: Balancing the Supply Chain with Customer Demand. The Educational and Resource Foundation of APICS, Falls Church, VA.

Lummus, R.R., Vokurka, R.J., 1999. Defining supply chain management: a historical perspective and practical guidelines. Ind. Manag. Data Syst. 99 (1), 11–17.

Maes, J., Vanelslander, T., 2012. The use of bicycle messengers in the logistics chain, concepts further revised. The Seventh International Conference on City Logistics. Procedia Soc. Behav. Sci. 39, 409–423.

Manyika, J., Lund, S., Bughin, J., Woetzel, J., Stamenov, K., Dhingra, D., 2016. Digital globalization: the new era of global flow. McKinsey Global Institute Report; Pennsylvania.

Markets and Markets Report, 2016. Material Handling Equipment Market by Product Type (AGV, ASRS, Automated Crane, Robotic System, Automated Conveyor and Sortation System), System Type, Software and Service, Operation, Application, and Geography—Global Forecast to 2022. Research and Markets.

Matopoulos, A., Vlachopoulou, M., Manthou, V., Manos, B., 2007. A conceptual framework for supply chain collaboration: empirical evidence from the agri-food industry. Supply Chain Manag. Int. J. 12 (3), 177–186.

Mentzer, J.T., DeWitt, W., Keebler, J.S., Min, S., Nix, N.W., Smith, C.D., Zacharia, Z.G., 2001. Defining supply chain management. J. Bus. Logist. 22 (2), 1–26.

Mirsane, S.A., Shafagh, S., 2016. A narrative review on fasting of pregnant women in the holy month of ramadan. J. Fasting Health 4 (2), 53–56.

Nair, V., 2013. Don't Judge a Book by its Price. Business Today Available from: http://www.businesstoday.net.my/dont-judge-a-book-by-its-price/&gt.

O'Neil, C., 2016. How Robotics will Change Supply Chains in the Next Decade. Innovation Enterprise Available from: https://channels.theinnovationenterprise.com/articles/how-robotics-will-change-supply-chains-in-the-next-decade&gt.

Patel, N., Vedula, N., 2006. Dabbawalas of Mumbai. MBA White Paper. University of North Carolina's Kenan-Flager Business School; North Carolina.

Pathak, G., 2010. Delivering the nation: the dabbawalas of Mumbai. South Asia J. South Asian Stud. 33 (2), 235–257.

Pew Research Center, 2014. Global Religious Diversity: Half of the Most Religiously Diverse Countries are in Asia-Pacific Region.

Prasad, S., Sounderpandian, J., 2003. Factors influencing global supply chain efficiency: implications for information systems. Supply Chain Manag. Int. J. 8 (3), 241–250.

Rashidvash, V., Mirak, F.M., 2015. Ethnic groups in Asia. Int. J. Humanit. Soc. Sci. Stud. 2 (3), 181–186.

Razmi, J., Sangari, M.S., Ghodsi, R., 2009. Developing a practical framework for ERP readiness assessment using fuzzy analytic network process. Adv. Eng. Softw. 40 (11), 1168–1178.

Reid, R.D., Sanders, N.R., 2013. Operations Management: An Integrated Approach, third ed. John Wiley & Sons Singapore Pte. Ltd.; Singapore (Chapter 4).

Ruiz-Torres, A., Mahmoodi, F., 2008. Outsourcing decision in manufacturing supply chains considering production failure and operating costs. Int. J. Integr. Supply Manag. 4 (2), 141–158.

Simatupang, T.M., Sridharan, S., 2005. An integrative framework for supply chain collaboration. Int. J. Logist. Manag. 16 (2), 257–274.

Stevenson, W.J., Sum, S.C., 2007. Operations Management: An Asian Perspective, ninth ed. McGraw-Hill Companies; Singapore.

Stock, J.R., Boyer, S.L., 2009. Developing a consensus definition of supply chain: a qualitative study. Int. J. Phys. Distrib. Logist. Manag. 39 (8), 690–711.

Verma, R., Boyer, K.K., 2010. Operations & Supply Chain Management: World Class Theory and Practice, International ed. South-Western, Cengage Learning; China (Chapter 14).

CHAPTER 7

Networking Strategies and Internationalization in the Asia Pacific

N. Udomkit
Mahidol University International College, Nakhon Pathom, Thailand

7.1 INTRODUCTION

Networks play an important role in the success of businesses in Asia, especially for small and medium enterprises (SMEs). Firms typically face limitations with their resources, management capabilities, and international experience, which makes thorough strategic planning a task beyond reality. Firms often have very limited or no information to support them to make informed and effective decisions to manage uncertainty. Social networks can influence a company's decision-making process in starting up new businesses or initiatives, and constitute a crucial mechanism for accessing necessary resources to undertake a business. Networks are a crucial mechanism to minimize the gap between "what firms need" and "what firms have" (Schreier et al., 2015).

In the context of internationalization, the network theory has become a widely used approach in understanding the internationalization process of entrepreneurial firms. Networks help firms initiate, enable, and sustain their internationalization process, and also navigate them to international markets through knowledge accumulation. Networks are a critical asset that helps firms minimize resource constraints, such as limited resources, and lack of information and market insights. In consequence, this creates awareness of international opportunities and promotes decisions on when and how to internationalize. It is important to note that most SMEs expand their businesses into specific countries as a result of the owner, the owner's relatives, close friends, or acquaintances having lived or worked in that particular country. The decision-making process in internationalization is therefore tactical rather than systematic (Schreier et al., 2015).

In Asia, networks play an enormous role in linking opportunities, assessing the possibilities and helping companies reach their goal; networks are

Internationalization and Managing Networks in the Asia Pacific
http://dx.doi.org/10.1016/B978-0-08-100813-3.00007-9

utilized in unique forms. For nonAsian entrepreneurs, failing to understand the roles and utilization of networks may result in frustration or failure to conduct business in the region. This chapter attempts to guide readers through networking and internationalization strategies within the Asia-Pacific zone. This chapter will start by exploring of the concept of social networks and their roles, particularly in the context of internationalization and network utilization in the Asia Pacific.

7.2 DEFINITIONS AND CLASSIFICATIONS OF NETWORKS

Several scholars have attempted to define and classify types and levels of networks. However, within the literature there is no universal agreement as to a precise definition of the term "network." The definition and classifications of network vary slightly by the context of the studies. For example:

Coviello and Munro (1997) view a network as a set of two or more linked exchange relationships.

Dollinger (2003) defines networking as the mechanism of expanding the entrepreneur's circle of trust.

Hoang and Antoncic (2003) describe social networks as a group of actors (individuals or organizations) and the relationships between these actors.

Neegaard and Madsen (2004) propose that networks are built on trust. Entrepreneurs aim to find "trusted alters" (people who share homogeneous beliefs, experiences, and patterns of association) when establishing networks. These people could be relatives, old friends, or former colleagues.

Coviello and Cox (2006) define a network as bonds between agents that can be individuals or organizations. This research classifies networks into personal, business, and institutional networks.

Zain and Ng (2006) describe a social network as the relationship between a company's executives and employees, with other stakeholders that enable the firm to expand its business operations to the international arena.

Zhou et al. (2007) define social networks as interconnections and relationships between persons established for securing favors and/or organizational activities.

Gartner and Bellamy (2009) interpret an entrepreneur's network as the total of his or her relationships, including all the ties a person has with other actors.

On network classifications, there is no consensus among researchers on the topic of social networks on how to classify the types of networks. For example, Senik et al. (2011) classify three types of networks. The first is the institution network, which represents the supporting government agencies; the second are the business associates, which include local/foreign SMEs or multinational corporations; and the third are personal networks, which include relatives, friends, and colleagues. The nature of a personal network is embedded in "personal relationships," where solid personal ties with other SME owners, friends, relatives, and colleagues play a significant role in the networking web.

In the study conducted by Kontinen and Ojala (2011), a network is categorized into formal, informal, and intermediary ties. A formal tie is an existent connection between particular business partners, where products or services are bartered or paid for. Informal ties refer to familial or friend relationships. An intermediary tie is a relationship where sellers and buyers have indirect communication through a middleman like an export promotion organization. Strong and weak ties differ according to levels of proximity, trust, mutual respect, and commitment. For a strong or tight tie, relationships between the firms are solid; hence the entry and exit of network members do not take place regularly. On the other hand, weak ties result in unclear roles of functional performance and frequent entries and exits.

In the study of Chen et al. (2015), a network is a group of people bonded by specific interpersonal relationships, which are fostered and sustained through trust, obligation, and reciprocity. A guanxi network is believed to consist of four relational bonds in Chinese society: family, business, community, and government ties.

Aldrich and Zimmer (1986) suggest that a "formal" network can almost be used in the same way as a "business" network. Other scholars include joint ventures, licensing agreements, strategic alliances, and joint marketing agreements in the term "network" (Groen, 2005).

In conclusion, networks are commonly embedded into a group or individual actors who provide interaction with some level of trust. This trust, existing in each relationship, provides access to a variety of resource types and also assists in overcoming institutional barriers.

7.3 ROLES OF NETWORKS IN THE INTERNATIONALIZATION PROCESS

Several studies have touched on the roles of networks in the internationalization process. As firms internationalize, the number and strength of relationships within the networks increase, correspondingly helping international extension. Therefore, networks are necessary for international development, as they promote the acquisition of experiential knowledge related to foreign markets and facilitate decision-making in terms of when and how to expand their operations internationally. They can also influence the mode of entry when internationalizing (Johanson and Mattsson, 1988; Johannisson, 2000; Johnsen and Johnsen, 1999; Ojala, 2009; Zain and Ng, 2006).

Leyden et al. (2014) highlight the significance of social networks in enhancing innovation and mitigating risks. Their research results show that this social dimension of entrepreneurship boosts the probability of entrepreneurial accomplishment. Their model is built on the assumption that entrepreneurs seek knowledge and the key to discovering knowledge lies in access to social networks. They concluded the importance of social networks by quoting the words of Granovetter (1973, p. 1378): "no luxury but of central importance." An entrepreneur's ability to search within and across sources of knowledge is determined by the size and heterogeneity of his or her effective networks; the greater the variety of social bonds and past knowledge and experiences, the more creative the entrepreneur will be (Leyden et al., 2014).

Prashantham and Birkinshaw (2015) identified two mechanisms that networks utilize for international expansion. The first is that connections provide the concrete links to clients and others with whom the company may do business, and also the intangible aspects of trust and amity between members that raise the willingness to share resources (Elango and Pattnaik, 2007; Hitt et al., 2006). Secondly, a network of relationships expedites the ability to grow and learn. Regular interaction promotes knowledge creation and transfer by reducing the barriers to incorporating and exchanging intellectual resources (Nahapiet and Ghoshal, 1998). The learning process creates value for both parties and supports the focal actor to gradually become one of the "insiders" in the targeted market (Johanson and Vahlne, 2009). Moreover, it is found that a company's network can become a "reference group" for normative guidance that formulates the managers' understanding of the firm's opportunities, and further constructs their future activities (Fiegenbaum et al., 1996; Fiegenbaum and Thomas, 1995).

7.4 NETWORKS IN ASIA

In the context of Asia, networks have played an enormous role in business management and are vital to the success of business. Methods of how networks in Asia are exercised and sample cases will be presented.

7.4.1 Guanxi Networks in China

A network that has gained increasing interest among researchers is the Chinese "guanxi." The term "guanxi" is translated as "relationship" or "connection," used to describe a unique interpersonal relationship that comprises elements of favor, trust, and interdependence. It is a special relationship bonded through trust, mutual obligation, and reciprocal exchange of favors. It commonly depends on solid ties of blood or marital relations, or social identifiers. Hence with strong trust, involvement of care, and empathy, it is difficult for the relationship to fall apart (Chen et al., 2015; Lee et al., 2001; Hammond and Glenn, 2004; Hutchings and Murray, 2002; Parnell, 2005).

According to Chen et al. (2015), there are four relational ties that a guanxi network in Chinese society consists of: family, business, community, and government ties. It was found that these networks impact business success via the mediating effects of resource availability and information accessibility. Chinese entrepreneurs create and use their networks to obtain information and resources for new ventures. Particularly, it was found that while family ties, business connections, and community bonds facilitate information accessibility, family and government ties enhance resource availability.

Several researchers observe that guanxi is influenced by the Chinese philosophy "Confucian ethics" (Hutchings and Murray, 2002; Vanhonacker, 2004). The Chinese do not view the guanxi obligation to repay as a "using" relationship, but rather as ethical behavior. But several critiques argue that guanxi creates high potential for relationships to cover up corrupt transactions, where it may be viewed as unethical in the business sense, especially with regard to the ties between government officials and businesspeople, which is argued to bring out an overlap of the guanxi and corruption, or Crony capitalism.

However, guanxi is critical for sustaining business in China, as the Chinese embed the use of guanxi networks in their business practices (Luo, 2000). Guanxi networks influence insider-based decision-making in business negotiations (Szeto et al., 2006) and enable economically effective exchanges in a disintegrated, weak-rule-of-law society. Frequently, connections are used to find employment, get promotions, establish businesses, and form strategic alliances.

7.4.2 Guanxi Networks in Other Asian Nations

As the Chinese have settled down across many Asian nations, there is a utilization of the strong influence of the Chinese ethnic network. Guanxi is therefore commonly exercised throughout Asia, which relies greatly on personal contacts or guanxi networks, generally related to ethnicity. Similarity in cultural attitudes also promotes trust and cooperation. These networks and relationships allow access or connections to local markets, local bureaucracies, business systems, and also effective business partners (Sim and Pandian, 2003).

The practices of guanxi are evident in Taiwan, as the country shares Confucian traditions, Chinese languages, and cultures. In order to invest in China, the strategy of Taiwanese investors is to build a business-to-business (B2B) guanxi and business-to-government (B2G) guanxi. B2B guanxi is seen as effective relational linkages with customers and local suppliers to guarantee their orders and low costs of supplying goods (Wong, 2012). B2G guanxi allows Taiwanese companies to utilize close relationships with local Chinese officials, having more flexibility in their negotiation and reducing the bureaucratic delay (Wong, 2012).

In Taiwan, there are groups of related businesses that practice a personal network; this is known as "guanxi qiye." The term "guanxi qiye" implies a group of companies that commonly share ownership through strong connections such as family members, marriage, and other forms of social ties (Hamilton, 1996). It is also uncommon to see the same person or their relatives being on the board of directors of two or more firms in their business group (Hamilton, 1996).

An important factor for finding a job in Taiwan and within the Chinese community is guanxi networks, in which the Taiwanese people attempt to create personal relationships with an employer to ensure that they will have a stable job (Hung and Ho, 2010). The Taiwanese people often provide gifts, tea, or coffee or ensure frequent interactions to maintain the guanxi network (Hung and Ho, 2010; Wang and Woods, 2013).

In addition to this, guanxi is sometimes represented in the form of social capital, which develops trust and binds individuals or firms together. There is clear evidence that Taiwanese firms utilize the guanxi network to internationalize. For instance, the study of Sim and Pandian (2003) illustrates the case of a Taiwanese textile company that was successful in expanding to the Philippines and China by using the guanxi network. This firm used the owner's personal network to build its first factory in the Philippines (Sim and Pandian, 2003). Moreover, in China, this Taiwanese firm focused on generating trust and cooperative relationships, which led to the joint venture with a local firm (Sim and Pandian, 2003).

In Singapore, the role of the guanxi network through old school ties is evident throughout. The people regularly keep in touch with high school and college associates in order to utilize future opportunities of the guanxi network (Bian and Ang, 1997; Gomez and Hsiao, 2012). Singaporeans do not involve social relationships between government officials and businesspeople, or so-called vertical guanxi, as much as other countries in the Southeast Asian region. The reason is that Singapore is a leading country that is proactive in promoting transparency in business. However, horizontal guanxi networks are vastly exercised in Singapore (Gomez and Hsiao, 2012). For example, Singaporeans often practice guanxi networks by hosting lunches or dinners, and giving presents in exchange for promises for doing future favors for each other (Bian and Ang, 1997). On job mobility, most employers deliberate recruitment through personal relationships because it is an effective way to obtain significant information such as trustworthiness and qualified candidates; this information is difficult to acquire using formal channels. Furthermore, using personal networks for hiring employees reduces recruitment costs, as recruitment through formal channels is both expensive and time-consuming. Singaporean firms' strategies for acquiring potentially reliable employees at comparatively low costs is to utilize guanxi networks by providing referral bonuses to current employees upon recommendation of a friend to a job interview (Bian and Ang, 1997).

Singapore's former prime minister, Lee Kuan Yew, also emphasized the importance of ethnic networking. It is viewed as an effective approach to compete with multinational enterprises, and also enhances the firms' abilities to anticipate profitable markets (Szeto et al., 2006). In Sim and Pandian (2003), their research presented a Singaporean textile firm that utilized its Chinese ethnic contacts in Africa to start a joint venture there. Another sample firm expanded to the international market using its family network. Hence it is clear that both example Singaporean firms utilized their personal networks or guanxi network to expand their businesses into the international market.

In Malaysia, there are a number of studies highlighting the utilization of networks for internationalization. These networks also influence the market selection, entry modes, and accession of resources (Jaafar et al., 2009; Senik et al., 2011; Zain and Ng, 2006).

The study of Jaafar et al. (2009) examined the use of social networks in the Malaysian housing and construction industries. It was found that new private housing developers depend heavily on their strong ties (family/relatives/close friends) for advice in selecting the most suitable contractor, consultant, and suppliers; while at the start-up and later stage, they gain more advice from weak ties (individuals from the same industry and their acquaintances). Private housing developers place their personal trust more on strong ties, which can provide information related to the contractor, consultant, and suppliers. Once it comes to the selection of a contractor, consultant, and suppliers, private housing developers give priority to nonsocial factors such as the lowest quotation and willingness to customize, as well as social factors such as past relationships and ethnicity.

In the works of Senik et al. (2011), they illustrated a case study firm in Malaysia that began its business in 1984 as a family-owned food company, which initially penetrated into Malaysian hypermarkets through the owner's personal contacts, resulting in expansions into Singapore and Hong Kong. Their work shows three cases of Malaysian software companies that heavily relied on networks to penetrate into the international market. Infosoft decided to expand its business to Japan because the exemployer of the firm's owner was located in Japan, which provided more security and credibility for the firm to overcome many barriers, including culture and language. Edusoft, another case study firm, also used its personal relationships, including friends, relatives, and contacts, to enter New Zealand, the United Kingdom, Australia, the United States, and Indonesia. The last case firm, Securesoft, also utilized personal connections or guanxi network to enter into Singapore; for example, the firm established a subsidiary in Singapore because the founder's relatives lived in Singapore.

7.4.3 Japanese "Keiretsu"

Keiretsu are networks of autonomous companies connected by tightly integrated ownership, management, and financial ties. The term "keiretsu" is commonly translated as a business group that was developed from the "zaibatsu" network (family-run holding companies) prior to World War II. The zaibatsu was vastly known by Westerners as a conglomerated business group in which people in the network are tied by trust and close relationships (Kienzle and Shadur, 1997).

There are two types of keiretsu—vertical and horizontal keiretsu. The horizontal (financial) keiretsu is formed around a Japanese bank through cross-shareholding connections with other firms. The bank serves the companies through a variety of financial services. The well-known "Big Six," a group of banks making up the leading Japanese horizontal keiretsu, include Dai-Ichi Kangyo, Mitsubishi, Mitsui, Sanwa, Sumitomo, and Fuyo. The relationships of a horizontal keiretsu comprise the Presidents' Council, a social event for member firms' presidents, cross-shareholding, trading of products and services among actors, credit and loans from the group's bank, and interlocking directorates (Knoke, n.d.).

Vertical (industrial) keiretsu connect one industry's distributors, producers, and suppliers. One or more affiliates are established for the benefit of the parent company. An example of this would be the supply chains of small firms that sell parts to a major manufacturer like Toyota, Sony, or Toshiba.

Through pooling and diversifying risk, keiretsu members have implicit insurance against bankruptcies and market breakdowns. The other members of keiretsu can assist distressed companies by rolling over old loans into financial aid packages, sending employees to these troubled companies, and enabling them to raise capital through the sale of cross-held shares (Knoke, n.d.).

The study of Aoki and Lennerfors (2013) explains why keiretsu is long-lasting and has proved to be tenacious in Japan. On the cost aspect, keiretsu helps manufacturers avoid hidden costs of unwillingness among manufacturers and suppliers to find the root causes of supply-chain issues. On the quality aspect, manufacturers depend on commitment and competence from their keiretsu suppliers, and hence have confidence in the quality of components. On the innovation aspect, with manufacture assistance, suppliers come up with product and process breakthroughs. In the "Anshin" (peace of mind) aspect, keiretsu offers mutual trust that as long as suppliers and manufacturers genuinely support each other, the relationship will be maintained.

In the present day, it can be recognized that this network's level of practicing is reducing; however, they implicitly engage in Japanese business networks. For SMEs in Japan, the government plays a momentous role in supporting them. In comparison to the Chinese network, there are interindustrial networks for technological activities where a grouping of firms in the industry is able to exchange information and technological know-how with other industries. It is an interpersonal tie between firms that extends their relationship horizontally. The Japanese are often less concerned with blood-related ties and conspire on relationships from various sources (Lincoln and Shimotani, 2009).

7.4.4 South Korea "Chaebol"

South Korea is another country that intensively incorporates personal relationships in business networks. The Korean chaebol is family based, applied in a circle of corporate ownerships between a family and its members. The relationships of families also exist within chaebols. Managerial positions and key responsibilities are allocated and concentrated among family members, where control is commonly limited to the founding family (Kienzle and Shadur, 1997).

Chaebol has a similar aspect to guanxi relationships in China in the sense that both are based on mutual trust and geared toward the blood-related or family members. Chaebol is also similar to the keiretsu network practiced in Japan (Kienzle and Shadur, 1997). Nevertheless, the chaebol varies from the keiretsu in terms of control and ownership. To delineate, chaebol is a network with fewer hands to reach out for other potential firms than the Japanese network; however, it emphasizes the specific recruitment of retired government officials or military representatives in order to exercise those people's power in lobbying the government and bureaucracy (Hamilton, 1996).

7.4.5 Thailand

Networks play a crucial role in operating business in Thailand. Building good relationships within the networks produces mutual benefits such as shared information, updated regulations, and market insight. Networks are viewed as high value for their businesses. Moreover, maintaining good relationships with their networks helps firms manage their business smoothly as they rely on interdependent relationships.

Thai SMEs commonly face a shortage of labor that has knowledge, skills, and adequate competencies for handling internationalization. A common solution for such a labor shortage during internationalization is to obtain assistance from family members and relatives. Close family members and friends are often in charge of major positions in the firms. The channel of recruiting new personnel is often done through recommendations and connections from existing staff. This type of channel binds everyone to work together, and employees are treated like family members.

SMEs lack information, market insights, and knowledge on international markets as key barriers to internationalizing their business. SMEs highlighted the importance of networks as prime sources for market insights. In other words, networks help SMEs overcome the key constraint of a lack of market insights. Equally important, networks were reported by all informants to be key sources for knowledge and management skills enhancement.

Networks are sources of referrals for new customers. Companies often gain new customers through their existing customer base, suppliers, and even their competitors. Moreover, networks can promote the credibility of companies in foreign markets. As competition in the market is high, being recommended or referred by a trustworthy party gives the companies some advantages.

Networks can also build and strengthen good practices among their members. If firms conduct malpractice, reputations can be destroyed. For example, companies in the Thai pharmaceutical distribution industry are very limited. This proves advantageous, as the chances of malpractice become minimal. Once a company in the pharmaceutical market engages in wrongdoings, news spreads throughout the market rapidly, making that particular company lose trust among its suppliers.

Evidence of networks' influence on market selection and entry mode illustrates that market selection at the early stage of internationalization depends solely on opportunities arising from their networks, which commonly begins by exporting. For more committed entry modes such as foreign direct investment (joint venture and wholly owned subsidiary) and licensing, these opportunities also arise from close network ties, such as family members, relatives, and friends. Examples of internationalization through close network ties are illustrated in Case 1.

CASE 1 Diamond for You

Diamond for You started its operation in Thailand in 1995 as a subsidiary of an Indian-based diamond manufacturing company. The history of the company dates back to 1975 in Mumbai, India, where it first began as a small family business, engaged in imports and exports of diamonds. With the growth in family size and determination to expand the business internationally, Diamond for You internationalized the business by establishing subsidiaries in Hong Kong, Italy, and Thailand. Currently, the parent company in India imports and polishes rough diamonds, and exports polished diamonds to its international subsidiaries and customers in countries like Belgium.

Diamond for You has evolved from a small family business to operating countless branches in multiple countries. Hong Kong was the first international market the company entered into, a well-established hub for trading business and one of Asia's busiest harbors. Entering Hong Kong benefits the company as the city facilitates an effective path for the company to transport and circulate its diamonds. Hong Kong is a free port; therefore it creates a valuable logistics chain between the headquarters in India and its branches. To export or import in Hong Kong, the process is

Continued

CASE 1 Diamond for You—cont'd

simple because the local government is supportive of international trade, hence making Hong Kong attractive for many foreign investments, especially in entering the Asian market.

After Hong Kong, the company opened its next branch in Thailand in 1995. The main drive for the company to enter Thailand at the time was its large market size compared to its neighboring countries. Moreover, jewelry has been a part of Thai culture and is a symbol of wealth and high social status. Thailand also has unique jewelry designs and unmatched craftsmanship, which emphasizes the importance of jewelry to the Thai culture. Taking the B2B approach, Diamond for You's Bangkok branch sells loose diamonds from India to jewelry manufacturers and retailers through jewelry exhibitions.

In comparison with Hong Kong, language barriers were a main concern. The management faced difficulties communicating with Thai employees who had insufficient English skills. As a result, the management had to learn Thai in order to effectively administer the business. Another obstacle encountered in Thailand was dealing with government policies, as they were more "complicated" than those in Hong Kong. As the Thai government did not focus on international trade, taxation was high, and necessary documents for diamonds were not easily approved.

The management spent four to five months surveying and familiarizing itself with the Thai market. After obtaining enough information on the local market, the company participated in major exhibitions such as the jewelry fairs, where it made contacts with large manufacturers.

The company's most recent expansion was to Italy, the jewelry capital of Europe. Just like other cross-border expansions, cultural barriers were some of the factors the company faced. Rules and regulations are far stricter in Italy than in Asian countries, which lengthens documentation processes. However, with accumulated internationalization experience from the previous two subsidiaries, the company was able to launch its Italian branch.

Because market information and business know-how in the diamond industry are confidential, networks play an essential role in the company's process of internationalization. The company relies on networks from family, friends, customers, and people in the same line of business to gain market insights. Considering the massive capital and high risks involved in the products' high value, one would need in-depth product and market knowledge to start up or expand a diamond business abroad. By taking advantage of it being a family-owned business, the company has transferrable business know-how and diamond knowledge within family members when establishing international branches, giving them an advantage over new entrants to the industry.

CASE 1 Diamond for You—cont'd

Family networks also influence the company's choice of international market entry. For instance, the company chose to expand its business into Italy because a family member had an Italian partner who was able to assist in overcoming language barriers and provide information on the local market.

The management views customer networking as one source of gaining market insights. While mainly doing business with large jewelry factories in Thailand and keeping a healthy relationship with people in the same line of business, the company is able to receive updated insights such as changes in price, market trends, or laws and regulations. The networks are well maintained through trust and personal engagement by occasionally dining in and playing sports with customers.

In Thailand, personal networks such as family members, relatives, and friends are primary sources. Businesses and government networks that were introduced through personal networks seem to be a second layer that Thai SMEs utilize at the initial stage of internationalization. The common business networks that SMEs utilize are trade associations, which provide updated information about market trends, regulations, and trade fairs or exhibitions in both Thailand and abroad.

Government institutes such as the Ministry of Commerce, particularly its Department of International Trade Promotion (DITP), play a crucial role in assisting SMEs to export to other countries. DITP helps connect them with relevant government agencies and trade associations, and provides advice on rules and procedures such as customs regulations. The majority of SMEs in this research joined trade fairs or business-matching missions organized by DITP, and built relationships with their business partners. It is evident that where entrepreneurs have problems setting up network relationships on their own, the establishment of entrepreneurial networks by governmental or other advising agencies is crucial.

It is interesting to note the evolving business relationships within networks. In Asia, business relationships have developed and evolved toward closer relationships—from business networks to personal networks. In other words, they have evolved from business partnerships to "friendships." In the context of Thailand, closer relationships can be developed by regular meetings, lunch or dinner arrangements, gifts to show respect, and paying visits on special occasions. Customers are often well taken care of when they visit Thailand. The term "friendship" is viewed as a strongly bonded relationship. Thais, and perhaps Asians, tend to develop and build networks by remaining close with business partners and creating a feeling of being more than pure business, and treating partners as friends. The following case firms 2 and 3 highlight the evolving network relationships.

CASE 2 World Premiums

World Premiums was established in 1995. It started as an import business selling an array of premium and home utilities from different countries, such as China, Taiwan, Hong Kong, South Korea, and Indonesia. Over the past decade, the company grew successfully and built its own factory in Thailand. The company is now the leader of gift premiums in Thailand, and supplies exclusive premiums for many leading companies. The company is renowned for supplying licensed cartoon characters such as Walt Disney, Sanrio, and nonlicensed products or products of the customer's own brand.

World Premiums' key competitive advantage is its low prices, top designs, fast production processes, punctual delivery, and ability to provide customers with one-stop service, from design to delivery. The company currently exports its products to Taiwan, Korea, and Malaysia, and plans to expand export channels to neighboring countries such as Vietnam, Myanmar, and Lao People's Democratic Republic.

As the company is a family-run business, internationalization shows a number of limitations, and thus relies on networks for knowledge, market insights, and know-how. For example, as the company imported plastic injection machines from China, the company relies on its Chinese partner for technical know-how. The company's Chinese supplier sends local technicians to work at the factory, and trains Thai employees. The company also sends Thai staff to China to learn about new production techniques.

For market expansion, the company is introduced to new markets and foreign distributors through current customers or business partners as well as the DITP. To build a new network, the company sources potential networks from trade fairs. Exhibitions that the company attends regularly take place in China and Hong Kong. This exhibition allows the company to search for new partners with business potential by studying their products and speaking with other participants.

Relationships are crucial in business, especially in China and other Asian countries. The company visits suppliers in China to build and strengthen relationships. It also has a very long-term relationship with its distributor, so when the distributor visits Thailand, the company ensures the highest quality of hospitality. This helps strengthen the friendship and creates the most trust between the company and suppliers, resulting in an ease of doing business such as sharing market information, providing support, and negotiation.

CASE 3 Thai Textile Group

Thai Textile Group is a vertically integrated textile manufacturing group located in Bangkok. It consists of four dominant firms involved in diverse stages of the textile production process, including the manufacturing and processing of yarn spinning, weaving, dyeing, and printing. Its product range includes yarns, apparel fabrics and uniforms, home furnishing fabrics, and automotive fabrics. It exports more than 80% of its production worldwide. Its key markets are Canada, the United States, Mexico, Central America, South America, the United Kingdom, Europe, Turkey, Mauritius, South Africa, New Zealand, Australia, the Middle East, India, Hong Kong, Japan, Korea, and Singapore.

In order to gain customers' confidence, Thai Textile Group places emphasis on customer service in two keys aspects: it keeps its promises and delivers, and it is honest with its customers. For instance, if products cannot be produced as requested, the company notifies buyers immediately. This has become the company's key strength. Though prices in China, India, Indonesia, and other countries may be lower, buyers still prefer Thai Textile Group because it fulfills what it promises. The company always delivers the identical quality of products seen in samples, ships products on time, and complies with sale terms and conditions. As a result, buyers have developed confidence and trust in the company's products and service.

The company acquires knowledge on foreign markets mainly from customers and sources on the Internet. Representatives of the company usually arrange meetings with foreign buyers abroad. This face-to-face meeting gives the company insights on markets as well as on the people with whom they are working.

The company maintains connections with potential buyers and companies in the same industry. They are key sources of valuable information on potential buyers and current market trends. Both parties can exchange information to gain insight on the nature of new buyers and new markets.

Thai Textile Group views networks as a source of referrals. The company gains new customers through companies in the same industry, customers, and even customers of its customers.

In order to manage and maintain trust within its networks, Thai Textile Group uses the same principles of how people expect to be treated by their friends—have regular conversations, exchange opinions, find time to meet, have dinners, and send greetings on special occasions. Most importantly, they are collaborative, help each other, and are honest with each other.

7.5 CONCLUSION

This chapter highlights the importance of networks in the Asia Pacific, which play a crucial role in assisting companies to internationalize. Networks provide expertise and information relevant to internationalization, such as market information, work procedures, rules and regulations, and referring key contacts for helping internationalization, as well as potential customers or business partners. Sharing information, market insights, and combined expertise in networks can drive companies to succeed in the internationalization process.

Networks are core to businesses in Asia. The concept of networks in specific cultures and evidence of utilization are pointed out, such as the guanxi networks in China, Taiwan, and Singapore; the Japanese keiretsu; the South Korean chaebol; and examples of networks in Thailand and Malaysia. Personal networks were found to have played the most prominent roles in the Asian business world.

It is interesting to point out the evolving business relationship within networks. In Asia, the business relationship has developed and evolved toward a closer relationship—from business network to personal network. In other words, the relationship has evolved from business partnership to friendship, where friendship is considered the greatest of all relationships in the trustworthy networks.

REFERENCES

Aldrich, H.E., Zimmer, C., 1986. Entrepreneurship through social networks. In: Sexton, D.L., Wilson, R.W. (Eds.), The Art and Science of Entrepreneurship. Ballinger, Cambridge, MA, pp. 154–167.

Aoki, K., Lennerfors, T.T., 2013. The new, improved keiretsu. Harv. Bus. Rev. 91 (9), 109–113. Available from: https://hbr.org/2013/09/the-new-improved-keiretsu#.

Bian, Y., Ang, S., 1997. Guanxi networks and job mobility in China and Singapore. Soc. Forces. 75 (3), 981–1005. http://dx.doi.org/10.1093/sf/75.3.981.

Chen, M., Chang, Y., Lee, C., 2015. Creative entrepreneurs' guanxi networks and success: Information and resource. J. Bus. Res. 68 (4), 900–905. http://dx.doi.org/10.1016/j.jbusres.2014.11.049.

Coviello, N., Cox, M., 2006. The resource dynamics of international new venture networks. J. Int. Entrep. 4 (2-3), 113–132. http://dx.doi.org/10.1007/s10843-007-0004-4.

Coviello, N., Munro, H.J., 1997. Network relationships and the internationalisation process of small software firms. Int. Bus. Rev. 6 (2), 1–26. http://dx.doi.org/10.1016/S0969-5931(97)00010-3.

Dollinger, M.J., 2003. Entrepreneurship: Strategies and Resources, third ed. Pearson Education, Inc., Upper Saddle River, NJ

Elango, B., Pattnaik, C., 2007. Building capabilities for international operations through networks: A study of Indian firms. J. Int. Bus. Stud. 38 (4), 541–555. http://dx.doi.org/10.1057/palgrave.jibs.8400280.

Fiegenbaum, A., Thomas, H., 1995. Strategic groups as reference groups: Theory, modelling and empirical examination of industry and competitive strategy. Strateg. Manag. J. 16, 461–476. http://dx.doi.org/10.1002/smj.4250160605.

Fiegenbaum, A., Hart, S., Schendel, D., 1996. Strategic reference point theory. Strateg. Manag. J. 17, 219–235. http://dx.doi.org/10.1002/(SICI)1097-0266(199603)17:3<219::AID-SMJ806>3.0.CO;2-N.

Gartner, W.B., Bellamy, M.B., 2009. Entreprise. Cengage/South-Western Publishing, Cincinnati, OH.

Gomez, E.T., Hsiao, H.M., 2012. Chinese Business in Southeast Asia. Routledge Curzon, London.

Granovetter, M.S., 1973. The strength of weak ties. Am. J. Sociol. 78 (6), 1360–1380. Available from: https://sociology.stanford.edu/sites/default/files/publications/the_strength_of_weak_ties_and_exch_w-gans.pdf.

Groen, A.J., 2005. Knowledge intensive entrepreneurship in networks: Toward a multi-level/multi dimensional approach. J. Enterp. Cult. 13 (1), 69–88. Available from:http://www.insme.org/files/1810.

Hamilton, G.G., 1996. Asian Business Networks. Walter de Gruyter, Berlin; New York.

Hammond, C.S., Glenn, M.L., 2004. E:CO. 6.The Ancient Practice of Chinese Social Networking: Guanxi and Social Network Theory. Emergent Publications, AZ. Available from: http://emergentpublications.com/ECO/ECO_other/Issue_6_1-2_6_AC.pdf.

Hitt, M.A., Tihanyi, L., Miller, T., Connelly, B., 2006. International diversification: Antecedents, outcomes, and moderators. J. Manag. 32 (6), 831–867. http://dx.doi.org/10.1177/0149206306293575.

Hoang, H., Antoncic, B., 2003. Network-based research in entrepreneurship - a critical review. J. Bus. Ventur. 18 (2), 165–187. http://dx.doi.org/10.1016/S0883-9026(02)00081-2.

Hung, W.S., Ho, S.H., 2010. A study of guanxi and employment in Taiwan. Available from: http://proj3.sinica.edu.tw/~tea/images/stories/file/WP0118.pdf.

Hutchings, K., Murray, G., 2002. Working with guanxi: An assessment of the implications of globalisation on business networking in China. Creat. Innov. Manag. 11 (3), 184–191. http://dx.doi.org/10.1111/1467-8691.00251.

Jaafar, M., Abdul-Aziz, A.R., Sahari, Md H., 2009. The use of social network theory on entrepreneur's linkages development. Theor. Empir. Res. Urban Manag. 4 (1s), 101–119. Available from: http://www.um.ase.ro/No1S/9.pdf.

Johannisson, B., 2000. Networking and entrepreneurial growth. In: Sexton, D., Landström, H. (Eds.), Handbook of Entrepreneurship. Blackwell, London, pp. 368–386.

Johanson, J., Mattsson, L.G., 1988. Internationalization in industrial systems – A network approach. In: Hood, N., Vahlne, J.-E. (Eds.), Strategies in Global Competition. Beckham, London, pp. 287–313.

Johanson, J., Vahlne, J.E., 2009. The Uppsala internationalization process model revisited: From liability of foreignness to liability of outsidership. J. Int. Bus. Stud. 49 (9), 1411–1421. http://dx.doi.org/10.1057/jibs.2009.24.

Johnsen, R.E., Johnsen, T.E., 1999. International market development through networks: The case of Ayrshire knitwear sector. Int. J. Entrep. Behav. Res. 5 (6), 297–312. Available from: http://dx.doi.org/10.1108/13552559910306114.

Kienzle, R., Shadur, M., 1997. Developments in business networks in East Asia. Manag. Decis. 35 (1), 23–32. Available from: http://dx.doi.org/10.1108/00251749710160151.

Knoke, D., n.d. It's different in East Asia. https://www.soc.umn.edu/~knoke/pages/It's_Different_in_East_Asia.pdf (accessed 05.04.16.).

Kontinen, T., Ojala, A., 2011. Network ties in the international opportunity recognition of family SMEs. Int. Bus. Rev. 20 (4), 440–453. http://dx.doi.org/10.1016/j.ibusrev.2010.08.002.

Lee, D.J., Pae, J.H., Wong, Y.H., 2001. A model of close business relationships in China (guanxi). Eur. J. Mark. 35(½), 51–69. http://dx.doi.org/10.1108/03090560110363346.

Leyden, D., Link, A., Siegel, D., 2014. A theoretical analysis of the role of social networks in entrepreneurship. Res. Policy 43 (7), 1157–1163. http://dx.doi.org/10.1016/j.respol.2014.04.010.

Lincoln, J.R., Shimotani, M., 2009. Whither the Keiretsu, Japan's business networks? How were they structured? What did they do? Why are they gone?: IRLE Working Paper No. 188-09. Available from: http://irle.berkeley.edu/workingpapers/188-09.pdf.

Luo, Y., 2000. Guanxi and business. Asia-Pacific Business Series. 1. Available from: https://books.google.co.th/books?hl=en&lr=&id=-GXVCgAAQBAJ&oi=fnd&pg=PR5&dq=Business+networking+in+Myanmar&ots=DOgdLN4_sl&sig=klrWb4i1MD1tgV8LOAb6F8u8xj4&redir_esc=y#v=onepage&q&f=false.

Nahapiet, J., Ghoshal, S., 1998. Social capital, intellectual capital, and the organizational advantage. Acad. Manag. Rev. 23 (2), 242–266. Available from: http://www.jstor.org/stable/259373.

Neegaard, H., Madsen, H., 2004. Knowledge intensive entrepreneurship in a social capital perspective. J. Enterp. Cult. 12 (2), 105–125. http://dx.doi.org/10.1142/S0218495804000063.

Ojala, A., 2009. Internationalization of knowledge-intensive SMEs: The role of network relationships in the entry to a psychically distant market. Int. Bus. Rev. 18 (1), 50–59. http://dx.doi.org/10.1016/j.ibusrev.2008.10.002.

Parnell, M.F., 2005. Chinese business guanxi: An organisation or non-organisation? J. Organ. Transform. Soc. Chang. 2 (1), 29–47. http://dx.doi.org/10.1386/jots.2.1.29/1.

Prashantham, S., Birkinshaw, J., 2015. Choose your friends carefully: Home-country ties and new venture internationalization. Manag. Int. Rev. 55 (2), 207–234. http://dx.doi.org/10.1007/s11575-015-0244-9.

Schreier, C., Udomkit, N., Dievernich, F.E.P., 2015. The roles of competencies, cultural intelligence, and intuition in SMEs internationalization. In: Conference Proceedings. The International Conference on Tourism and Business.

Senik, Z., Scott-Ladd, B., Entrekin, L., Adham, K., 2011. Networking and internationalization of SMEs in emerging economies. J. Int. Entrep. 9 (4), 259–281. http://dx.doi.org/10.1007/s10843-011-0078-x.

Sim, A.B., Pandian, J.R., 2003. Emerging Asian MNEs and their internationalization strategies—Case study evidence on Taiwanese and Singaporean firms. Asia. Asia Pac. J. Manag. 20, 27–50. Available from: http://www.mmt3000.dk/Upload/K16%20sim%20emerging%20asian%20mnes%20olavs.pdf.

Szeto, R., Wright, C.P., Cheng, E., 2006. Business networking in the Chinese context: Its role in the formation of guanxi, social capital and ethical foundations. Manage. Res. News 29 (7), 425–438. http://dx.doi.org/10.1108/01409170610690880.

Vanhonacker, R.W., 2004. Guanxi networks in China: How to be the spider, not to fly. China Bus. Rev. 48–53. Available from: http://mabrito.net/spring14/420/Guanxi%20in%20China.pdf.

Wang, C.M., Woods, M., 2013. The role of guanxi in rural social movements: Two case studies from Taiwan. J. Agrar. Chang. 13 (2), 197–212. http://dx.doi.org/10.1111/j.1471-0366.2012.00359.x.

Wong, J.M., 2012. The guanxi strategies of Taiwanese firms in China's economic reforms. J. Glob. Bus. Manage. 8, 111–115. Available from: http://www.jgbm.org/page/15%20Jeng-Min%20Wong.pdf.

Zain, M., Ng, S.I., 2006. The impacts of network relationships on SMEs' internationalization process. Thunderbird Int. Bus. Rev. 48 (2), 183–205. http://dx.doi.org/10.1002/tie.20092.

Zhou, L., Wu, W., Luo, X., 2007. Internationalization and the performance of born-global SMEs: The mediating role of social networks. J. Int. Bus. Stud. 38 (4), 673–690. http://dx.doi.org/10.1057/palgrave.jibs.8400282.

CHAPTER 8

Internationalization Through Investor, Advisory Board, and Accountant Networks: An Exploratory Study of Australian SMEs

C.R. Graves*, P-S. Seet†
*The University of Adelaide Business School, Adelaide, SA, Australia
†Edith Cowan University, Joondalup, WA, Australia

8.1 INTRODUCTION

In recent years, in line with globalization trends, small and medium enterprises (SMEs) have been encouraged to internationalize their activities in order to survive and grow (Coviello and McAuley, 1999; Lu and Beamish, 2001b). As a result, researchers have sought to understand the internationalization process of SMEs, which has resulted in the development of theories such as the Uppsala model (Johanson and Vahlne, 1990) to explain patterns of internationalization. Other existing theories (e.g., network theory, resource-based view theory) have been drawn on to understand why some firms are more successful than others in internationalizing their operations. Increasing attention is being given to factors ("enablers") that assist SME internationalization (Love and Roper, 2015), and these fall broadly into two categories: internal enablers (e.g., skills, leadership, research and development) (Freel, 2005; Harris and Moffat, 2011), and external enablers (e.g., links or networks, government support, and the role of customers) (Eckaus, 2008; Love and Roper, 2015). The focus of this study is on external enablers—specifically, an SME's network ties with external investors, external advisors, and advisory boards, and whether such ties influence the firm's likelihood to internationalize.

Research has found that network ties can provide firms with access to resources essential for internationalization (Kontinen and Ojala, 2010). This is especially critical among smaller firms that typically have limited resources,

Internationalization and Managing Networks in the Asia Pacific
http://dx.doi.org/10.1016/B978-0-08-100813-3.00008-0

whereby network ties act as an enabler to foreign markets (Johanson and Mattsson, 1988). In such cases, network ties of individuals, especially among key actors associated with the SMEs, play a significant role in terms of supporting SMEs in their internationalization processes (Coviello, 2006; Coviello and Munro, 1997; Crick and Spence, 2005; Ghauri et al., 2003). SMEs not only use internal knowledge and networks of the owner-manager and the top management team (TMT), but also the external knowledge and networks of partners (e.g., suppliers, customers, and investors) (Fernhaber et al., 2009). Family SMEs have been found to engage less in external networking activities, which may explain why their internationalization lags behind that of their nonfamily counterparts (Graves and Thomas, 2006, 2008).

The role of external network ties of SMEs has been a particular focus in research on the rapid growth of new international ventures (Coviello, 2006; Zhou et al., 2007). The effect of leveraging the networks of key external partners of SMEs is relatively underresearched (Manolova et al., 2010). Little is known, for example, whether external network ties encourage SMEs to venture from a domestic market focus and whether different types of external network ties are more influential than others. This study aims to further understanding on the effect of three different types of external network ties (external investors, advisory boards, and external accountants) on the likelihood of SMEs to venture beyond their domestic market.

8.2 THEORETICAL BACKGROUND

This section provides an overview of the concept of networking and discusses its potential enabling role in the internationalization of a firm. Second, we briefly discuss the internationalization of SMEs. Third, we examine research on how key external partners, namely investors, advisory boards, and accountants, can have an impact on SME internationalization.

8.2.1 Networks, SMEs, and Internationalization

The term "network" is loosely defined in SME research, but generally involves sets of two or more connected exchange relationships (Axelsson and Easton, 1992), which can be formal or informal in nature. This includes individuals and firms that are linked through interactions that consist largely of social interactions (Kiss and Danis, 2008). The premise that underlies much of the research on SME networks is that they provide access to much-needed resources and thereby enable SMEs to overcome their resource constraints (BarNir and Smith, 2002; Madhok, 2002) and the liability of "smallness" (Aldrich and Auster, 1986; BarNir and Smith, 2002).

Recent research suggests that firms increasingly rely on relationships rather than "arms-length," contractual arrangements (Chesbrough, 2003; Cooke et al., 2004; Seely-Brown and Duguid, 2001). These relationships may be formal (Hagedoorn et al., 2000), informal, or based on social relationships with acquaintances that individuals within organizations possess (Gulati, 1998; Oliver and Liebeskind, 1998). Furthermore, formal organizational-level relationships are often underpinned by informal, interpersonal relationships among members of different organizations (Perkmann and Walsh, 2007). In the SME context, networks and contacts with other people provide social sources of opportunity-relevant information, which can then be acted on by the owner-manager (Ozgen and Baron, 2007). Social networks have been found to be important in opportunity recognition (Singh, 2000), and the larger the entrepreneur's or owner-manager's social networks, the more opportunities they recognize (Singh et al., 1999).

Johanson and Mattsson's (1988) model of internationalization follows a similar argument but in the context of foreign market entry, as it was observed that in the 1980s, the incremental internationalization models were not able to fully explain how firms entered foreign markets. They argued that it was important for firms to develop network ties with other firms in a foreign market, as this will facilitate entry to these markets by acting as "bridges" or "insiders" (Chetty and Blankenburg Holm, 2000; Johanson and Vahlne, 1990). For the majority of SMEs, the networks they have are predominantly domestic; in terms of internationalization, unless the SME owner-manager has personal network ties to these foreign networks, they will be treated as "outsiders." As SMEs have limited financial and managerial resources available for international expansion (Chetty and Campbell-Hunt, 2003), they need to leverage their relationships with other firms (Chetty and Wilson, 2003) or with partners to gain entry and develop these international business relationships.

The strength of ties refers to the "combination of the amount of time, the emotional intensity, the intimacy and the reciprocal services that characterize the tie" (Granovetter, 1973: 1361). The relative strength of ties in a network has become an important source of research in terms of explaining differences in outcomes from a network perspective. In terms of internationalization, close geographic proximity is assumed to facilitate strong relational ties between firms (Granovetter 1973), and SMEs in general have relatively stronger ties domestically than internationally. Specifically, geographic closeness facilitates repeated interactions among firms and helps organizations develop the mutual trust and reciprocity needed to maintain relationships (Etzioni and Etzioni, 1999; Harrison, 1992; Rosenfeld, 1997). To that end, while SME owner-managers may lack strong ties with foreign markets, they could make up for this by leveraging their domestic partners who may have ties in these foreign markets, thereby capitalizing on what Granovetter has called the "strength of weak ties." The extent to which SMEs rely on weak or strong ties when pursuing international opportunities remains uncertain (Kiss and Danis, 2008). However, it is common that SMEs rely on partners that are able to help act as bridges; these may be in the form of domestic customers, suppliers, collaborators, investors, advisors, government agencies, and any firm or person that may be part of the SME's value chain (Corral de Zubielqui et al., 2015). In that sense, these may be a form of what Söderqvist and Chetty (2013) have called an "equally strong as weak relationship," whereby stronger relationships may dominate but they play an important broker role to link with other unconnected networks.

Most of the research on networks focuses on interorganizational (business-to-business) linkages (Coviello and McAuley, 1999; Jones, 1999). Limited research has been conducted on the social network ties of the key decision makers within SMEs (usually the owner-manager), as the extent to which they rely on such networks is complex and varies significantly across countries and institutional contexts (Kiss and Danis, 2008). As we will discuss further, social network relationships developed by SME owner-managers can be formal or informal, and include business professionals (e.g., accountants, advisors, financiers, and lawyers) and government officials, in addition to those with family and friends. This study is concerned with the network ties that owner-managers have with investors and two advisor groups, and whether such networks influence the likelihood of an SME to internationalize its operations.

8.2.2 Investor, Advisory Board, and Accountant Networks

Leveraging other people within a firm's network for information and other resources can assist in recognizing and exploiting opportunities (Aldrich, 1999; Ardichvili et al., 2003). Within these networks, relationships can be divided into formal and informal ones (Rialp et al., 2005; Westphal et al., 2006). Formal relationships are related to business activities between two or more actors in the networks, while informal relationships refer to personal relationships between family members and friends (Coviello and Munro,

1997). It is sometimes unclear whether the formal-informal distinction can be clearly applied to the SME context. For example, external investor(s) and advisory board members of SMEs may also be personal friends of the owners. Similarly, the firm's external accountant may have been working with the firm over a long time and therefore built a personal relationship with the owner-manager. Notwithstanding this, the relationships with regard to investors, boards, and accountants are governed by contractual and regulatory requirements. While much research has been conducted on these relationships in terms of corporate governance (Wright et al., 2007) and SME finance (Bygrave et al., 2003; Seet and Graves, 2010), there appears to be little done on how SMEs could use the less formalized roles with these external partners in facilitating internationalization (Tanewski and Carey, 2007).

Based on this, Agndal et al. (2008) would claim that given that these are not the core functions of these external partners (e.g., investors are mainly there to provide finance, and accountants are mainly there to facilitate auditing and financial reporting), they therefore are "serendipitous" roles of social capital in terms of facilitating internationalization, and as such are less important in early phases of internationalization. In contrast, we argue that these supplementary roles of external partners play an important "efficacy" role, especially in terms of facilitating foreign market entry.

Research has also shown that it is not just the reliance on one external network partner that is enough, but rather that the diversity of the external partner network will offer benefits of enhanced opportunity recognition (Manolova et al., 2014). Relationships with different partners can provide SMEs opportunities to learn about a greater number of markets, their degree of attractiveness, their local competitive conditions, and their sociocultural and institutional environments, thus facilitating the internationalization process (Eriksson et al., 1997, Kiss and Danis, 2010). So in the context of our research, SMEs that rely on more than one of their external partners (e.g., financial investor, advisory board, or external accountant) may be able to leverage their networks and resources to internationalize more effectively.

8.2.3 SME—Investor Ties and Internationalization

Research has found that SME owner-managers have difficulty engaging with external financial investors because of the existence of finance gaps, knowledge gaps, and empathy gaps between the two parties (Seet et al., 2010). While research has shown that it is important for SMEs in relatively undeveloped financial markets to cultivate links with foreign investors to raise finance (Hymer, 1976), when external investors take on a value-added role beyond that of merely providing financing, and especially if they develop a form of mentorlike relationship with the owner-manager, they are able to bring significant knowledge and experience to the SME or start-up and thereby help them be alert to more opportunities (Kaish and Gilad, 1991; Ozgen and Baron, 2007).

As Manolova et al. (2014) argue, external investors who have good networks are able to offer benefits beyond that of merely securing financial resources for growth. Leveraging financial networks can potentially yield more than just the finance that is exchanged (Uzzi and Gillespie, 2002), and research has shown that in the context of raising venture capital or private equity (PE) financing, the "extra-financial" value may be more distinctive than the functionally equivalent investment capital secured (Hsu, 2004). These value-added benefits may include important contacts in the investor's networks that could provide business referrals, mentoring, or nonfinancial assistance that may be instrumental in the internationalization process (Manolova et al., 2014). Value-adding investors, like venture capitalists and PE investors, focus on growing the businesses they invest in as a whole, which broadens the applicability of their knowledge to the entire business and facilitates internationalization (Fernhaber et al., 2009). Therefore these investors can contribute to SME internationalization via their expert knowledge (De Clercq and Dimov, 2008), experience in strategy and decision-making (Maula et al., 2005), recruiting relevant talent (Hellmann and Puri, 2002), and network contacts (Busenitz et al., 2004). Besides providing "know-what," "know-why," "know-how," and "know-who" to facilitate SME internationalization (Park et al., 2015), external financial investors can also support SME internationalization by conferring legitimacy (LiPuma, 2006), which is sometimes especially important for firms entering new markets. A study of Turkish SMEs found that smaller firms sought to form alliances with foreign capital providers in order to access foreign markets and expand production capacity (Ulubaşoğlu et al., 2009).

Hence, besides gaining access to financial capital, there could be reduced information acquisition costs and improved knowledge of foreign market opportunities, thereby reducing the learning curve and potential transaction costs for SMEs, which would result in increased internationalization (Zhou et al., 2007). Hence we hypothesize that:

H1: The internationalization status of SMEs is positively associated with their investor networks.

8.2.4 SME—Advisory Board Ties and Internationalization

An agency-based view of a board's role is to act as a check and balance for the executive. However, board members can play a broader role to help owner-managers avoid the traps of success and maintain the entrepreneurial drive that builds their companies and their reputations, and therefore protect themselves against inertia-inducing conservatism (Brunninge et al., 2007; Ranft and O'Neill, 2001). Based on the resource-based view of the firm, board members' experience, knowledge, expertise, and networks are valuable, rare, inimitable, and nonsubstitutable resources that make up the "advisory" board potential (Barroso et al., 2011). Nadler et al. (2011) further contend that a board can not only be involved in strategic decisions, but also provide input into the strategy implementation process. In line with this, Kim et al. (2009) assert that board members can inject a strategic perspective into the decision-making processes that enhances TMTs' strategic action capabilities. They also argue that today's competitive landscape should call for both an internal (e.g., between strategy and structure) and an external (e.g., between structure and environment) fit that provide a basis for competitive advantage. Others have found that a board with a high percentage of independent directors provides greater independence and will become more involved in strategic decision-making (Kaymak and Bektas, 2008; Osma, 2008).

Following this line of argument, the considerable risk and significant managerial challenges that internationalization brings increase demands on corporate mechanisms to govern top managers (Musteen et al., 2009). Because international markets are highly complex and dynamic (Sanders and Carpenter, 1998), advisory board members who may possess relevant information, resources, and international experience could be exploited to enhance the TMT capabilities in terms of internationalization (Finkelstein et al., 2009; Luo, 2007). Chen (2011) finds positive associations of TMT tenure and international experience are stronger as more independent directors are included on the board, suggesting that boards that act as monitors and resource providers may offer better advice and counsel to executives and enhance their strategic action capabilities in moving toward internationalization.

However, there is still relatively little research into how advisory boards and top executives are interrelated in shaping firm strategies (Brunninge et al., 2007; Wu, 2008), and especially so in terms of internationalization strategies (Chen, 2011). Our research aims to fill this research gap by highlighting the potential influence of advisory boards in facilitating SME internationalization.

In the limited research on boards and their influence on SME internationalization, advisory boards have been found to be an important strategic resource contributing to SME internationalization expansion (Calabro et al., 2009). In their research on Norwegian family SMEs, Calabrò and Mussolino (2013) found that boards provided assistance in the selection and implementation of internationalization strategy through an "interdependence" relationship between family board members who had intimate knowledge of the internal workings of the firm and independent board members who had more experience on external markets and opportunities. This reinforced earlier research that found that family SMEs that move beyond family-dominated governance to establishing a board that is "advisory" in nature are more likely to be international (Calabro et al., 2009).

Hence we hypothesize that:

H2: The internationalization status of SMEs is positively associated with whether they have an advisory board.

8.2.5 SME—External Accountant Ties and Internationalization

Like external financial investors and advisory boards, SMEs can leverage the advice of their external accountant, and research has shown that where this advice was used, SMEs reported better performance (Berry et al., 2006). In an Australian study of SMEs, it was found that accountants, banks, other business operators, and family/friends were the most commonly consulted services, while lawyers, government agencies, industry associations, and management consultants were only infrequently used (Jay and Schaper, 2003). This is in line with other studies in other countries that found that the most common external resource for SME owner-managers is their accountant, as roughly 75%–95% of all SMEs rely on an external accountant for services and advice (Bennett and Smith, 2002; Berry et al., 2006; Chrisman et al., 2009b; Jay and Schaper, 2003; Robson and Bennett, 2000).

Other research suggests that external accountants of small and medium-sized family business owners are the first port of call when seeking advice on planning for significant change (e.g., exit, succession, or alternative financing) (Seet and Graves, 2010). One reason may be that SME owner-managers are able to more willingly and comfortably confide in their accountant on sensitive issues and ask them for additional advice regarding business strategies, personnel issues, and much more. Consequently, there have been many cases where clients have reportedly told their accountants information that they have not shared with their spouses (Vago, 1998). While external accountants have been dubbed the small and medium-sized family firm's "most trusted advisor" and are commonly regarded as "one-stop shops" for advice (Chrisman et al., 2009a; Strike, 2013), this is also seen to apply generally among nonfamily SMEs, where the majority seek advice from accountants if they only have one source of external advice (Bennett and Robson, 1999).

However, SME owner-managers do not normally see their accountants as a potentially important point of entry into wider ecosystems or new markets (Smallbone et al., 1993), and adopt a very narrow "bookkeeper" relationship with their external accountants (Nandan, 2010). While some SMEs may make extensive use of external accountants as business advisors, a substantial proportion uses them only to a minor degree (Gooderham et al., 2004). This is because the SME-accountant relationship is characterized by a very specific institutional framework of self-regulation, whereby accountants are seen as mainly implementers of statutory audit requirements (Bennett and Robson, 1999). This practice is reinforced by SMEs mainly engaging small accounting practices as their favored advisors for reasons of keeping costs down (Arnold et al., 1984). This is in line with what resource-based theory would also lead us to suppose—that the use small firms make of their accountants as sources of business advice will be a function of the resources at the disposal of the firm. That is, the more resources (tangible and intangible) a firm disposes, the more likely it is that the accountant will be used as a business advisor (Gooderham et al., 2004). Smaller accountant practices also lack expertise and training in areas beyond routine compliance work (mainly the preparation of financial statements and taxation returns, and audits) (Kirby and King, 1997; Nandan, 2010).

However, as Seet et al. (2010) found, beyond compliance work, there is an expectation among other stakeholders in the industry that SMEs need to seek the services of mid- to upper-tier accounting firms that have broader and deeper experience, for example in the complexities around succession, exit, and external funding. Based on this, there should be a similar link between SMEs that are planning to internationalize, given that larger accountancy practices have increasingly "depicted themselves as multidisciplinary practices, one-stop shops for an extensive array of services, including financial advisory, management consulting, and legal services" (Greenwood et al., 2002: 58). In spite of this, there is limited research on whether SMEs do seek out the services of larger external accountants when they wish to access foreign markets.

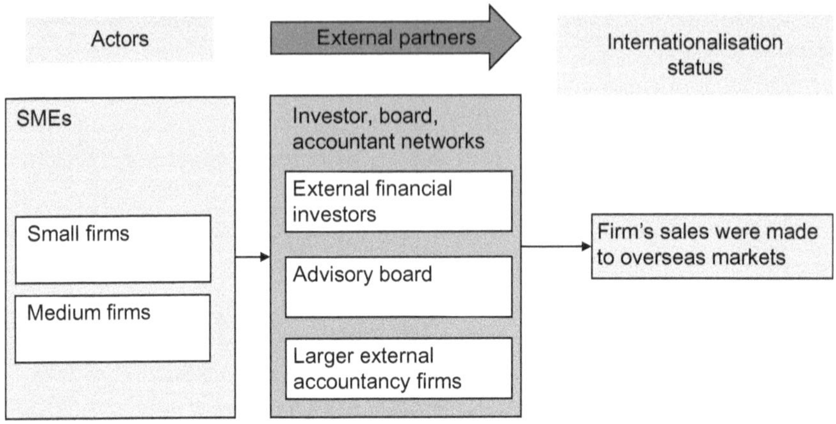

Fig. 8.1 Conceptual model.

Hence we hypothesize that:

H3: The internationalization status of SMEs is positively associated with the size of the external accounting firm they use.

8.2.6 Conceptual Framework

Fig. 8.1 presents the conceptual framework derived from external investor, advisory board, and external accountant network factors that may influence SME internationalization.

8.3 RESEARCH METHOD

8.3.1 Sample, Data Collection, and Respondents

Data was collected through a survey of firms. Drawing on survey instruments developed in previous academic research, a 240-item questionnaire was developed with the assistance of business researchers, business owners, and advisors. The questionnaire contained six sections: firm and owner characteristics, firm performance, management and strategic issues, practices and attitudes to financing alternatives, succession and exit plans, and sources of advice for business and financing issues.

The population used in this study was of Australian SMEs, which is defined as businesses that employ between 5 and 200 employees (Australian Bureau of Statistics, 2002). To avoid geographical bias, using the Dunn and Bradstreet database, 2300 Australian privately owned (i.e., unlisted) SMEs were randomly selected from two states in Australia that represented regions of high and low economic growth and private investment activity (Victoria and South Australia). The questionnaire was sent to the chief decision maker (the chief executive officer) together with a cover letter that explained the purpose of the study and outlined an incentive to encourage participation (donation made to charity). A follow-up letter was sent 3 weeks after the initial questionnaire was distributed, which resulted in 385 completed questionnaires (response rate of 16.7%). After removing invalid questionnaires (incomplete, non-SMEs <5 or >200 employees), a total of 325 usable questionnaires remained.

8.3.2 Dependent Variables—Internationalization Status

As highlighted in the introduction section, this study focuses on the influence of investor and advisor networks on the internationalization of SMEs. There has been a lack of consensus over the measurement of internationalization, particularly of large firms (Lewis and Minchev, 2001; Sullivan, 1996). However, as mentioned earlier, as exporting is considered the most common foreign market entry mode of SMEs (Leonidou and Katsikeas, 1996), the most common measurement of SME internationalization is the ratio of foreign sales to total sales (Bell et al., 2001; Lu and Beamish, 2001a; Westhead et al., 2001). As this study focuses on determinants of being internationally active (vs. domestically focused), internationalization was measured in terms of whether any of the firm's sales were made to overseas markets. Specifically, internationalization status (DV1) was measured using a dichotomous variable to indicate whether a firm was internationally active (foreign sales dollars >0 = "1," otherwise "0").

8.3.3 Independent Variables—Investor Networks, Advisory Board Networks, External Accountant Networks

This study focuses on the influence of three types of networks on internationalization: external investor networks, advisory board networks, and external accountant networks.

Given that we are studying external investment in SMEs that generally have little access to public investment markets, we focused on providers of outside PE financing, which forms a growing part of the external investment in the SME sector (ABS, 2010; Ahn et al., 2011; AVCAL, 2013). We utilize a broad definition of external PE financing that encompasses a range of potential sources of outside equity. Specifically, we define PE as an investment by a person (e.g., business angel) or an intermediary (e.g., managed investment fund, venture capital/PE firms), excluding funds provided by owners, family, relations, and friends (i.e., excluding "insiders"). To ascertain their links to outside PE networks, we asked the key decision maker whether he or she had experience with or previously used outside PE investment from individuals (e.g., business angels) (yes/no) or from intermediaries (e.g., PE/venture capital firms) (yes/no). Firms where the key decision maker had experience with/previously used outside PE from both individuals and intermediaries were coded "2," coded "1" if they had experience with/previously used one source but not the other, while those that had not experienced/used either source were coded "0."

Another influential and trusted source of advice is that from a board. For most SMEs, there is no legal requirement to establish a formal board of directors. However, some will choose to establish an independent board (i.e., board comprising outside directors) because of the perceived value from accessing particular advice, expertise, and the broader networks of board members. SMEs commonly establish an "informal" board (often referred to as an "advisory board") as part of the journey toward establishing an independent board of directors. Although both boards are similar in that they comprise "outsiders" with the requisite expertise and networks, only formal boards are recognized as having legal rights and responsibilities by Australian Corporations Law. Regardless of whether an SME has established an informal board or a formal board, both can play an important role in accessing needed outside expertise and oversight for the SME. For the purposes of this study, both types of boards are referred to as "advisory boards." The use of an advisory board was measured using an ordinal measure. Specifically, the key decision maker was asked whether the firm had an advisory board or an independent board of directors in place. SMEs with no board in place were coded "0," currently putting a board in place were coded "1," while those with an established board were coded "2."

External accountants have traditionally been regarded as the "most trusted" advisor to SME owners (Khadem, 2013). However, as previously discussed, external accountants are not a homogeneous group, and one of the key distinguishing features is the size (and consequently resources and expertise) of the accounting firms they work for. Traditionally, accounting firms have been grouped according to the "Big 4" (EY, PwC, Deloitte, and KPMG), "second-tier firms" (medium-large accounting firms), and "third-tier firms" (small local firm/sole practitioner). The bigger the accounting firm, the more it is able to advise on a broader range of issues (including international expansion) because of the diverse knowledge resident among its employees and strategic alliances. In this survey, the size of the accounting firm used by the SME was measured using an ordinal measure. Specifically, the key decision maker was asked whether the SME predominantly utilized a "small local firm/sole practitioner" (coded "1"), "medium/large firm" (coded "2"), or "Big 4 international firm" (coded "3") for their external accounting and business advisory needs.

8.3.4 Control Variables

The following control variables were included in the study when examining the influence of external investor, advisory board, and external accountant networks on internationalization:

Age of firm: The process perspective of internationalization argues that knowledge and experience are associated with internationalization (Johanson and Vahlne, 1977). Because older firms are more likely to accumulate greater knowledge and experience, this study controlled for the influence of firm age. Specifically, firm age was measured at the number of years the firm had been in existence since establishment.

Size of firm: Prior research has used firm size as a proxy for the amount of resources available for internationalization (Zahra, 2003). The total number of full-time equivalent employees was used to measure firm size.

Past performance: Firms with superior performance have a greater ability to expand internationally for several reasons, such as retained profits to fund expansion. As a consequence, the key decision maker was asked six questions to assess how the firm performed over the past 12 months. Specifically, using a five-point Likert scale ranging from "strongly disagree" (coded "1") to "strongly agree" (coded "5"), respondents were asked questions such as "our firm has been very profitable" and "our performance has been very satisfactory." An overall composite measure of past performance was calculated by adding the responses to the six questions on performance.

Family business status: Whether the SME was a family business was controlled for because such firms have been shown to have a lower propensity to internationalize (Graves and Thomas, 2004). Although a single agreed definition of a family firm still remains elusive, there is general consensus that a business owned and managed by a nuclear family is a family business (Chua et al., 1999). Others studies (Sonfield and Lussier, 2004; Westhead et al., 2002) included perception as a "family business" because this identification by owners as a "family" in "business" (i.e., family "matters") is what influences their behavior and distinctiveness when compared to nonfamily firms. For the purposes of this study, a family business was defined as one that was (1) perceived by the key decision maker to be a family business, with (2) at least 50% of the firm owned or controlled by a single family group related by blood or marriage.

Industry: An SME's primary industry was controlled for because not all industries lend themselves to global expansion. SMEs were classified into one of the following five industry groups: primary industries (i.e., agriculture), construction, manufacturing, retail and wholesale trade, and service-based industries. The service-based industry category was used as the reference category when undertaking the statistical analysis. That is, the other four industry categories were included in the regression models used ($n-1=4$ categories included).

Respondent characteristics: To control for the potential influence of respondent characteristics on the dependent variable, their highest level of education (ranging from "primary school" coded as "1" to "postgraduate degree" coded as "7") was included as a control variable.

In summary, the following model was used to test the influence of external investor, advisory board, and external accountant networks on the internationalization status of SMEs while controlling for firm-level and respondent-level variables:

$$\begin{aligned}\text{Internationalization status} &= \beta_0 + \beta_{1-3}(\text{Investor networks, advisory board, accounting firm size}) \\ &\quad + \beta_4(\text{firm age}) + \beta_5(\text{firm size}) + \beta_6(\text{past performance}) \\ &\quad + \beta_7(\text{family business status}) + \beta_{8-11}(\text{firm industry}) \\ &\quad + \beta_{12}(\text{respondent's education}) + \varepsilon\end{aligned}$$

8.4 DATA ANALYSIS

As outlined, as the dependent variable was measured using a dichotomous variable, logistic regression analysis was used to examine the influence of investor and advisor networks on the internationalization status of SMEs, while controlling for firm age, firm size, past performance, family business status, principal industry, and respondent's level of education.

To ascertain concerns regarding multicollinearity between independent and control variables, the Pearson matrix was used. Table 8.1 indicates there are no correlation values between explanatory variables that reach 0.3. Second, potential multicollinearity is further examined through estimation of the variance inflation factor (VIF). As reported in Table 8.1, VIF values of all the independent and control variables are below eight. Based on these two tests, there are no concerns regarding the possible effect of multicollinearity on the regression results.

Table 8.1 Correlation matrix

	Variables	VIF	1	2	3	4	5	6	7	8	9	10	11	12
1	Investor networks	1.227	1.00											
2	Accounting firm size	7.677	0.01	1.00										
3	Advisory board	1.524	0.182**	0.03	1.00									
4	Firm age	3.489	−0.06	0.11	0.02	1.00								
5	Firm size	2.103	0.05	0.121*	0.04	0.199**	1.00							
6	Past performance	7.169	−0.05	−0.02	−0.06	0.05	0.115*	1.00						
7	Family business status	2.329	−0.11	0.03	−0.197**	0.119*	−0.06	−0.11	1.00					
8	Industry—construction	1.471	0.04	−0.02	−0.07	−0.03	0.10	0.10	−0.01	1.00				
9	Industry—manufacturing	1.47	−0.06	0.01	0.12	0.11	0.00	−0.10	0.04	−0.156**	1.00			
10	Industry—primary industries	1.206	0.04	−0.04	0.08	0.178**	−0.06	−0.166**	0.144**	−0.10	−0.11	1.00		
11	Industry—retail/wholesale	1.575	−0.04	−0.01	−0.12	−0.08	0.00	0.04	0.08	−0.193**	−0.203**	−0.131*	1.00	
12	Respondent—education level	4.082	0.06	0.05	0.200**	−0.04	0.117*	−0.169**	−0.234**	−0.04	0.03	0.06	−0.08	1.00

Correlation matrix relates to 325 respondents and presents the correlations between independent and control variables included in the ordinal regression modeling presented in Table 8.3.
Significance level: $*P<.10$; $**P<.05$; $***P<.01$ (two-tailed P-values are used in determining significance).
VIF refers to the variance inflation factor. The critical value of the VIF to test for multicollinearity is 10. Ghauri et al. (2003) suggests that there is no evidence of multicollinearity unless the VIF of a variable exceeds 10. All values used in this study were below this critical level.

8.5 RESULTS

8.5.1 Descriptive Statistics

Table 8.2 presents the descriptive statistics of the variables used in this study. Of the 325 firms included in the study, around 27% had internationalized (mean value of internationalization status). Concerning the three independent variables, most SMEs had little to no investor networks (mean investor networks <1 where 1 corresponded to experience/prior use of one source of outside equity). On average, SMEs surveyed were most likely to use a medium-large accounting firm (mean score of 2.113, where 2 corresponds to medium/large accounting firms). Most SMEs did not have an advisory board in place, nor were they implementing one (mean score <1 where score of 1 = currently putting a board in place, 2 = have board in place).

The remainder of this section discusses the descriptive statistics of the control variables used in this study. On average, SMEs surveyed were 24 years old (ranging from 1 to 84 years of age) and employed around

Table 8.2 Descriptive statistics

Variables	Mean	Median	SD	Min	Max
Internationalization status	0.271	0.000	0.445	0.000	1.000
Investor networks	0.133	0.000	0.409	0.000	2.000
Advisory board	0.405	0.000	0.724	0.000	2.000
Accounting firm size	2.113	2.000	0.719	1.000	3.000
Firm age	23.984	21.000	17.985	1.000	151.000
Firm size	20.442	11.000	27.701	1.000	193.000
Past performance	20.765	22.000	5.582	6.000	30.000
Family business status	0.588	1.000	0.493	0.000	1.000
Industry—construction	0.129	0.000	0.336	0.000	1.000
Industry—manufacturing	0.142	0.000	0.349	0.000	1.000
Industry—primary industries	0.065	0.000	0.246	0.000	1.000
Industry—retail/wholesale	0.200	0.000	0.401	0.000	1.000
Industry—service	0.459	0.000	0.499	0.000	1.000
Respondent—education level	3.740	3.000	1.882	1.000	7.000

Internationalization status, family business status, and industry variables are dichotomous variables (1, 0). As a consequence, their mean scores indicate the % of firms with a positive state. For example, 27.1% of firms sampled are selling their product overseas (internationalization status mean = 0.271).
Investor networks, accounting firm size, advisory board, and respondent—education level are ordinal variables.
Firm age and firm size are continuous variables.

21 full-time-equivalent employees (ranging from 1 to 193 employees). SMEs reported an average performance rating of 20.765 (out of a possible 30, and ranging from 6 to 30) and around 60% were identified as family businesses (mean of 0.588 for family business status). With regard to industries, most SMEs principally operated in service-related industries (mean of 0.459, or 45.9%), followed by manufacturing industries (mean of 0.142, or 14.2%). The median education level of the key decision makers (the respondents) was 3, which corresponds to a technical or trade qualification [ranging from 1 (primary school) to 7 (postgraduate university degree)].

Using the results of the ordinal regression analysis, the following sections highlight what variables were found to have a significant influence on the internationalization status of SMEs.

8.5.2 Control Variables

Model (i) in Table 8.3 examines the association between the control variables and internationalization status without the inclusion of the independent variables. The results highlight that industry type has a significant association with the internationalization status of SMEs. Specifically, SMEs operating in the construction industry were significantly ($P<.10$) less likely to internationalize. With regard to the characteristics of the key decision maker (the survey respondent), education level had a significant ($P<.01$) positive association with the internationalization status of SMEs. Specifically, the more educated the key decision maker, the more likely an SME is to internationalize.

As highlighted in Table 8.3, the influence of these control variables appears to be consistent across the three models that include the independent variables (Models 1, 2, and 3). That is, firm industry-type and the education level of the key decision maker are significantly associated with the internationalization status of an SME.

8.5.3 Results From Modeling

Model 1 presents the results of the ordinal regression modeling of the influence of the independent variable "external investor networks" (H1) on the internationalization status of SMEs, while controlling for other variables. Models 2 and 3 in Table 8.3 present the results of the ordinal regression modeling of the influence of the independent variables "advisory board" (H2) and "accounting firm size" (H3) on the internationalization status of SMEs.

Table 8.3 Ordinal regression results

Variables	Internationalization status			
	Model *i*	**Model 1**	**Model 2**	**Model 3**
	β	β	β	β
Constant	−2.932***	−3.257***	−2.81***3	−2.778***
Independent variables				
Investor networks		1.19***		
Advisory board			0.473**	
Accounting firm size				0.006
Control variables				
Firm age	0.001	−0.002	−0.001	−0.003
Firm size	0.002	0.001	0.002	0.002
Past performance	0.029	0.032	0.017	0.025
Family business status	−0.132	0.035	0.228	−0.085
Industry—construction	−0.993*	−1.054*	−0.711	−1.025
Industry—manufacturing	0.635	0.684*	0.673	0.559
Industry—primary industries	−0.164	−0.171	0.124	−0.176
Industry—retail/wholesale	0.291	0.504	0.541	0.279
Respondent—education level	0.319	0.334	0.265	0.32
Model diagnostics				
−2 log likelihood	323.634	298.448	250.596	318.959
Chi square statistic	31.280	41.730	23.77	30.226
Pseudo *R*-square: Nagelkerke statistic	0.141	0.193	0.141	0.139

The table reports the following ordinal regression model:

$$\begin{aligned}\text{Internationalization status} = \beta_0 &+ \beta_{1-3}(\text{Investor networks, advisory board, accounting firm size})\\ &+ \beta_4(\text{firm age}) + \beta_5(\text{firm size}) + \beta_6(\text{past performance})\\ &+ \beta_7(\text{family business status}) + \beta_{8-11}(\text{firm industry})\\ &+ \beta_{12}(\text{respondent's education}) + \varepsilon\end{aligned}$$

where internationalization status (dependent variables) = whether the firm sells product overseas; Investor networks (independent variable, Model 1) = key decision maker had experience/previously used outside private equity; advisory board (independent variable, Model 2) whether firm had advisory board/board of directors; accounting firm size (independent variable, Model 3) = size of SME's accounting firm—small/medium/large; firm age (control variable) = years since foundation; firm size (control variable) = FTE employees; past performance (control variable) = past SME performance based on composite score of six questions; family business status (control variable) = if SME is majority family-owned and perceived as a family business; firm industry (control variable) = whether belongs to one of four industry categories (service industry excluded as used as reference category); respondent—education level (control variable) = highest level of education of key decision maker in the firm (the respondent). Two-tailed *P*-values are used in determining significance: $^*P<.10$; $^{**}P<.05$; $^{***}P<.01$.

As highlighted in Model 1, "investor networks" was significantly ($P < .01$) and positively associated with internationalization status. This provides support for hypothesis H1, namely, that firms with investor networks are significantly more likely to internationalize the firm. Model 2 highlights that "advisory board" was significantly ($P < .05$) and positively associated with internationalization status. This provides support for hypothesis H2, namely, that firms with an advisory board are significantly more likely to internationalize the firm. As highlighted in Model 3, accounting firm size was not significantly associated with internationalization status. Therefore H3 is not supported.

8.6 DISCUSSION OF RESULTS

The study reinforced earlier research but also differed in the following ways:

First, while prior studies have found evidence that SMEs could leverage these external partners in terms of their networks and knowledge, our study reinforced findings from earlier research. In terms of external investors, the study reinforces findings from earlier research that show that external investors enhance the international knowledge and network capabilities of SME owner-managers and also confer legitimacy in terms of entering new foreign markets (LiPuma, 2006; Park et al., 2015; Ulubaşoğlu et al., 2009). In terms of board network effects, the study also found similarities with earlier research studies that found that effective boards can improve internationalization capabilities of TMTs through enhanced information, experience, and resources (Chen, 2011; Finkelstein et al., 2009; Luo, 2007).

Second, this study attempted to study whether SMEs seek out the services of larger external accountants when they wish to access foreign markets. As there was limited research in this area and in spite of the larger accountancy practices offering these additional services, there was no significant link between accessing these larger accountancy practices with internationalization among Australian SMEs. This points to SMEs, even those who are internationalizing, mainly using external accountants, regardless of their size, for mainly routine financial and tax compliance work as noted by previous research (Kirby and King, 1997; Nandan, 2010), and not accessing them as business advisors as claimed by some researchers (e.g., Gooderham et al. (2004)).

Third, from the model testing, the study found that the external partners contributed to different degrees in terms of SME internationalization. External investors had the most significant effect on internationalization ($P < .01$)

as compared to advisory board members ($P < .05$) and external accountants (no significance). The results in terms of external investors and external accountants is paradoxical in that earlier research comparing SMEs accessing external investment versus external accountants showed that accountants are the main advisor for SME owner-managers in contrast to the significant barriers between SME owner-managers and external investors (Seet et al., 2010). Hence it may be that SME owner-managers believe that external investors would be able to help them gain access to foreign markets and internationalize more effectively, but due to finance, knowledge, and empathy gaps (Seet, 2011), they are unlikely to consider external investors. Likewise, SME owner-managers may trust their external accountant and use him or her as their preferred advisor, but this may not stretch beyond more standard compliance-related advice into nontraditional aspects like internationalization, even when these accountants may be from larger firms and part of very extensive international accounting networks.

8.7 CONCLUSIONS, IMPLICATIONS, AND LIMITATIONS

This study examined whether an SME's external network ties, namely those with external investors, advisory boards, and external accountants, influence the firm's likelihood to internationalize. Results suggest that investor networks and advisory boards play a significant role in the internationalization of SMEs.

8.7.1 Research Contributions

This research contributes in the following aspects. First, our research focuses on external network partners that are relatively under-studied in terms of their contribution to internationalization. Second, in terms of theory, our research enhances network-based internationalization theory by moving beyond a simple examination of which external partner contributes to internationalization, revealing the relative extent to which three important external party networks contribute to SME internationalization by studying the perceived relative contributions of external investors, advisory boards. and external accountants from the SME owner-managers' perspective.

8.7.2 Limitations and Future Research

This study is subject to some limitations. First, this study focused on Australian SMEs only, and may not be generalizable in other contexts. Second, this research is cross-sectional, and as a consequence it is possible that the cause-and-effect relationships between networks and internationalization are opposite to that argued (e.g., internationalization of the SME creates the need to establish an advisory board). Future research would benefit from longitudinal studies to examine the dynamic nature of the different factors and their interrelationships. Third, this research only focused on three potential external network partners and left out potentially important ones (e.g., government agencies, business groups, etc.). Future research should examine these.

8.7.3 Implications for Practice

This study has implications with respect to supporting SME internationalization. As previously highlighted, while SME owner-managers acknowledge and perceive that external investors can and should bring with them resources, networks, and expertise to facilitate internationalization, there may be significant barriers between SMEs and external investors. Similarly, the research indicates that there may be knowledge and perception gaps in terms of SMEs capitalizing on their accountants in the internationalization process. What is positive is that there is a positive role for advisory boards in the process, which can form an important bridge between SMEs and external investors and/or accountants in building internationalization capabilities. Given that most SMEs do not have advisory boards, this means that there is an important role for other stakeholders (e.g., policy makers, small business associations, and industry associations) to help SMEs understand the need for and develop effective advisory boards, as well as bridge knowledge and perception gaps with potential external advisors and accountants.

ACKNOWLEDGMENTS

This research was supported by a research grant from CPA-Australia and it is gratefully acknowledged.

REFERENCES

ABS, 2010. Venture Capital and Later Stage Private Equity (2008–2009). Australian Bureau of Statistics, Canberra.

Agndal, H., Chetty, S., Wilson, H., 2008. Social capital dynamics and foreign market entry. Int. Bus. Rev. 17, 663–675.

Ahn, J., Bhagat, C., Honda, K., Kwan, I., Lind, F., Pandit, V., Poullet, J.-M., Roy, B., Ye, T., 2011. Private equity Asia-Pacific: rebounds, glocalization, and other tales. In: Private Equity & Principal Investing. McKinsey, New York.

Aldrich, H., 1999. Organizations Evolving. Sage, London.

Aldrich, H., Auster, E.R., 1986. Even dwarfs started small: liabilities of age and size and their strategic implications. Res. Organ. Behav. 8, 165–186.
Ardichvili, A., Cardozo, R., Ray, S., 2003. A theory of entrepreneurial opportunity identification and development. J. Bus. Ventur. 18, 105–123.
Arnold, J.L., Cherry, A.A., Diamond, M.A., Walker, J.A., 1984. Small business: an area ripe for practice development. J. Account. 158, 74–82.
Australian Bureau of Statistics, 2002. Small Business in Australia 2001. Australian Bureau of Statistics, Canberra.
AVCAL, 2013. 2013 Yearbook. Australian Private Equity & Venture Capital Association, Sydney, NSW.
Axelsson, B., Easton, G., 1992. Industrial Networks: A New View of Reality. Routledge, London.
BarNir, A., Smith, K.A., 2002. Inter-firm alliances in the small firm: the role of social networks. J. Small Bus. Manag. 40, 219–232.
Barroso, C., Villegas, M.M., Pérez-Calero, L., 2011. Board influence on a firm's internationalization. Corp. Gov. 19, 351–367.
Bell, J., McNaughton, R., Young, S., 2001. Born-again global firms: an extension to the born global phenomenon. J. Int. Manag. 7, 173–189.
Bennett, R.J., Robson, P.J.A., 1999. The use of external business advice by SMEs in Britain. Entrep. Reg. Dev. 11, 155–180.
Bennett, R.J., Smith, C., 2002. The influence of location and distance on the supply of business advice. Environ. Plan. A 34, 251–270.
Berry, A.J., Sweeting, R., Goto, J., 2006. The effect of business advisers on the performance of SMEs. J. Small Bus. Enter. Dev. 13, 33–47.
Brunninge, O., Nordqvist, M., Wiklund, J., 2007. Corporate governance and strategic change in SMEs: the effects of ownership, board composition and top management teams. Small Bus. Econ. 29, 295–308.
Busenitz, L.W., Fiet, J.O., Moesel, D.D., 2004. Reconsidering the venture capitalists' "value added" proposition: an interorganizational learning perspective. J. Bus. Ventur. 19, 787–807.
Bygrave, W., Hay, M., Ng, E., Reynolds, P., 2003. Executive forum: a study of informal investing in 29 nations composing the Global Entrepreneurship Monitor. Ventur. Cap. 5.
Calabrò, A., Mussolino, D., 2013. How do boards of directors contribute to family SME export intensity? The role of formal and informal governance mechanisms. J. Manag. Gov. 17, 363–403.
Calabro, A., Mussolino, D., Huse, M., 2009. The role of board of directors in the internationalisation process of small and medium sized family businesses. Int. J. Glob. Small Bus. 3, 393–411.
Chen, H.-L., 2011. Does board independence influence the top management team? Evidence from strategic decisions toward internationalization. Corp. Gov. 19, 334–350.
Chesbrough, H.W., 2003. Open Innovation: The New Imperative for Creating and Profiting From Technology. Harvard Business School Press, Cambridge, MA.
Chetty, S., Blankenburg Holm, D., 2000. Internationalisation of small to medium-sized manufacturing firms: a network approach. Int. Bus. Rev. 9, 77–93.
Chetty, S., Campbell-Hunt, C., 2003. Explosive international growth and problems of success amongst small to medium-sized firms. Int. Small Bus. J. 21, 5–27.
Chetty, S.K., Wilson, H.I.M., 2003. Collaborating with competitors to acquire resources. Int. Bus. Rev. 12, 61–81.
Chrisman, J.J., Chua, J.H., Sharma, P., Yoder, T.R., 2009a. Guiding family businesess through the succession process: a step-by-step guide for CPA advisors. CPA J. 79, 48–51.

Chrisman, J.J., Chua, J.H., Sharma, P., Yoder, T.R., 2009b. Guiding family businesses through the succession process. CPA J. 79, 48–51.
Chua, J.H., Chrisman, J.J., Sharma, P., 1999. Defining the family business by behavior. Enterp. Theory Pract. 23.
Cooke, P., Heidenreich, M., Braczyk, H., 2004. Regional Innovation Systems: The Role of Governance in a Globalised world. Routledge, London.
Corral de Zubielqui, G., Jones, J., Seet, P.-S., Lindsay, N., 2015. Knowledge transfer between actors in the innovation system: a study of higher education institutions (HEIS) and SMES. J. Bus. Ind. Mark. 30, 436–458.
Coviello, E.N., 2006. The network dynamics of international new ventures. J. Int. Bus. Stud. 37, 713–731.
Coviello, N.E., McAuley, A., 1999. Internationalisation and the smaller firm: a review of contemporary empirical research. Manag. Int. Rev. 39, 223–256.
Coviello, N., Munro, H., 1997. Network relationships and the internationalisation process of small software firms. Int. Bus. Rev. 6, 361–386.
Crick, D., Spence, M., 2005. The internationalisation of 'high performing' UK high-tech SMEs: a study of planned and unplanned strategies. Int. Bus. Rev. 14, 167–185.
De Clercq, D., Dimov, D., 2008. Internal knowledge development and external knowledge access in venture capital investment performance. J. Manag. Stud. 45, 585–612.
Eckaus, R.S., 2008. An Inquiry into the determinants of the exports of China and India. Chin. World Econ. 16, 1–15.
Eriksson, K., Johanson, J., Majkgård, A., Sharma, D.D., 1997. Experiential knowledge and costs in the internationalization process. J. Int. Bus. Stud. 28, 337–360.
Etzioni, A., Etzioni, O., 1999. Face-to-face and computer-mediated communities, a comparative analysis. Inf. Soc. 15, 241–248.
Fernhaber, S.A., McDougall-Covin, P.P., Shepherd, D.A., 2009. International entrepreneurship: leveraging internal and external knowledge sources. Strateg. Entrep. J. 3, 297–320.
Finkelstein, S., Hambrick, D.C., Cannella, A.A., 2009. Strategic Leadership: Theory and Research on Executives, Top Management Teams, and Boards. Oxford University Press, New York.
Freel, M.S., 2005. Patterns of innovation and skills in small firms. Technovation 25, 123–134.
Ghauri, P., Lutz, C., Tesfom, G., 2003. Using networks to solve export-marketing problems of small- and medium-sized firms from developing countries. Eur. J. Mark. 37, 728–752.
Gooderham, P.N., Tobiassen, A., Døving, E., Nordhaug, O., 2004. Accountants as sources of business advice for small firms. Int. Small Bus. J. 22, 5–22.
Granovetter, M.S., 1973. The strength of weak ties. Am. J. Sociol. 78, 1360–1380.
Graves, C., Thomas, J., 2004. Internationalisation of the family business: a longitudinal perspective. Int. J. Glob. Small Bus. 1, 7–27.
Graves, C., Thomas, J., 2006. Internationalization of Australian family businesses: a managerial capabilities perspective. Fam. Bus. Rev. 19, 207–224.
Graves, C., Thomas, J., 2008. Determinants of the internationalization pathways of family firms: an examination of family influence. Fam. Bus. Rev. 21, 151–167.
Greenwood, R., Suddaby, R., Hinings, C.R., 2002. Theorizing change: the role of professional associations in the transformation of institutionalized fields. Acad. Manag. J. 45, 58–80.
Gulati, R., 1998. Alliances and networks. Strateg. Manag. J. 19.
Hagedoorn, J., Link, A.N., Vonortas, N.S., 2000. Research partnerships. Res. Policy 29.
Harris, R., Moffat, J., 2011. R&D, Innovation and Exporting. SERC, London. SERC Discussion Paper.
Harrison, B., 1992. Industrial districts: old wine in new bottles? Reg. Stud. 26, 469–483.

Hellmann, T., Puri, M., 2002. Venture capital and the professionalization of start-up firms: empirical evidence. J. Financ. 57, 169–197.
Hsu, D.H., 2004. What do entrepreneurs pay for venture capital affiliation? J. Financ. 59, 1805–1844.
Hymer, S., 1976. The International Operations of National Firms: A Study of Direct Foreign Investment. MIT Press, Cambridge, MA.
Jay, L., Schaper, M., 2003. Which advisers do micro-firms use? Some Australian evidence. J. Small Bus. Enterp. Dev. 10, 136–143.
Johanson, J., Mattsson, L.-G., 1988. Internationalisation in industrial systems—a network approach. In: Hood, N., Vahlne, J.-E. (Eds.), Strategies in Global Competition. Croon Helm, London, pp. 287–314.
Johanson, J., Vahlne, J.-E., 1977. The internationalization process of the firm—a model of knowledge development and increasing foreign market commitments. J. Int. Bus. Stud. 8, 23–32.
Johanson, J., Vahlne, J.-E., 1990. The mechanism of internationalisation. Int. Mark. Rev. 7, 11–24.
Jones, M.V., 1999. The internationalization of small high-technology firms. J. Int. Mark. 7, 15–41.
Kaish, S., Gilad, B., 1991. Characteristics of opportunities search of entrepreneurs versus executives: sources, interests, general alertness. J. Bus. Ventur. 6, 45–61.
Kaymak, T., Bektas, E., 2008. East meets West? Board characteristics in an emerging market: evidence from Turkish Banks. Corp. Gov. 16, 550–561.
Khadem, N., 2013. Why SMEs Still Trust Accountants Over Financial Planners, Australian Financial Review. Fairfax, Sydney.
Kim, B., Burns, M.L., Prescott, J.E., 2009. The strategic role of the board: the impact of board structure on top management team strategic action capability. Corp. Gov. 17, 728–743.
Kirby, D.A., King, S.H., 1997. Accountants and small firm development: filling the expectation gap. Serv. Ind. J. 17, 294–304.
Kiss, A.N., Danis, W.M., 2008. Country institutional context, social networks, and new venture internationalization speed. Eur. Manag. J. 26, 388–399.
Kiss, A.N., Danis, W.M., 2010. Social networks and speed of new venture internationalization during institutional transition: a conceptual model. J. Int. Entrep. 8, 273–287.
Kontinen, T., Ojala, A., 2010. The internationalization of family businesses: a review of extant research. J. Fam. Bus. Strat. 1, 97–107.
Leonidou, L.C., Katsikeas, C.S., 1996. The export development process: an integrative review of empirical models. J. Int. Bus. Stud. 27, 517–551.
Lewis, G., Minchev, T., 2001. Methodological Issues in Researching Internationalisation Strategies of Australian Firms. The Flinders University of South Australia, Adelaide, SA. Working Paper: School of Commerce Research Seminar Series.
LiPuma, J.A., 2006. Independent venture capital, corporate venture capital, and the internationalisation intensity of technology-based portfolio firms. Int. Entrep. Manag. J. 2, 245–260.
Love, J.H., Roper, S., 2015. SME innovation, exporting and growth: a review of existing evidence. Int. Small Bus. J. 33, 28–48.
Lu, J.W., Beamish, P.W., 2001a. The Internationalization and Performance of SMEs. Strateg. Manag. J. 22, 565–586.
Luo, Y., 2007. Global Dimensions of Corporate Governance. Wiley-Blackwell, Malden, MA.
Madhok, A., 2002. Reassessing the fundamentals and beyond: Ronald Coase, the transaction cost and resource-based theories of the firm and the institutional structure of production. Strateg. Manag. J. 23.

Manolova, T.S., Manev, I.M., Gyoshev, B.S., 2010. In good company: the role of personal and inter-firm networks for new-venture internationalization in a transition economy. J. World Bus. 45, 257–265.
Manolova, T.S., Manev, I.M., Gyoshev, B.S., 2014. Friends with money? Owner's financial network and new venture internationalization in a transition economy. Int. Small Bus. J. 32, 944–966.
Maula, M., Autio, E., Murray, G., 2005. Corporate venture capitalists and independent venture capitalists: what do they know, who do they know and should entrepreneurs care? Ventur. Cap. 7, 3–21.
Musteen, M., Datta, K.D., Herrmann, P., 2009. Ownership structure and CEO compensation: implications for the choice of foreign market entry modes. J. Int. Bus. Stud. 40, 321–338.
Nadler, D.A., Behan, B.A., Nadler, M.B., 2011. Building Better Boards: A Blueprint for Effective Governance. Wiley, San Francisco, CA.
Nandan, R., 2010. Management accounting needs of smes and the role of professional accountants: a renewed research agenda. J. Appl. Manag. Account. Res. 8, 65–77.
Oliver, A.L., Liebeskind, J.P., 1998. Three levels of networking for sourcing intellectual capital in biotechnology: implications for studying inter-organisational networks. Int. Stud. Manag. Organ. 24, 76–103.
Osma, B.G., 2008. Board independence and real earnings management: the case of R&D expenditure. Corp. Gov. 16, 116–131.
Ozgen, E., Baron, R.A., 2007. Social sources of information in opportunity recognition: effects of mentors, industry networks, and professional forums. J. Bus. Ventur. 22, 174–192.
Park, S., LiPuma, J.A., Prange, C., 2015. Venture capitalist and entrepreneur knowledge of new venture internationalization: a review of knowledge components. Int. Small Bus. J. 33, 901–928.
Perkmann, M., Walsh, K., 2007. University-industry relationships and open innovation: towards a research agenda (review article). Int. J. Manag. Rev. 9, 259–280.
Ranft, A.L., O'Neill, H.M., 2001. Board composition and high-flying founders: hints of trouble to come? Acad. Manag. Exec. 15, 126–138.
Rialp, A., Rialp, J., Knight, G.A., 2005. The phenomenon of early internationalizing firms: what do we know after a decade (1993–2003) of scientific inquiry? Int. Bus. Rev. 14, 147–166.
Robson, P.J.A., Bennett, R.J., 2000. SME growth: the relationship with business advice and external collaboration. Small Bus. Econ. 15, 193–208.
Rosenfeld, S.A., 1997. Bringing business clusters into the mainstream of economic development. Eur. Plan. Stud. 5, 3–23.
Sanders, W.G., Carpenter, M.A., 1998. Internationalization and firm governance: the roles of CEO compensation, top team composition, and board structure. Acad. Manag. J. 41, 158–178.
Seely-Brown, J., Duguid, P., 2001. Knowledge and organization: a social-practice perspective. Organ. Sci. 12, 198–213.
Seet, A.-M., 2011. Teleconversation Between the Group Members and Dr. Ai-Mee Seet on 17 July 2011. Adelaide, Singapore.
Seet, P.-S., Graves, C., 2010. Understanding the Barriers to and Opportunities for Access to Private Equity: For Small-to-Medium Sized Family-Owned Enterprises (SMFEs). CPA Australia Ltd., Southbank, VIC. pp.1–44.
Seet, P.-S., Graves, C., Gustafson, P., Hadji, M., Schnackenberg, A., 2010. The effect of finance, knowledge and empathy gaps on the use of private equity amongst family-owned SMEs. Int. J. Entrep. Small Bus. 11, 85–104.

Singh, R.P., 2000. Entrepreneurial Opportunity Recognition Through Social Networks. Garland, New York.
Singh, R.P., Hills, G.E., Lumpkin, G., Hybels, R.C., 1999. The entrepreneurial opportunity recognition process: examining the role of self-perceived alertness and social networks. In: Academy of Management Proceedings: Academy of Management, pp. G1–G6.
Smallbone, D., North, D., Leigh, R., 1993. The use of external assistance by mature SMEs in the UK: some policy implications. Entrep. Reg. Dev. 5, 279–295.
Söderqvist, A., Chetty, S.K., 2013. Strength of ties involved in international new ventures. Eur. Bus. Rev. 25, 536–552.
Sonfield, M.C., Lussier, R.N., 2004. First-, second-, and third-generation family firms: a comparison. Fam. Bus. Rev. 17, 189–202.
Strike, V.M., 2013. The most trusted advisor and the subtle advice process in family firms. Fam. Bus. Rev. 26, 293–313.
Sullivan, D., 1996. Measuring the degree of internationalisation of a firm: a reply. J. Int. Bus. Stud. 27, 179–192.
Tanewski, G., Carey, P., 2007. Determinants of value adding business advice provided by external accountants to SME clients. In: 52nd International Council for Small Business World Conference, Turku, Finland.
Ulubaşoğlu, M.A., Akdiş, M., Kök, S.B., 2009. Internationalization and alliance formation: evidence from Turkish SMEs. Int. Small Bus. J. 27, 337–361.
Uzzi, B., Gillespie, J.J., 2002. Knowledge spillover in corporate financing networks: embeddedness and the firm's debt performance. Strateg. Manag. J. 23, 595–618.
Vago, M., 1998. Multiple roles in serving families in business. Fam. Bus. Rev. 11, 261–266.
Westhead, P., Wright, M., Ucbasaran, D., 2001. The Internationalization of new and small firms: a resource-based view. J. Bus. Ventur. 16, 333–358.
Westhead, P., Howorth, C., Cowling, M., 2002. Ownership and management issues in first generation and multi-generation family firms. Entrep. Reg. Dev. 14, 247–269.
Westphal, J.D., Boivie, S., Ming Chng, D.H., 2006. The strategic impetus for social network ties: reconstituting broken ceo friendship ties. Strateg. Manag. J. 27, 425–445.
Wright, M., Burrows, A., Ball, R., Scholes, L., Meuleman, M., Amess, K., 2007. The Implications of Alternative Investment Vehicles for Corporate Governance: A Survey of Empirical Research. Centre for Management Buy-out Research, Nottingham University Business School, Nottingham.
Wu, H.-L., 2008. How do board-CEO relationships influence the performance of new product introduction? Moving from single to interdependent explanations. Corp. Gov. 16, 77–89.
Zahra, S.A., 2003. International expansion of U.S. manufacturing family businesses: the effect of ownership and involvement. J. Bus. Ventur. 18, 495–512.
Zhou, L., Wu, W.-P., Luo, X., 2007. Internationalization and the performance of born-global SMEs: the mediating role of social networks. J. Int. Bus. Stud. 38, 673–690.

CHAPTER 9

Managing Networks in the Asia Pacific

N. Thirawat
Mahidol University International College, Nakhon Pathom, Thailand

9.1 INTRODUCTION

Firm-specific advantages gained from mutual relationships and integrated network structures can greatly contribute to value creation and the addition of activities embedded in multiple product lines, including various internationally geographical markets. The collaboration within a network helps network members (or firms, in this case) access limited or innovative resources and information critical for the advancement of new products, research and development (R&D) initiatives, and cross-border market expansions (Chen and Jaw, 2014). Being part of a network can also enhance the performance of small firms through exploration opportunities and international exploitation because it can lower barriers such as a firm's small size, lack of resources, and distance from markets. Above all, networks can also promote product commercialization overseas and increase a firm's competitiveness on a global scale (Vasilchenko and Morrish, 2011). Therefore it is clear that networks are necessary for internationalization. This chapter will explore network management strategies with regard to international expansion, focusing on case studies in the Asia-Pacific region.

According to Ratajczak-Mrozek (2014), a network is "a structure where a number of nodes, which are companies and their counterparts, are related to each other by a particular organization of relationships formulated by mutual benefits such as tangible and intangible resources." In his work entitled "Companies' Simultaneous Embeddedness in Local, International and Global Networks: A Conceptualization from the Perspective of Local Enterprises and their Degree of Internationalization," the author defined a "network" as a system of relationships that can be either formal or informal, and further stated that there are various types of networks in which firms can position themselves in any of them, or a number of them, simultaneously. Hence, it can be concluded that a network is a complex structure. Another

Internationalization and Managing Networks in the Asia Pacific
http://dx.doi.org/10.1016/B978-0-08-100813-3.00009-2

study written by Vasilchenko and Morrish (2011) provides a similar definition in which the network is a set of operators connected by relationships that can generally be categorized as "social or business networks," which refers to "informal networks." These are built upon personal relationships and "formal networks" that concern regular economic exchange. In their research, a network is also considered a "central figure" that can be administered or mobilized by an individual or a group of people.

More specifically, Ratajczak-Mrozek (2014) defined a "business network," or an industrial network, as a set of repeated shared business activities formulated by interconnected factors such as agents, resources, and activities. This kind of network aims to facilitate the flow of information, resources, and commitment among network members. Similarly, Chen and Jaw (2014) defined a business network as a group of enterprises that are legally and independently allied by their formal and informal ties in order to accomplish a common goal. Another study conducted by Vasilchenko and Morrish (2011) provides the definition of a business network from a marketing perspective in which a business network is an assortment of two or more affiliated business relationships between collective actors such as competitors, suppliers, customers, distributors, and the government. In other words, this kind of network requires a goal-oriented collaboration among multiple firms, including the mutual exchange of resources and accomplishments for resolving problems toward formal agreements and long-term relationships established in international business activities. In terms of internationalization, business networks can help firms gain experiences and knowledge about international markets as well as increase chances to exploit international opportunities. Business networks could play a significant role in terms of eliminating foreign market entry barriers (Ibid).

Another important term relevant to the international business network is "embeddedness." According to Chen and Jaw (2014), embeddedness refers to "the process by which social relations shape economic actions." In the same study, embeddedness also indicates the exchange system in which companies coordinate in networks in order to increase their survival rate. Strictly speaking, embeddedness can enhance a business's economic performance towards interfirm cooperation, resource sharing, and conformed adjustment. In relation to business networks, embeddedness plays a crucial role in linking network members altogether toward shared equity, family, and friendship. According to Ratajczak-Mrozek (2014), embeddedness is a sociological concept in which firms cooperate with each other in the form of a network comprising personal (social) and cultural relationships. Local embeddedness refers to better access to resources, involving knowledge and innovation from such relationships in a specific location. Based on the same study, there are three types of organizational embeddedness: relational embeddedness, structural embeddedness, and position embeddedness. Relational embeddedness is the by-products of adhesive bonds between social actors as a result of trust or previous encounters. The second type, structural embeddedness, refers to relationships maintained with one another, whereas position embeddedness refers to how the position of the actors and objective factors formulate business relationships in the overall network structure.

According to Ge and Wang (2013), "internationalization" is defined as an aggregate process in which business ties are continuously created, sustained, developed, and disintegrated in accordance with the organization's goal. Likewise, Johanson and Vahlne (1992) stated that internationalization refers to a gradual process in which business relationships are established and preserved over time and derived from interactions between network members. Network ties with diverse key suppliers, financial institutions, and local governments play a significant role in international expansion because it forms the platform where firms can access foreign markets and explore opportunities (Sharma and Johanson, 1987). Jones (1999) also affirmed that the rate of internationalization derives from knowledge and experience obtained through network relationships.

Another study conducted by Vasilchenko and Morrish presented the definition of a social network in the area of entrepreneurship, coined by Gilmore and Carson (1999) as "a group of individuals, who may or may not know each other, but contribute to each and every business in the network passively, reactively, or proactively." They also explained that social networks are developed from personal connections and industrial events that allow exploration of internationalization opportunities. As such, they can lead to formal cooperation and become business networks, influencing a firm's foreign market selection and entry. Ge and Wang (2013) defined a "social network" in their study, as it is highly valuable for cross-border investment by multinationals from emerging markets and developing countries. They called social networks "the infomediaries" who play a significant role in facilitating the exchange of beneficial information and broadening international vision. In other words, social networks can provide in-depth information and advice about foreign markets and business practices necessary for international expansion and performance enhancement. Based on their research, social networks can initiate trust and solidarity toward cooperative alliances that lead to legitimacy and credibility for economic transactions with other parties.

9.2 NETWORK-RELATED THEORIES

Regarding relevant theories to the formulation of networks in the field of business management, this section presents an overview of theories explaining networks and their importance, ranging from classic school to contemporary school as follows.

9.2.1 Motives Theory and International Production Network Theory

According to the traditional theory of internationalization (or "motives theory") developed by Johanson and Vahlne (1977) and Dunning (1988), multinationals have a number of typical motives for expanding production and establishing production subsidiaries in foreign markets. These include transaction and transportation cost reduction, product development and adaptation to the local environment and tastes, and trade barriers diminution, for instance. Nonetheless, if firms aim to enhance performance of the whole production system, the strategic plan makers should broaden their scope from the access to a specific market to the entire series of production locations controlled by the firm. This is because an international production system settled in diverse locations can support capitalization and exploitation in multiple countries simultaneously. Studies showed that multinational corporations are able to exploit factor cost differentials between countries and reduce the risk of falling factor costs resulting from cost minimization of geographic organization in their production and distribution process (Fisch and Zschoche, 2012). Tan (1996) also asserted that having network economies is a theoretical explanation for the preentry decision-making process. This includes installments of production plants in different locations. In short, international networks in multiple host countries can increase a firm's flexibility and option value.

9.2.2 Resource-Based View Theory and New Venture Internationalization Theory

Pfeffer and Salancik's (1978) research regarding the resource dependency theory states that organizational networks are composed of partnerships, cooperative bodies, customer-supplier relationships, competitions, and social-legal instruments, which are used for setting and identifying the nature and scope of the business networks. In other words, networks in their perspective consist of a nonstatic structure and a variety of relationships. However, in order to keep the networks running, critical resources are needed (Shaner and Maznevski, 2011). According to Oviatt and McDougall (as cited by Vasilchenko and Morrish, 2011), networks are a dominant resource-preserving choice for internationalization. Firms should not only engage in network activities, but also arrange their network in diverse environments whenever the firms shift their focal direction, in order to maximize the benefits from such networks. Examples of benefits are greater prospects for analyzing cross-border opportunities for a specific product and better access to resources necessary for enabling entry into foreign markets. In the same study, it was concluded that inadequate resources are a major challenge to international expansion, particularly for firms that seek global existence. In spite of huge investments, having a network exchange structure can reduce the constraints resulting from a financial burden or insufficient resources, widening the firm's adaptability to new environments. Vasilchenko and Morrish's (2011) study stated clearly that studies proved networks to be highly significant for businesses from Denmark, New Zealand, and the three Scandinavian states, in terms of international expansion.

9.2.3 Network Model of Internationalization

According to Ratajczak-Mrozek (2014), the network model of internationalization is a concept explaining inward connections proceeding from imports, collaboration, and competition within a firm's internationalization process. That is to say, firms tend to successfully set up and develop their positions in foreign networks through connections with their counterparts toward international extension, penetration, and integration. In a similar manner, the study conducted by Winch (2014) stated that multinationals generally work in "constellations," which are groups of firms interacting with each other directly and mutually in order to provide complex services or products in a limited time period. The study suggested two main strategies for participating in constellations. First, it said that firms usually accumulate specialization and skills toward various demanding tasks that accommodate exploration and exploitation of learning opportunities. Second, it suggested that firms tend to pursue collective benefits by establishing stable relationships arranged by cooperation and mutual reinforcement.

9.2.4 Social Network Theory

Social network theory is a theory that supports the role of social networks as an instrument facilitating global commercialization of innovation, due to the fact that social relationships built upon organizational behaviors and human actions unavoidably become part of business practices (Vasilchenko and Morrish, 2011). Entrepreneurial networks potentially motivate the firms' internationalization direction, especially in the early stages of global commercialization when firms tend to retrieve information about favorable circumstances for business in international markets or promising foreign business partners (Johanson and Vahlne, 2003). In the same manner, Coviello and Munro (1997) asserted that firms generally select their international markets based on the location of their social networks because they can approach local markets by utilization of personal and business contacts.

9.2.5 New International Division of Labor Theory

Since the 1960s, new international divisions of labor have increasingly emerged in developing countries, significantly in the area of transnational corporations' strategic investment plans. Originally, traditional international divisions of labor were established by transnational corporations from Europe, North America, and Japan. As explained by the new international division of labor theory proposed by Frobel et al. (1980), in order to cope with decreasing profitability rates in terms of production, market saturation, and underconsumption in their home countries, such enterprises started joining labor-intensive export platforms commonly named "newly industrializing economies" (NIEs) in order to adjust their production from their cores to lower-cost production areas, which were the NIEs in this case. By doing this, products were eventually exported back to the original markets from the offshore plants. Today, new NIEs in South America, Eastern Europe, Africa, and Asia have become bases for labor-intensive production (Coe et al., 2013a).

9.3 NETWORK MANAGEMENT STRATEGIES

This section examines how multinational enterprises (MNEs) manage their networks for internationalization, using various forms of relationships.

9.3.1 Multinational Enterprise-Small and Medium Enterprise Networks

In Buckley and Prashantham's (2016) study, to regulate processes of large enterprises, cospecialization or interfirm networks of multinational enterprises (MNEs) and small and medium enterprises (SMEs) is acknowledged. This includes mutual dependence and spatial heterogeneity implanted in the relationships between advanced and emerging economies. This division of entrepreneurial labor embodying the engagement of smaller companies in worldwide business networks helps businesses plan and analyze their strategies effectively, integrating spatial perspectives crucial for understanding the universal nature of modern business networks. For network management, the MNE-SME relationship emphasizes the contribution of all members in the global business network rather than exceedingly focusing on the central firm. According to the study, this type of network had three main elements: the "who," the "how," and the "where." The "who" refers to differentiation between SMEs and MNEs in regard to exploration and exploitation capabilities, as well as potential for value creation in these interfirm networks. The "how" indicates how such potential of each participant in the networks is realized through interdependence, assisted by network organization and collaboration. The "where" addresses the worldwide adaptation across space, aiming to institutionally support entrepreneurship in both advanced and emerging economies.

The study suggests that the benefit of MNE-SME relationships is proactiveness, such as opportunities in new niches and settled markets and better policy-making judgment; this means the market is an integration of multiple niches, and the main mission of entrepreneurs is to create markets where they have not formerly existed. Both MNEs and SMEs have their own unique competencies; MNEs have greater necessary means to enhance their positions in existing markets, while SMEs generally have higher entrepreneurial enthusiasm to find and label new market niches. Correspondingly, MNEs tend to play the role of "ecosystem developers" that integrate innovation and lead the platform, while SMEs generally play the role of "ecosystem participants." With respect to innovation, MNEs and SMEs also have different strengths in their value chain activities. For example, case studies showed that alliances between small biotech ventures and big pharmaceutical MNEs enabled SMEs to effectively engage in upstream activities and MNEs to downstream activities (Buckley and Prashantham, 2016). In risk management, MNEs and SMEs can productively compensate for each other's deficiencies. To illustrate, with their smaller size and recent existence, SMEs can heighten their flexibility, but would need to be faced with the lack of legitimacy in exchange. On the other hand, MNEs' enormity and longevity offer resources to a greater degree, but less flexibility. Therefore, SMEs' illegitimacy issue could be lessened by partnering with high-status MNEs, where MNEs could augment flexibility and mitigate possible risks by engaging with active and elastic SMEs (Buckley and Casson, 1998).

According to Dhanaraj and Parkhe (2006), there are three essential activities that multinationals should accomplish: knowledge mobility management; innovation management; and more importantly, network stability management. Another study conducted by Buckley and Prashantham (2016) affirmed that any MNE operator must have run two important innovative activities based on two different dimensions. First, in the technological dimension, MNEs must establish platforms where external companies (including SMEs) can create their own equivalent products and services. Second, in the organizational dimension, MNEs must expand their organized networks' entry points through the installation of partner programs. Additionally, SMEs may be attracted to develop technology and have the ability to enhance sales along with their partners through these programs. Network management consists of progressive policies that MNEs use to build up a range of links within the global value chain. Within the system, SMEs must decide whether to engage in an MNE ecosystem or not. This means the SMEs have two options to join the network: to continuously develop their products and services in accordance with a specific MNE's technology development, or create products and services before deciding which MNE ecosystem to join. Nonetheless, this kind of network relationship would bring about risks related to ecosystem building and partner selection. As a result, it is necessary for MNEs to manage the aftermath of possible rebellion or the risk of partners becoming competitors, while SMEs should adopt forms of protection concerning intellectual property and business secrecy while enhancing their own capabilities (Buckley and Prashantham, 2016).

As reported in the study entitled "Aligning Interests of SMEs and a Focal Firm (MNE) in a Global Supply Chain Setup" written by Morya and Dwivedi (2009), SMEs play a significant role in MNEs' networks due to globalization, which drives the growth of foreign markets integrating into a large single market. From MNEs' standpoint, global sourcing is necessary to reduce production costs as well as expand opportunities in the retail industry. In other words, global sourcing facilitates access to SMEs or new suppliers who can supply quality goods and services at lower costs across the world. In the research, a case study illustrated that Indian enterprises in advanced fields such as business process outsourcing and the biotechnology industries are perceived as modern firms that are aware of the competition and are able to utilize advanced technologies. This kind of SME has the potential to supply products and services to leading MNEs globally. Though low in quantity, their growth is highly visible in the MNE ecosystem. For example, large companies like General Electronics chiefly rely on suppliers located in India and other developing states to produce and distribute their products and services to clients worldwide.

In the same manner, Punyasavatsut (2010) explained the rapid development of global business networks in Southeast Asia, which involve SME participation. The arrival of MNEs in overseas markets granted international knowledge and other competitive advantages to the domestic suppliers that were mostly SMEs. However, to promote and strengthen such international networks and alliances (including industrial clusters) requires numerous policies and programs. Such policies can revolve around productivity enhancement and innovation development for SMEs. In Thailand's case, recent measures magnifying networks consisted of business alliances and SME cluster establishments, support for the application of technological infrastructure and reinforcement of linkages between technology developers and users, advancement in efficiency and productivity through better management and skills, stimulation of readiness for trade liberalization to reduce unfavorable effects, and enrichment in quality and standards of goods in agreement with market demands. In Thailand, the agency acting as the intermediary unit to organize programs supporting such activities has been the Office of SME Promotion. The study affirmed that approximately 60%–70% of responding SMEs had received assistance from the agency.

A case study from "SMEs in the Thai Manufacturing Industry: Linking with MNES" written by Punyasavatsut (2008) illustrates the interplay between Thai SMEs and Japanese MNEs in the Thai automobile part industry, namely promotion of mutual internationalization. According to the Thai Automotive Industry Association (as cited by Punyasavatsut, 2008), in 2002, Thailand auto parts suppliers consisted of large and medium enterprises joining through foreign joint ventures and local suppliers from supporting industries. The study confirmed that Thailand's 1978 local content policy pushed forward linkages between MNEs and local companies, almost entirely SMEs, through subcontracting terms. This emergence of condensed local enterprise networks enticed foreign automakers to the country in the 1990s. Correspondently, there was an increase of automobile manufacturers and enormous movement of Japanese MNEs to Thailand. Though the local content policy was terminated as planned in the early 21st century, having been considered a challenge for trade liberalization, it had become the base for developing MNE-SME networks in the Thai automobile sector. Connections between suppliers and assemblers were multipliers; this means a single supplier procures auto parts to a number of assemblers at the same time (Maruhashi, 1995). This system is a "cross-supplier network," which promotes economies of scale, more spill-over effects, and extension beyond national boundaries (Fujita and Hill, 1997). Another benefit of MNE-SME networks as proved by the case study is that foreign assemblers brought technical assistance and training to the local suppliers in the host country to enhance their manufacturing processes.

9.3.2 Business Networks

As stated in the research entitled "The Role of Entrepreneurial Networks in the Exploration and Exploitation of Internationalization Opportunities by Information and Communication Technology Firms" written by Vasilchenko and Morrish (2011), if MNEs are eager to pursue opportunities for international expansion, they must be able to formulate and exploit their business network relationships and utilize diverse forms of partnerships that match their particular needs. There are four main methods enabling and facilitating MNEs' internationalization: acquiring credibility in foreign markets, gaining local market knowledge, expanding customer bases, and mitigating resource scarcity. According to Vasilchenko and Morrish (2011), implementing business networks is a productive means to acquire initial credibility when entering a new market, as well as local market knowledge that facilitates effective exploitation of internationalization opportunities. Moreover, business networks can help MNEs access local customers and reduce risks related to foreign market entry. In a case study of Xero, an MNE from New Zealand found in the study written by Vasilchenko and Morrish (2011), business networks benefit the company in many forms. First, the authors asserted that Xero had gained credibility in the local market from its business networks. As reported by the authors, Xero's plan of action for making an entrance to the United Kingdom and Australian markets was established on the use of partnership opportunities. As Xero's major product was consultancy, partnerships with local enterprises were essential to obtain authorization and credibility among clients in target areas. It is also confirmed that the partnering program that helped Xero sell its service through its partners allowed the company to gain more growth opportunities as well as lower costs of sale. Furthermore, Xero had acquired local market knowledge and customers, including regulatory and industry-specific knowledge of competitors and leading players, from its business partners in host countries. An interviewee who worked for Xero affirmed that the company's earlier settled bonds in the market were the source of initial insights in the UK accounting market. Partnerships with various stakeholders were another important approach for Xero's internationalization to Australia. The company collaborated with two of Australia's leading banks in order to obtain daily bank information, and partnered with a major Australian software provider that gave the firm smooth access to local customers.

Welch and Welch (1996) stated that the growth of business networks and their application highly contributes to a firm's learning process, which influences its internationalization as a whole. To elaborate the statement, according to Ge and Wang (2013), there are three main hypotheses that support the reason behind a company's decision to formulate business networks for internationalization purposes. It can first be concluded that as business networks expand, MNEs will make their first foreign market entry. In doing so, they lay foundations for joint ventures and/or strategic alliances with foreign partners, which equip the MNEs with priceless international information and market knowledge necessary for early entry. Furthermore, network bonds with miscellaneous levels of government can also ameliorate the MNEs' internationalization, boost their administrative processes, and reduce costs associated with information on the local markets and product standards (Tsui and Farh, 1997). Second, when firms achieve larger business networks, they are likely to internationalize faster. This can be explained by the fact that internationalizing companies or MNEs can use their social capital to access their network partners' overseas market information and know-how, as a firm's knowledge is usually gained and sustained through actors in its networks. In other words, having business networks allows the MNEs to use their connections with the suppliers, distributors, and even competitors who have been well established in the foreign markets; hence it enables MNEs to rapidly label their market opportunities across borders and accordingly go after them in a short period of time (Ge and Wang, 2013). It can also be seen that the wider the extent of business networks, the higher the resource commitment MNEs desire to make to overseas markets. Because interpersonal connections and networking can reduce risks and uncertainties caused by external dependences, MNEs in network ecosystems are willing to commit more resources to overseas operations. To illustrate, international venturing usually demands large amounts of financial or capital investment, but it is difficult for MNEs to obtain loans from local banks, as they lack credibility and legitimacy. However, MNEs can use their business network relationships to obtain external legitimacy, which is a resource for organizations to acquire and exchange important resources. To do so, they can initially foster relationships with government agencies and officials that regulate resource allocations, as there is a greater possibility for MNEs to be granted loans from banks and other financial institutions once considered legitimate and credible (Ibid).

In the study conducted by Ge and Wang (2013), formal business network ties with foreign-invested companies provided Chinese MNEs opportunities to internationalize rapidly. It illustrated that network relationships with different levels of government connections can enhance the internationalization process of MNEs, particularly for the reason that foreign trade and investment in China have been greatly regulated by state-owned enterprises since the beginning of China's economic reforms. These ties with the government cannot only improve an MNE's performance to boost managerial processes, but they also decrease costs accompanied with information on overseas markets and product standards. Another case firm found in the research is Huawei Technologies, a supreme privately owned telecommunications equipment producer in China. To expedite its internationalization, Huawei decided to develop global partnerships with major players in the business to internalize its partners in order to enhance its partners' technology—a more cost-effective and productive approach than promoting in-house technology. Xero, another case firm from New Zealand, also exploited its business contacts with formal business network actors, such as consultants and government bodies, which allowed it to gain in-depth information and regulatory knowledge. When the firm entered the United Kingdom, it accessed the market through a New Zealand Trade and Enterprise-launched program called "UK Beachhead program," which was designed for developing business networks between New Zealand Trade and Enterprise members and successful businesspeople, to facilitate each other's market entry and growth in major export markets (Vasilchenko and Morrish, 2011).

Other evidence of formal business networks in the Asia-Pacific region can be found in the study conducted by Mazzarol (2003). The survey showed that 44% of the responding firms from the information and communications technology (ICT) sector in Western Australia reported engagement in formal business networks, and stated that their level of export activities and investment in R&D had increased considerably. Other than the production layer, another significant layer of formal business networks, like resource network layers, is also crucial for Western Australian ICT MNEs in internationalization. Conventional actors within resource networks are financial institutions (including banks and venture capital firms), insurance providers, logistics agencies, storage and communications bureaus, and educational and training institutions. These also involve research centers and supporting industries that can supply complimentary products and services or transfers of technology (e.g., packaging companies).

Similar to formal business networks, informal business networks are also highly prized to MNEs in initiating international expansion. Based on Ge and Wang's (2013) study, three hypotheses were once again proposed. First, they suggested that if the MNEs broaden their personal networks, they would enter foreign markets earlier. Personal ties cultivated through informal social networks can support early entrance, as this gives more accurate and credible information to the MNEs for decision-making relevant to internationalization. Ethnic ties, particularly rooted in foreign countries, are also useful sources of information for MNEs to determine business opportunities. Second, as soon as MNEs have developed their informal business networks, the study said they would be able to run their internationalization activities at a more accelerated pace. Ethnic ties can be considered alternative financial resources, especially when the MNEs face funding difficulties through conventional channels; this increases the MNEs' flexibility and enables them to respond to both new and unstable circumstances promptly. Third, they said MNEs would be more willing to make more resource commitment once they have widened their informal business networks. Domestic and overseas personal networks through family members and friends can work as an alternative source of funding because MNEs tend to have greater availability of investment capital from their relatives or those who have similar social backgrounds.

Mazzarol (2003) confirmed that social interactions, especially at an informal level between personnel from the firms within the international networks across production and resource network layers, were an essential source of innovation due to the sharing of new ideas and tacit knowledge. In his study, face-to-face communication with key customers and major suppliers commonly occurred within Western Australian ICT MNEs. These informal contacts between the enterprises' senior managers and lead customers took place monthly with 54% of responding firms, and weekly with 11%. Similarly, there were monthly informal communications between predominant customer companies and 43% of technical, marketing, and sales staff of the responding firms. Email and telephone contacts accounted for 86% and 79% of the firms' interactions with their main clients on a daily or weekly basis. Furthermore, 52% of respondents perceived that informal network communications were important sources for information on new knowledge and technology, and even more significant than formal research and conferences or contacts via newsletters or at trade shows. Another 28 case firms asserted that social networks were their source of innovation and business development. Senior managers from 60% to 70% of responding companies stated that they had locally, nationally, and internationally maintained professional networks with an array of groups such as financial institution staff, venture capital providers, university researchers, government officers, and new technology developers via telephone, email, traveling abroad, and other direct contact channels. A chief executive officer from a case firm reported that his employees were active members of many associations and sporting clubs where they sustained contacts and communications with key customers, military, and government officers; these old ties could be further developed into more formal relationships.

As another illustration, Ge and Wang (2013) studied the positive effects of informal network ties on Chinese MNEs' international expansions. First, they claimed that to gain accurate and credible market information to prevent potential risks from early foreign market entry, personal ties established through informal social networks are needed. This is because in China, foreign trade is controlled by bureaucratic hierarchies. As a result, public information such as government policies and regulations on foreign trade and investment has limited accessibility. Ethnic and family ties can also provide financial aid for early entry to the Chinese MNEs that would like to invest or run a business. Cardoza and Fornes (2011) proved that financial support from private sources are an essential element for Chinese MNEs because it can enable the companies to make more resource commitment to foreign ventures. Similarly, another case study of Chinese firms from a feature article entitled "Entrepreneurial Orientation, Social Capital, and the Internationalization of SMEs: Evidence from China" written by Zhang et al. (2012) illustrated the importance of social networks. The research found that there were three major benefits for internationalization that Chinese MNEs gained from social networks, particularly ties with managers in other companies; these included information on foreign market opportunities, experiential learning, and referral trust. These competitive advantages helped Chinese firms accumulate social capital, quality materials, credit guarantee, sales channels, and much more, which further reduced exchange and production costs because they provided indirect access to the assets of their business partners. From the interviews with some Chinese responding firms, the results showed that informal business networks had major contributions to the MNEs' business practices, ranging from financial support to market access channels. An interviewee stated that when they dealt with financial difficulties and had to pay suppliers for the ordered goods, they would ask their partners to wait until money could be collected from customers who owed them, and that their business partners would agree. The interviewee said it would have been impossible to do so without past informal connections. Another interviewee also added that during the process of expanding their business internationally, existing clients were the major contributors. According to Ge and Wang (2013), the case of SimWorks, one of the world's leading developers in mobile applications from New Zealand, demonstrated the application of past industry connections to enter Australia's market. With these contacts, the company could adapt its products to the local market and partner with Australia's biggest mobile operator.

9.3.3 Global Production Networks

According to Coe et al. (2013a), global production networks refer to the networks coordinated and regulated by MNEs that involve interconnections between foreign affiliates, strategic partners, main customers, and nonfirm organizations. This shows that the global production network system is not a simple process, but comprises the production network configuration. Configuration means the decisive setting of value-added activity locations along the commodity chains; this includes the decision-making on production sites in the firms' key markets in different regions. From all of the above, it can be assumed that MNEs would engage in some segments of the production network and create contractual relationships with other bodies or companies as part of an immense system. Coe et al. (2013a) called these kinds of relationships "externalized transactions." These transactions are business relationships that emerge from interconnections between independent MNEs. They are market based, as they can put some pressure over the price competition as well as other factors beyond the control of a specific firm. For instance, Nokia from Finland and Sanyo from Japan had formed an interfirm transaction when Nokia bought lithium batteries for its mobile handsets from its supplier, which was Sanyo at the time. These global production networks consist of the overlaps in corporate functions and geographical locations in order to formulate complex systems of internal and external relationships that cannot be completed by a single entity in a commodity chain. Based on the same study written by Coe et al. (2013a), internal and external relationships or intrafirm and interfirm relationships are the basic building blocks of global production networks.

Starting with internal relationships, the internal divisions of labor within MNE networks generally result from the combination of organizational/technological dynamics and location-specific determinants embedded in three main types of organizational units: corporate and regional headquarters, R&D facilities, and transnational operational units. Corporate and regional headquarters are the core centers of MNEs where important decisions and plans are made, such as finance and investment decisions, product choice, and market specialization. R&D facilities refer to activities found in production and service areas used for maintaining the competitiveness of the MNEs in the marketplace, whereas transnational operating units are the bodies covering a wide range of activities from production sites and facilities to sales and marketing offices, and more (Coe et al., 2013a).

The aforementioned study shows that there are four approaches to organize transnational production units among MNEs in a global production network. The first method is called "globally concentrated production," which is the mode of cross-border production utilized for resource extraction and manufacture because MNEs may have more control over their subsidiaries and be able to gain spatial-geographic concentration during their early years when they tend to locate their manufacturing plants in their home countries and export their products to the rest of the world. For example, Toyota's Lexus series is wholly produced in Japan and exported to other parts of the world. The second mode of organization is the "host-market production structure," which is applied when the exports are not accessible in host countries due to trade barriers. It is therefore necessary to customize their products to the tastes and preferences of local markets or grant the autonomy to local subsidiaries or units, like the case of HSBC in Asia versus HSBC in the United States. Third, "product specialization for a global or regional market" is a mode of organizing global production networks that is mainly applicable to the manufacturing industries, as the production autonomy is in the hands of global or macroregional production units. For instance, even though Hewlett Packard's (HP) computer servers are still coordinated by its global headquarters in California, its global mandate for all HP printers is arranged by its regional headquarters in Singapore due to Singaporean teams' excellence in design and engineering. Lastly, the fourth mode of global production network organization is "transnational vertical integration," which is the most developed and coordinated compared to the other approaches. This mode requires high management expertise and control for ensuring the production responsibilities across the MNEs' worldwide operations. To illustrate, the global production networks of Sony and Sharp are well established in Japan, China, and many Southeast Asian countries in order to maximize the efficiency and quality of their televisions based on the specialization of each production location; in this case, Japan is the center for producing core components, Chinese units are responsible for assembly and testing, and Southeast Asian countries take care of modular components and subassembly (Coe et al., 2013a).

As opposed to the intrafirm global production networks, interfirm global production networks do not only regulate their own internal webs of overseas subsidiaries and affiliates, but also administrate condensed external networks of independent contractors, suppliers, and the like. According to Coe et al. (2013a), there are three major approaches to organizing interfirm relationships in the market: subcontracting and outsourcing, strategic alliances and joint ventures, and franchising and cooperative agreements.

International subcontracting and outsourcing embrace the engagement between independent enterprises to manufacture products particularly for the parent company; these include commercial and industrial subcontracting. Commercial subcontracting has production mostly or fully subcontracted by another enterprise (the supplier) outside the country, while industrial subcontracting has more product specifications in order to meet technological and marketing requirements. For the latter, if there is a full subcontracting, brand management must be emphasized in order to handle their brand name. As an illustration, many leading laptop companies such as HP and Dell are clients of Taiwanese contract producers like Quanta and Wistron. Second, in highly competitive business environments, MNEs tend to participate in specific interfirm relationships called strategic alliances or joint ventures. Many MNEs decide to become mutual competitors in the same product lines and ally with each other at the same time. Especially in the service and retail industries, this kind of interfirm relationships is common. For example, Wal-Mart formed strategic alliances with Hong Kong-based Li & Fung in order to reduce costs, enhance product quality, and expand its global exposure. The last mode, franchising and cooperative agreements, comprises franchising, which occurs when an enterprise grants the franchisee, mostly overseas, rights to use its trademark and intellectual property; this helps the MNE mitigate risks from the new business environment as well as the financial burden that might result from huge capital investment (Coe et al., 2013a).

According to Hiratsuka (2011), the hard disk drive (HDD) industry's international production networks and industrial clusters in Asia not only offered insightful information on the integrated East Asian economy, but also lowered transportation costs to the MNEs in the networks. International production networks in the HDD industry had been well established, as

HDD components and parts were supplied from more foreign suppliers than from local suppliers. Because transportation costs involved in the HDD industry were lower than in the automobile industry, international production networks and intermediate trade in the HDD industry were more developed. The same study found that the majority of foreign suppliers in neighboring countries were located near the main assembler plants. For instance, factories in Thailand were predominantly procured by Indonesian, Malaysian, Filipino, and Singaporean suppliers due to the fact that their engineers were able to facilely travel to solve problems proceeding from production deficiencies. This supported the fact that international production networks were generally created among neighboring countries.

Another example of global production networks is the macroregional integration in Southeast Asia. It is clear that the integration processes in the area regulated by the Association of Southeast Asian Nations (ASEAN) have driven MNEs from Japan and South Korea for the most part. According to the United Nations Conference on Trade and Development (2011), Japanese and other automakers in the automobile and automotive component industries consolidated their manufacturing in the region and adopted macroregional production network strategies and production specialization to deal with their ASEAN Free Trade Agreement market. Leading automobile companies like Toyota and Nissan had a diversity of network operations that involved various activities such as regional headquarters, finance, training, components provision, and assembly. To supply the ASEAN market, Ford adopted a regional strategy of specialization. For example, the company installed a plant specialized in pickup truck production in Thailand, while it positioned passenger car production specifically in the Philippines. Likewise, global production networks in the electronics industry in ASEAN were also well developed. Samsung from South Korea settled a tube glass factory in Malaysia called Samsung Corning (Malaysia) to serve as a production site for color picture tubes in the country. This plant also supplied intermediate goods and parts to Samsung Electronics (Thailand) and subsidiaries in Indonesia, Malaysia, and Vietnam. This evidently shows a model of global production networks strengthening macroregional integration through manufacture and supply linkages.

9.3.4 Preclusterization

Based on the study conducted by Hatani (2009), preclusterization is an ad hoc entry strategy for international expansion of MNEs that helps competitive suppliers in a well-established network enter a new market and set up clusters in the target areas before full entry into the host country. The researcher defined preclusterization as a deep-rooted form of network-based foreign entry occurring when supplier companies in a business network enter an emerging market and start to cluster in the area that the core enterprise aims for before fully entering the market. Originally, MNEs in a network constructed vigorous entry processes that are more productive due to shared experience and capabilities to adapt to new business environments (Chang, 1995; Delios and Henisz, 2000). In other words, for production networks, it is highly important to continuously persist and survive in a competitive market, and building up supply clusters is an answer to the issue. Porter (1998) defined a cluster as a "geographic congregation of annexed enterprises and institutions in a specific area, while a network is the interactions between companies regardless of location." Benefits of positioning operations in a certain location with suppliers in the same industry or related industries (or "clusterization") include decisive sourcing inputs, productive transportation, useful information sharing, and interdependency with cluster members (Hatani, 2009). Above all, to successfully enter into host countries, MNEs need to reconsider their timing of entry thoroughly (Luo and Peng, 1998). It can be concluded that MNEs that arrive in foreign markets early often benefit from technological leadership, infringement of limited assets, and entry barriers for latecomers (Kerin et al., 1992). Luo and Peng (1998) suggested that early movers achieved better performance in many areas, such as higher profitability, stability, and long-run market extension. In the same manner, Chandler (1977, 1980) coined the term "economies of speed," which refers to comprehensive capital utilization and early coordination that can speed up the MNEs' entry pace based on their gained knowledge about the markets—so-called "experiential knowledge." Hence, forming clusters with the locals earlier is critical for MNEs.

As illustrated in his research entitled "Pre-clusterization in Emerging Markets: the Toyota Group's Entry Process in China," Hatani (2009) proved the significance of establishing networks or strategic collective actions when dealing with demanding competition and risks in the emerging market context by using a case study of the Toyota Group in China. Different from its entry process in the United States, Toyota Group began its entry into China by creating contractual ties with local enterprises and then preclusterizing with key suppliers instead of establishing wholly owned transplants. Afterward, the group built up joint assembly plants and reinforced the local supply network by foreign direct investment follow-up. In addition to key suppliers' proactive operations,

Toyota Group had made a number of commitments with China toward pre-clusterization. Though Toyota's full entry to China was late, the firm had made a lot of preparation, including the establishment of technical schools, training centers, and authorized service stations near its target areas in China in the 1980s. Toyota Group had also implemented its informal supplier management system to organize suppliers without physical production connections by settling a locally based liaison group in the host country called Tianjin Kyoho Liaison Group in 1995. This liaison group allowed Japanese MNEs in any field operating in the Tianjin area to expedite a broader array of information exchange and networking opportunities. The number of Tianjin Kyoho Liaison Group members unwaveringly rose as the foreign direct investment of Japanese MNEs increased in the area. In 2000, there were already 24 business units of Japanese multinationals registered to the group before Toyota gained permission for producing passenger cars in China from the Chinese government. Furthermore, Toyota Group also established a liaison office in Shanghai in order to set up local meetings to accommodate the rising number of Japanese MNEs in the area. Thanks to the liaison office and routine meetings, suppliers in the networks were able to sustain their close communication and information sharing with each other, even though there was no Toyota assembly factory in Shanghai at the time. These informal meetings were nothing new for the Toyota Group, but they were highly crucial for member firms in terms of local operation improvement and credibility building. The case study demonstrated that suppliers in a well-integrated network could enter an overseas market even before the installation of the core firm's assembly unit by establishing supply clusters near the promising target area. By having preclusterization, MNEs in the network could assure that the core enterprise's supply chain would be ready before local production began. This means it would be easier for the core firm that was a latecomer to overcome disadvantages from its late arrival and quickly become comparable to its competitors who already entered the market beforehand.

9.3.5 Ethnic Businesses and Clusters

Coe et al. (2013b) also studied the role and importance of ethnic networks in terms of internationalization in Chapter 14, "Ethnic Economies: Do Culture have Economies?" in their book "Economic Geography: A Contemporary Introduction." This section will summarize and interpret their perceptions toward ethnic businesses and clusters by examining the advantages of ethnic enterprises and the notion of transnationalism.

Before discussing the economic geographies of MNEs' ethnic networks, it is crucial to understand the positive sides of ethnic enterprises for international expansion. Network and organizational structure in ethnic networks usually increase the management capacity and offer ethnic resources to MNEs. The examples of ethnic resources mentioned here are investment funds, know-how, and market information. This means the MNEs have more opportunities to access protected markets and make successful business transactions. To maintain the aforementioned benefits, the MNEs are required to keep close ties with their home countries; these collective bonds are globally widespread but accessible at all times, and thus so-called "transnationalism." Initially, transnationalism refers to the social, economic, political, and cultural linkages with the countries that the immigrants sustain. There are three main reasons behind the rise in transnationalism. First, there has been an increase in the number of temporary and permanent immigrants. In addition to this, technological advancements have facilitated the perpetuation of strong ties, for instance lower transportation costs, cheaper telephone calls, and social network tools. Lastly, transnational activities have become increasingly promoted by institutional structures. It is evident that many governments acknowledge and support the maintenance of the bonds between overseas citizens and both home and host countries, for example, through provision of dual citizenship (Coe et al., 2013b).

From all of the above, transnational ethnic enterprises have grown exponentially. According to Landolt et al. (1999), there are four different types of transnational migrant enterprises that later form the MNEs' international ecosystem. These comprise circuit firms, cultural enterprises, ethnic enterprises, and return migrant microenterprises. Circuit firms are the agencies providing services transporting or transmitting products and remittances. This includes services facilitating the migration process. In addition to this, cultural enterprises refer to the companies importing and selling cultural products such as magazines and music. Ethnic enterprises are the firms supplying goods such as cooking ingredients and clothing from home countries, whereas return migrant microenterprises are the companies founded by returnees to their home countries, which use contacts acquired abroad to establish business networks. To illustrate, Chinese entrepreneurs have been highly successful in establishing Chinese business communities across the world, especially in the Asia-Pacific region. Chinatowns in Thailand, Singapore, Australia, and other parts of the globe are clear examples of the Chinese global networks framed by coethnic ties (Coe et al., 2013b).

More specifically, there are some distinctive features of Chinese business networks, called "guanxi" or "relationships" in Chinese, that other varieties of formal networks may not be able to mimic or exercise in order to adapt to the global economy competition. These competitive advantages include family ties, cultural affinities, familial and cultural relationships, ability to raise capital, and exchange of market intelligence. Family ties are key to Chinese business management. Many top Chinese MNEs are regulated by male family members, which facilitates quick decision-making processes across the networks. Various forms of cultural affinity such as place-based identities, common language, and collective social norms can facilitate business transactions outside the family loop and thus develop business relationships into mutual trust and reciprocity. Familial and cultural relationships are also enormously crucial for building trust and reputation in business practices that are globally widespread, with or without legal contracts. These involve the relationships between the firms and their competitors, contractors, suppliers, employers, employees, and other stakeholders. Informal networks like the ethnic enclave economy offer immense flexibility for raising the capital necessary for new business ventures, such as informal sources of credit and easy loans. Finally, the exchange of market intelligence as well as gifts and favors in the form of information creates indebtedness within the business relationships among MNEs and their stakeholders in the networks (Coe et al., 2013b).

The case study from Sim (2006) illustrates the significance of ethnic networks to internationalization in Asia. The first example is the case of a Singaporean textile firm that originally enlarged its foreign operations across borders via boundless family networks in the region. The firm capitalized its ethnic networks in Asia to formulate an Asian ecosystem for the whole business processes and collaborations. Another case firm is a Malaysian textile company with large connections to suppliers and other businesses in its region for a long period of time. All electronic enterprises in the study demonstrated their application of ethnic networks in the Southeast Asian region and China to cross-border business operations. To illustrate, Creative Technology, a case firm from the Singaporean electronics industry, formed ethnic-based alliances on licensing joint ventures to expand its extensive global network to more than 80 countries, including 5 different overseas production locations. A diversified MNE from Malaysia named Lion Group worked with its Chinese ethnic partners to localize its networks and gain market knowledge in China as well as implement its future plans to restructure its China focus on retailing. According to the author, the enterprise, especially its chief executive officer, had fostered large guanxi connections and political networks in China for a very long time.

9.4 CONCLUSION

This chapter has reassessed the importance of different kinds of networks influencing successful international expansion strategies of MNEs, including MNE-SME networks, business networks (both formal and informal), global production networks, preclusterization, and ethnic networks. In accordance with the conceptualizations of related subjects and theories from both classic and contemporary schools, networks provide a collection of mutual benefits and interests among the network members, ranging from in-depth information and knowledge to cost reduction. In this chapter, a number of case studies from various countries in the Asia-Pacific region are used as empirical evidence to illustrate each type of network, such as India, Thailand, Japan, China, Taiwan, New Zealand, Australia, the Philippines, Singapore, and Malaysia.

REFERENCES

Buckley, P.J., Casson, M.C., 1998. Models of the multinational enterprise. J. Int. Bus. Stud. 29 (1), 21–44.

Buckley, P.J., Prashantham, S., 2016. Global interfirm networks: the division of entrepreneurial labor between MNEs and SMES. Acad. Manag. Perspect. 30 (1), 40–58.

Cardoza, G., Fornes, G., 2011. The internationalization of SMEs from China: the case of Ningxia Hui autonomous region. Asia Pac. J. Manag. 28 (4), 737–759.

Chandler, A., 1977. The Visible Hand: the Managerial Revolution in American Business. Belknap/Harvard University Press, Cambridge.

Chandler, A., 1980. The growth of the transnational industrial firm in the United States and the United Kingdom: a comparative analysis. Econ. Hist. Rev. 33 (3), 396–410.

Chang, S.J., 1995. International expansion of Japanese firms: capability building through sequential entry. Acad. Manag. J. 38 (2), 383–407.

Chen, Y.Y., Jaw, Y.L., 2014. How do business groups' small world networks effect diversification, innovation, and internationalization? Asia Pac. J. Manag. 31, 1019–1044.

Coe, N.M., Kelly, P.F., Yeung, H.W.C., 2013a. The transnational corporation: how does the global firm keep it all together? In: Coe, N.M. et al., (Ed.), Economic Geography: A Contemporary Introduction. Wiley, New York, pp. 294–329.

Coe, N.M., Kelly, P.F., Yeung, H.W.C., 2013b. Ethnic economies: do culture have economies? In: Coe, N.M. et al., (Ed.), Economic Geography: A Contemporary Introduction. Wiley, New York, pp. 432–462.

Coviello, N.E., Munro, H.J., 1997. Network relationships and the internationalization process of small software firms. Int. Bus. Rev. 6 (4), 361–386.

Delios, A., Henisz, W., 2000. Japanese firms' investment strategies in wmerging economies. Acad. Manag. J. 43 (3), 305–323.

Dhanaraj, C., Parkhe, A., 2006. Orchestrating innovation networks. Acad. Manag. Rev. 31 (3), 659–669.

Dunning, J.H., 1988. The eclectic paradigm of international production: a restatement and some possible extensions. J. Int. Bus. Stud. 19, 1–31.
Fisch, J.H., Zschoche, M., 2012. The role of operational flexibility in the expansion of international production networks. Strateg. Manag. J. 33, 1540–1556.
Frobel, F., Heinrichs, J., Kreye, O., 1980. The New International Division of Labor. Cambridge University Press, Cambridge.
Fujita, K., Hill, R.C., 1997. Auto industrialization in Southeast Asia. National strategies and local development. ASEAN Econ. Bull. 13 (3), 312–332.
Ge, G.L., Wang, H.Q., 2013. The impact of network relationships on internationalization process: an empirical study of Chinese private enterprises. Asia Pac. J. Manag. 30, 1169–1189.
Gilmore, A., Carson, D., 1999. Entrepreneurial marketing by networking. N. Engl. J. Entrep. 2 (2), 31–38.
Hatani, F., 2009. Pre-clusterization in emerging markets: the Toyota group's entry process in China. Asia Pac. Bus. Rev. 15(3).
Hiratsuka, D., 2011. Production Networks in Asia: A Case Study from the Hard Disk Drive Industry. ADBI Working Paper 301, Asian Development Bank Institute, Tokyo.
Johanson, J., Vahlne, J., 1977. The internationalization process of the firm: a model of knowledge development on increasing foreign commitments. J. Int. Bus. Stud. 23–32.
Johanson, J., Vahlne, J.E., 1992. Management of Internationalization. Institute of International Business, Stockholm School of Economics, Sweden.
Johanson, J., Vahlne, J.-E., 2003. Business relationship learning and commitment in the internationalization process. J. Int. Entrepreneurship. 1 (1), 83–101.
Jones, M., 1999. The internationalization of small Hi-tech firms. J. Int. Mark. 7 (4), 15–41.
Kerin, R.A., Varadarajan, P.R., Peterson, R.A., 1992. First-mover advantages: a synthesis, conceptual framework, and research propositions. J. Mark. 56 (4), 33–52.
Landolt, P., Autler, L., Baires, S., 1999. From hermano lejano to hermano mayor: the dialectics of salvadoran transnationalism. Ethn. Rac. Stud. 22, 290–315.
Luo, Y., Peng, M.W., 1998. First mover advantages in investing in transitional economies. Thund. Int. Bus. Rev. 40 (2), 141–163.
Maruhashi, H., 1995. Japanese Subcontracting System in Thailand: A Case Study of the Thai Automobile Industry (Unpublished Master thesis). Faculty of Economics, Thammasat University, Bangkok.
Mazzarol, T., 2003. Strategic networking among small high technology firms: evidence from the Western Australian ICT sector. In: Paper Presented at the ANZAM Conference 2003, 2-5 December, Fremantle, WA.
Morya, K.K., Dwivedi, H., 2009. Aligning interests of SMEs and a focal firm (MNE) in a global supply chain setup. J. Supply Chain Manag. 6 (1), 49–59.
Pfeffer, J., Salancik, G.R., 1978. The External Control of Organization: A Resource Dependence Perspective. Harper & Row, New York.
Porter, M.E., 1998. Clusters and the new economics of competition. Harv. Bus. Rev. 76 (6), 77–90.
Punyasavatsut, C., 2008. SMEs in the Thai manufacturing industry: linking with MNES. In: Lim, H. (Ed.), SME in Asia and Globalization. pp. 287–321. ERIA research project report 2007-5.
Punyasavatsut, C., 2010. Integrating SMEs into East Asia production networks: Thailand. In: Vo, T.T., Narjoko, D., Oum, S. (Eds.), Integrating Small and Medium Enterprises (SMEs) into the More Integrate East Asia. ERIA, Jakarta, pp. 262–297. ERIA research project report 2009-8.
Ratajczak-Mrozek, M., 2014. Companies' simultaneous embeddedness in local, international and global networks – a conceptualization from the perspective of local enterprises and their degree of internationalization. Econ. Rev. 14 (1), 31–47.

Shaner, J., Maznevski, M., 2011. The relationship between networks, institutional development, and performance in foreign investments. Strateg. Manag. J. 32, 556–568.
Sharma, D.D., Johanson, J., 1987. Technical consultancy in internationalization. Int. Mark. Rev. 4 (4), 20–29.
Sim, A.B., 2006. Internationalization strategies of emerging Asian MNEs – case study evidence on Singaporean and Malaysian firms. Asia Pacific Business Review 12 (4), 487–505.
Tan, J., 1996. Regulatory environment and strategic orientations in a transitional economy: a study of Chinese private enterprises. Enterp. Theory Pract. 21, 31–46.
Tsui, A.S., Farh, J.L., 1997. Where guanxi matters: relational demography and guanxi in the Chinese context. Work. Occup. 24 (1), 56–80.
United Nations Conference on Trade and Development, 2011. World Investment Report 2011: Non-equity Modes of International Production and Development. UNCTAD, Geneva.
Vasilchenko, E., Morrish, S., 2011. The role of entrepreneurial networks in the exploration and exploitation of internationalization opportunities by information and communication technology firms. J. Int. Mark. 19 (4), 88–105.
Welch, L.S., Welch, D.E., 1996. The internationalization process and networks: a strategic management perspective. J. Int. Mark. 4 (3), 11–28.
Winch, G., 2014. Strategic business and network positioning for internationalization. Serv. Ind. J. 34 (8), 715–728.
Zhang, X., Ma, X., Wang, Y., 2012. Entrepreneurial orientation, social capital, and the internationalization of SMEs: evidence from China. Thund. Int. Bus. 54 (2), 195–210.

CHAPTER 10

Contemporary Issues in Internationalization of Asia Pacific Companies

N. Thirawat
Mahidol University International College, Nakhon Pathom, Thailand

10.1 INTRODUCTION

In the era of globalization and intensified competition, firms are forced to enter a new realm of business management, called "international business," toward greater risks and overseas activity expansion. Internationalization is considered a significant measure for enhancing performance and competitiveness at both domestic and international levels (Korsakiene, 2014). Advantages of business internationalization range from growth reinforcement, market size increase, dependence reduction, economies of scale, and higher competitiveness to long-term sustainability. It also offers greater opportunities for withstanding global competitors in host and home markets as well as achieving the demand of national and international customers, regardless of the size of the firm (Xie and Suh, 2014; Dewan and Singh, 2015). However, there are a number of possible challenges as well as institutional pressures that firms have to handle throughout their internationalization process. These include barriers to internationalization, such as cultural, political, and economic differences, which have been gaining growing attention. This chapter will examine contemporary issues associated with overseas operations, embedded in the internationalization process of multinational enterprises (MNEs) in the Asia-Pacific region.

According to Rajendran (2015), *internationalization* refers to the geographical growth of business operations across borders. In the same study, the author includes a wide range of activities perceived as components of internationalization, such as exports, imports, foreign direct investment, international subcontracting, technical collaboration, and more. This also involves relationships between small and medium enterprises (SMEs) and foreign partners. To elaborate, *SME internationalization* is SME's strategic

Internationalization and Managing Networks in the Asia Pacific
http://dx.doi.org/10.1016/B978-0-08-100813-3.00010-9

international expansion and export behavior attracting wider interest alongside the reduction of trade barriers.

Xie and Suh (2014) defined *barriers to internationalization* as problems limiting the anticipation of the opportunities and practicality in terms of foreign operation expansion. These barriers to internationalization or *export barriers* are constraints that obstruct firms from being able to launch, develop, or maintain their foreign operations (Lakew and Chiloane-Tsoka, 2015). Based on the same study, export barriers are classified into internal and external constraints that hinder MNEs from international expansion of their business. These include inadequate knowledge and information, and insufficient strategic resources to initiate export activities.

As stated in Leonidou (2004), *barriers to export* refer to the constraints that handicap the firm's performance in terms of market entry, operational development, and sustainability. Furthermore, export barriers can be categorized into internal and external barriers, where internal barriers relate to organizational resources and/or capabilities, and a company's approach to exporting products and services. On the other hand, external barriers are limitations associated with home and host environments found in the locations where the firm conducts its business activities.

Emerging markets are countries undergoing accelerated economic development, with their economic institutions experiencing expeditious adaptation to free market philosophy (Dixit and Yadav, 2008). Intense competition and recent opportunities escorted by globalization have influenced firms in emerging markets to expand their business operations across borders. However, businesses from these markets usually encounter a number of constraints in order to achieve internationalization.

10.2 RELATED THEORIES

In the field of international business management, a number of theories are used for explaining the internationalization of firms as an economic phenomenon, especially in regard to its drives and barriers. In this research, four main theories are selected to rationalize the emergence and evolvement of barriers to internationalization; these include the process of internationalization, network, resource-based view, and capabilities theories.

10.2.1 Process of Internationalization Theory

Johanson and Vahlne (1977) conceptualized stages of internationalization as the pace and direction of gaining and managing international experience and knowledge. As explained by Leick (2011), the main idea of the internationalization process theory relies on the concept of cultural distance. Cultural distance or "psychic distance" refers to a variety of qualitative factors influencing sociocultural homogeneity or heterogeneity between host and home markets, such as linguistic differences, business practices, and political and legal systems. These factors construct the intensity of commitment and affect a firm's decision-making process, both domestically and internationally. According to the model designed by Johanson and Vahlne (1990), it can be seen that before entering a foreign market, firms need to gain sufficient experience with and knowledge of their domestic markets. Afterward, they start to seek culturally comparable markets, such as countries with identical ethnic ancestors or business customs. With the acquired knowledge of the possible host markets and accumulated experience, companies hence increasingly boost their commitment and investment in the foreign markets or expand their business operations to the markets with a wider cultural distance. This conforms to Vernon's product life cycle theory (1966), which demonstrates that foreign direct investment tends to pursue several stages, starting from exporting, establishing overseas production bases, product standardization, and relocation once firms reach the saturation point. Process of internationalization theory is also similar to Rogers' (1962) innovation-related model because both emphasize the orientation of behaviors in which decisions and actions are assumed to be taken serially at the time that firms gain new knowledge and experiences (as cited by Abdelzaher, 2012).

10.2.2 Network and Social Network Theories

As stated in the research conducted by Ratajczak-Mrozek (2014), international networks are the inbound connections arising from imports, cooperation, and competition engaged in the internationalization process. In other words, MNEs are likely to establish and prosper their positions in cross-border networks by the bonds they make with their partners toward foreign expansion, infiltration, and integration. Correspondingly, Winch (2014) suggested that firms tend to formulate networks where they come across to interact with each other in order to supply a service or product in a definite period of time. In order to achieve successful networking, firms must also develop unique capabilities and skills to fulfill overseas demands and create opportunities for exploration and exploitation. It is also necessary for them to build up durable connections toward mutual collaboration and reinforcement in order to gain collective benefits altogether. Moreover, social network theory explains the role of social networks as a tool to facilitate firms' internationalization, by which firms can utilize their personal and business contacts to approach local markets and retrieve information about positive conditions and environments for business from their capable foreign partners (Vasilchenko and Morrish, 2011). Thus, to surpass numerous internationalization barriers, firms should focus on establishing networking relationships.

10.2.3 Resource-Based View Theory

According to Barney (1986, 1991), the resource-based perspective highlights how firms can gain sustainable competitive advantages from their possession of priceless, unfavorably imitable or substitutable, and rare resources in order to perform more economically and better fulfill customer needs. Hence management strategies tend to revolve around important components, which are identifying, developing, and utilizing resources effectively and efficiently. In the same manner, Hitt et al. (2001) define a *firm* as a compilation of unique resources and capabilities that supports its own strategy's development. These resources are the assimilation of diverse physical, human, and intangible resources. According to Barney (1991), resources are primarily classified into tangible and intangible resources. Intangible resources refer to the resources formulated and/or accumulated over time starting from the businesses' establishment; they are largely embedded in specific patterns of routines. Examples of intangible resources are knowledge-based resources, human resources, reputational resources, and research and development resources (Hitt et al., 2001). On the other hand, tangible resources are visible, measurable, physical resources such as factories and machinery, whereas financial resources and organizational resources include information technology (IT) systems, for example (Ibid). Having such resources can contribute to business success in the marketplace, but managing them is not simple. Additionally, Grant (1996) insisted that knowledge is one of the most strategically significant resources in the marketplace. Nevertheless, managing the value gained from knowledge acquisition remains a challenge for firms, especially when the world economy continues to evolve technologically. Similarly, experimental knowledge that is difficult to imitate by rivals is also required for driving internationalization of firms, but is not easy for firms to accumulate quickly (Barney et al., 2001). For this reason, resource management alongside the growing world economy and technological advancement should be considered an issue to study for internationalization.

10.2.4 Capabilities Theory

According to the capabilities theory suggested by Golgeci and Arslan (2014), in order to overcome barriers to internationalization, firms must acquire a series of capabilities; in other words, without dynamic and adaptive, marketing and supply chain, relational, and information acquisition capabilities, it is highly challenging for firms to expand their international operations successfully. To start, dynamic capabilities refer to MNEs' potential to systematically solve problems, constituted by their inclination to recognize opportunities and threats, to make market-oriented decisions at the right time, and to modify their resource base; strictly speaking, it is necessary for firms to be able to implement internationalization strategies in agreement with external context analysis (Barreto, 2010). Simultaneously, this also conforms to the idea of the evolutionary theory of marketing, which suggests that regardless of the firm's size, the most adaptable entities always get through obstacles and unfavorable environments; therefore adaptive capabilities represent the flexibility to rapidly fit and perform in overseas markets through creativity, responsiveness, and tolerance to the host countries, clients, and institutional preconditions (Tellis and Crawford, 1981; Yiu et al., 2007). In addition to this, marketing and supply chain capabilities signify the essential driving forces behind MNEs' performance in competitive global markets where product and marketing differentiations are emphasized (Morash and Lynch, 2002). Relational capabilities indicate the firms' competency to formulate, govern, and leverage relationships with supply chain partners that provide firms with potential to create value and competitive advantages. These relationships with suppliers and customers offer firms a wide range of resources and knowledge via network membership, which helps reduce problems and challenges embedded in foreign markets and greatly contributes to international expansion (Dyer and Hatch, 2006). Finally, many firms suffer from the lack of mandatory insights on market, customer, and institutional environments in host countries; hence firms are required to gain information-acquisition capabilities to collect, absorb, and integrate information in order to effectively perform and make appropriate strategic decisions in the global arena (Flint, 2004; Lu et al., 2009). In short, it can be concluded that if a firm lacks any of the aforementioned capabilities, it would be burdensome for it to expand its cross-border business operations.

10.3 PROBLEMS AND CHALLENGES OF FIRMS' INTERNATIONALIZATION

It is necessary for SMEs to "go global" as an institutional response to extrinsic tensions in their home countries. Research conducted by Reuber and

Fischer (1997) stated that knowledge and experience are essential elements for SMEs to internationalize. In comparison with large MNEs, SMEs generally face more limited resources and have fewer market entry modes from which to choose. According to Xie and Suh (2014), SMEs tend to confront various challenges and barriers when expanding their cross-border operations, such as restricted capabilities and resources, inadequate administrative procedures and practices, insufficient planning and management, and lack of expertise and access to foreign distribution channels. This corresponds to the study written by Holmlund and Kock (1998) stating that SMEs, in general, are deficient in acquiring knowledge about marketing, manufacturing, and finance in the markets; hence they are incapable of entering foreign markets and developing overseas activities that demand comprehensive resources and know-how. This phenomenon can be explained by the fact that most SMEs do not have a well-developed mechanistic approach to information and/or lack investment in knowledge management because they principally depend on their CEO's decision-making (McAdam and Reid, 2001)

Based on the study conducted by Dewan and Singh (2015), SMEs have a high tendency to be challenged by two major consequences of international integration: property rights protection and barriers to entry. According to a survey on SMEs' internationalization carried out by Szabo (2002), the most dominant barriers to internationalization for SMEs are the lack of entrepreneurial, managerial, and marketing skills, followed by bureaucratic dilemmas, defective approaches to information and knowledge, difficulties in gaining financial resources, poor accessibility to investment (particularly in technology and know-how), standardization discrepancies, differences in the range of product and service use, language and cultural differences, risks of selling overseas, competition of domestic enterprises, inappropriate behavior of multinationals against local companies, complicated trade documentation (including packaging and labeling), lack of government incentives for internationalization, and inadequate intellectual property protection, respectively. In the same manner, another survey conducted by Korsakiene (2014) compared noninternationalized SMEs and internationalized SMEs. It concluded that internationalized SMEs are more likely to face the following barriers: inaccessible market information, bureaucracy (such as long administrative procedures and laws and regulations), intense competition overseas, foreign government restrictions, disparities in consumer habit and standards, start-up costs, limited capital and funds, limited management skills, lack of marketing knowledge, and communication problems.

Empirical research has divided internationalization barriers into five main areas: financial and resource based, managerial or functional, market based (including both the domestic and international markets), industry specific, and firm specific (Campbell, 1996; Leonidou, 1995; Katsikeas and Morgan, 1994; Morgan, 1997). Shaw and Darroch (2004) summarized internationalization barriers according to the analyzes. First, in terms of financial and resource-based barriers, firms are generally challenged by the lack of resource availability, costs of operating abroad, and restricted access to capital and credit. In regard to managerial and functional barriers, firms usually have problems with managerial attitudes, lack of international experience and skills, lack of commitment, and partnership difficulties. Furthermore, market-based barriers include the liability of foreignness, environmental perception, government regulations such as tariffs and nontariff barriers, economic conditions, lack of market knowledge, cultural differences/psychic distance, access to distribution, and strong domestic market position. In addition to this, industry-specific barriers involve industrial competition and technological dilemmas, whereas firm-specific barriers comprise their newborn nature, limited resources, and size.

According to Xie and Suh (2014), barriers to internationalization can be generally categorized into internal and external barriers. Internal barriers are likely to be relevant to informational and functional deficiencies as well as marketing challenges, while external barriers usually refer to procedural, governmental, and environmental issues. Similarly, Leick (2011) distinguished internal barriers from external barriers by classifying internal barriers as limitations relevant to informational deficits and internal resources of firms, such as financial issues or a shortfall of experienced personnel for foreign ventures caused by size and organizational pressures. On the other hand, external barriers are macroeconomic factors such as the legal and administrative environment and problems associated with collaboration, including contradictory cooperative goals, specifications of contracts, and network risks. Tesfom and Lutz (2006) also proposed that external barriers to internationalization are divided into three main types: home-based market barriers, host-based market barriers, and industry-level barriers. Accordingly, these barriers are more evident among SMEs, especially those from developing countries. According to key findings from research conducted by the Organization for Economic Co-operation and Development (OECD) in 2009, SMEs tend to have limited resources and international contacts, and a lack of required managerial knowledge. They also face issues with factors within the external environment such as network and supply links, social ties, immigrant links, and so on. Another similar approach to classify the barriers to internationalization, especially in terms of export, is to divide them into two main categories, which are internal and external barriers, but with different classifications of barrier types under each category. Leonidou (2004) suggested that there are three kinds of barriers that fall into the internal barriers section, which are informational, functional, and marketing, while there are four types of barriers identified within the external barriers section, which are procedural, governmental, environmental, and task. Marketing barriers include issues revolving around product, price, distribution, logistics, and promotion, and environmental barriers can be further broken down into economic, political-legal, and sociocultural barriers.

Based on the aforementioned assumptions, this section will divide the problems and challenges of internationalization among Asia-Pacific firms, especially SMEs, into two main areas, which are internal and external barriers, with further subsections. However, to avoid overlap between subsections, the selected factors can be identified and studied distinctively from the others, and then recombined together under each major category. Therefore the barriers to internationalization that are particularly reviewed in this study are classified into internal and external barriers, with regrouped subsections, as illustrated in Fig. 10.1.

10.3.1 Internal Barriers to Internationalization

As presented in Fig. 10.1, internal barriers to internationalization consist of financial and resource-related barriers, managerial and functional barriers,

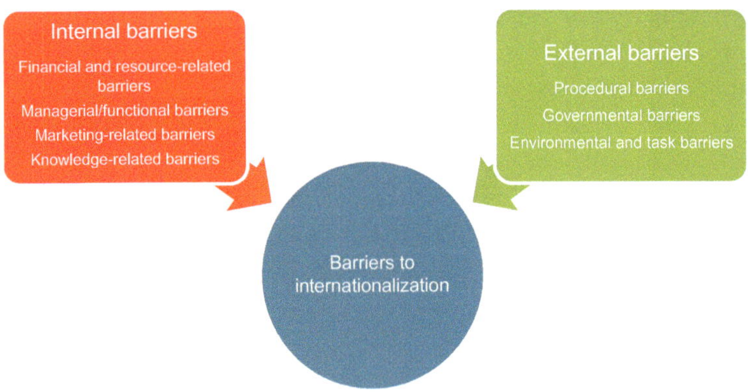

Fig. 10.1 Barriers to internationalization.

marketing-related barriers, knowledge-related barriers, and firm-specific barriers, as explained next in detail.

10.3.1.1 Financial and Resource-Related Barriers

It is clear that many MNEs have extensively highlighted financial and physical resource poverty as one of their core barriers to internationalization (Messina, 2015). Spyropoulou et al. (2011) argued that financial resources are competitively advantageous for firms in terms of export ventures such as brand advantage, marketing strategy adaptation, and better performance. According to Okpara (2010), internal financial and resource challenges indicate the requirements for firms to acquire capital and resources necessary for commencing export activity. In his study, the author suggested that the following factors are recognized as internal financial and resource barriers: difficulties in acquiring crucial funds for financing cross-border activities, problems with obtaining and using letters of credit for international transactions, lack of experienced and export-knowledgeable personnel to devote time to overseas operations, insufficient production capacity, and high costs of labor. These factors align with barriers mentioned in the research entitled "Top Barriers and Drivers to SME Internationalization," which was conducted by the OECD (2009). The study showed evidence supporting the notion that limitations in finance and relevant physical resources are the most dominant constraints to the internationalization of SMEs. The study ranked the shortage of working capital to finance exports and inadequate quantity of and/or untrained personnel for internationalization as the first and the seventh biggest challenges for firms' internationalization, respectively. These cause disadvantages to new venture projects or early-stage exporters due to unaffordable operations or inaccessible term loans. As reported in the same survey, the lack of capital requirements and limited resources and access to essential infrastructure are primary problems for Australian, Chinese, Indian, and Indonesian businesses. More importantly, when considering the impact of financial pressures on internationalization strategies specifically, firms tend to face cash-in-advance dilemmas that involve a lack of internal funding set-up costs that need to be paid before production and revenue distribution; hence firms may not be able to make decisions on setting up an overseas affiliate and exports timely or accurately (Arndt et al., 2012).

Apart from financial resources, other resources like physical production resources and personnel resources also play a huge role in firms' internationalization. Barney (1991) stated that physical production or "physical capital," including the design and development of manufacturing, are crucial for firms to find a strong base overseas. Likewise, human capital, especially catered with skills and experiences, is highly influential in MNEs' internationalization because it enables them to fulfill the customers' needs in a complex international business environment. One of the main challenges for firms in terms of international expansion is the limited number of managers or owners who have sufficient knowledge to cope with the diversity in business practices (Karagozoglu and Lindell, 1998). In addition to this, engagement in overseas expansion demands far-reaching expenditures in researching foreign markets, visiting customers abroad, and improving marketing strategies, which cause tremendous financial burdens for firms.

An example of financial barriers to internationalization in the Asia-Pacific region is the case of Haier. Haier is a Chinese company operating in overseas markets, particularly the US market; this means the firm has to confront not only diversities in culture, language, and tax laws, but also direct and indirect costs of doing business in the host countries. In Haier's case, its Camden plant in the United States was required to pay 10 times for local workers compared to normal Chinese wages. Nonetheless, the profits compensated for the costs. Employing local workers is unavoidable because firms need to accommodate themselves to local designs, manufacturing, distribution, and after-sales services. Despite the greater costs of labor, this plant helped Haier save on the significant transportation costs of huge refrigerators from its home country (Duysters et al., 2009). Another case study is a firm in the Indian pharmaceutical industry, found in the study conducted by Dixit and Yadav (2008). The interviewee from the firm, coded "PTR" in the survey, affirmed that having sufficient infrastructure facilities ready for its operations in the host market is crucial. It was unavoidable for the firm to spend money on upgrading its existing plant and allocating separate plants for exports. Likewise, Siawsurat and Önel (2011), who also studied internationalization stages of Thai SME exporters and their export barriers, found that a case firm's owner was required to spend an enormous amount of money to invest in machinery and product development for his business; thus he needed to get bank loans equivalent to 70% of the investment. Moreover, the process to request loans from the bank was highly complex and time-consuming, especially in terms of preparing documents. The owner also disclosed that although Thailand had a large supply of the main material (i.e., coconut) used in the company's production process, the company was still confronted with some periods of supply shortages. Also, because the company did not have enough coconut farms, the owner tried to surpass the problem by making contracts with farmers.

10.3.1.2 Managerial and Functional Barriers

As stated in the research conducted by the OECD (2009), managerial and functional factors play a huge role in firms' internationalization because they affect the level of focus, ambition, commitment, and effort to expand their businesses internationally. The study further suggested that complications emerging from managerial risk perceptions are the main psychological barriers, which are also reasons why firms decided not to engage in international trade. In other words, the lack of managerial knowledge and experience in overseas markets, along with the magnitude of managers' psychological opposition to internationalization, are the prominent challenges to the launch of exporting operations. Furthermore, Vozikis and Mescon (1985) defined functional barriers as inabilities in terms of operating firms' activities, such as problems in human resources management, production, and export financing.

Concerning management and function issues, there are two typical barriers that are highly emphasized: insufficient managerial time and low production capacity (Leonidou, 2004). First of all, there is limited managerial time to deal with cross-border operations in many cases. Management is very important in terms of choosing, accessing, and enlarging firms' international activities in foreign markets. It also affects the firms' export-marketing strategic plans and overseas customer service. This kind of situation is more noticeable among firms with managers or owners who correlate exporting with greater risks, lesser profits, and higher costs compared to the local business. Therefore firms are required to spend enough time, resources, and efforts to manage their internationalization. Second, the lack of adequate production capacity can obstruct the initiation and expansion of firms' internationalization. Many firms tend to perceive internationalization as a minor business operation that will be launched only if there are extra production resources.

To illustrate, in terms of international expansion, small business in Sri Lanka tended to lack inherent managerial capabilities as well as human resource development (HRD) interventions. This is partly because of the negligence of the HRD needs and lack of vision among the owners and managers (Hewapathirana, 2014). Another case study of managerial barriers in the Asia-Pacific region is the case of Daewoo Motor Company, a South Korean MNE in the automobile industry. According to the survey conducted by Oh et al. (1998), the ambitious drive for success to establish a chairperson was the main factor behind the expeditious development of the company. The CEO of the group emphasized the significance of managerial awareness and role models for the employees. When Daewoo's shipbuilding section was impacted by the financial crisis in the 1980s, he went to live in the shipyard to give operational instructions himself. The study also suggests that Daewoo's business was successful thanks to high risk-taking policies and unique approaches to problem-solving.

10.3.1.3 Marketing-Related Barriers

Marketing-related problems and challenges can be classified into two main areas: market entry and marketing mix barriers. Market entry barriers refer to incapability to recognize foreign business opportunities, generate new sales leads, gain foreign representation, acquire access to distribution routes, sustain control over intermediaries, and set up repeat business (Kaniya, 2013). In addition to market entry barriers, numerous studies include a marketing mix adaptation deficiency as a major barrier to internationalization. These particular barriers involve product modification to respond to different end users' needs, promotion approach selection, and pricing strategy assessment (Ibid). To a greater extent, Leonidou (2004) comprehensively sorted marketing barriers into different categories, including (1) product and price barriers and (2) distribution and logistics barriers.

There are multiple problems and challenges posed by the product and price issues for firms that would like to expand their business operations abroad. In terms of product issues, it is not easy to develop new products for overseas markets. That is why many firms hesitate to perform foreign operations, especially when there is a diversity of customer preferences in different countries. In contrast with bigger companies, it is more burdensome for small firms to develop innovative products for the foreign markets due to lack of managerial expertise, insufficient research and development capabilities, and scarce financial resources (Leonidou, 2004). To solve this problem, small firms may have to establish strategic alliances with other companies that are capable of launching new products to international markets. Firms are also required to adapt or modify their product design and style to dissimilar conditions of usage, disparities in purchasing power, different consumer tastes, and varied sociocultural settings in agreement to each foreign market. These can pose problems for the firms, such as increases in unit costs owing to the lack of economies of scale, fragile administration and authority over cross-border operations, and uncertainty in marketing support activities overseas (Terpstra and Sarathy, 2000). Similarly, in the matter of promotion, it is also difficult for firms to adjust their promotional activities because there are diversities in the target audience, inappropriate content of the advertising messages, deficiencies of advertising media, limitations in the frequency and/or duration of advertising, and inadequate approaches to evaluate advertising effectiveness abroad. Furthermore, product adaptations may be mandatory to meet quality standards and specifications as well as packaging and labeling requirements in each international market. This is a typical problem in some countries where the local consumers look for better quality than that offered in their domestic market. Foreign governments often implement special legislation aiming to protect the health and safety of their own population as well as safety during transportation, storage, and handling. Large geographic distances can also cause delays and escalate costs when providing technical and/or after-sale services in which firm personnel have to visit host countries regularly or establish service stations in the locations. Regarding price barriers, many SMEs face problems offering satisfactory prices to customers in foreign markets. Firms tend to face pricing issues due to additional costs aroused by product/service modifications and greater expenditures related to administration, operations, and transportation. It is also difficult to match competitors' prices in overseas markets because there are diversities in the cost structure of manufacturing, distribution, and logistics. Credit risks may also be brought in by customers who are from countries with a large psychic distance or unstable political-economic circumstances, or who have no past experience with the company.

As an illustration, in terms of product adaptation and new product development, Siawsurat and Önel (2011) showed in their study the internationalization stages of Thai SME exporters and the export barriers that exist in expanding their international operations successfully, where the case firms had to pass a number of product quality standard requirements posed by the host country authorities. For example, if the companies' major markets were in the European Union, they had to follow the commission regulations in order to get exporting permission. These regulations are usually complicated and the implementation process is time-consuming, for instance, REACH regulations for product safety, which require chemical registrations, assessments, and authorization. In the same study, the researchers mentioned that one of the case firms was confronted with product adaptation and new product development problems, especially when selling goods to the United States and Canada. To illustrate, Company A's target groups are Europe and Asia, where they already adjusted their plastic injection moldings for house design products to different electricity systems. However, the firm did not export its products to Canada and the United States because it was not worthwhile to struggle with additional product adaptations on another continent at that time.

Regarding quality and credibility, according to a survey on firms' internationalization barriers in India conducted by Dixit and Yadav (2008), a case firm coded "SLC" attempted to improve its image in terms of quality suppliers by inviting officials of regulatory authorities to visit the factory and organize technical discussions with experts. In the same study, most case firms were required to formulate standard operational procedures to administer quality assurance and control different activities, including input purchases and product delivery. Thus the firms had to organize training programs to enhance employees' comprehension of the procedures and instructions. Siawsurat and Önel (2011) also showed that new-entry firms tend to have credibility problems. For example, a case firm in their study hardly gained profits; as customers in new foreign markets usually order small quantities to test them first, it would not be profitable due to potential fixed costs like shipping and documentation.

Likewise, distribution and logistics are also considered major challenges to internationalization of businesses. Respecting distribution barriers, there are complicated foreign distribution channels not only between the host and home countries, but also between foreign markets. This is particularly the case for firms from emerging markets because there are smaller area sizes of retailing outlets and distribution channels, which usually comprise many complex layers across countries (Terpstra and Sarathy, 2000). In addition to complexity, accessibility to distribution channels hinders firms from successful internationalization. In other words, these distribution channels may already be occupied by competitors, too costly to manage, or controlled by certain distributors at various levels of the system (Czinkota and Ronkainen, 2001). It is also challenging for firms to obtain reliable representation, which would meet various requirements such as physical facilities, logistical capabilities, market reputation, relationships with government, and so on. Thus firms need to enter a foreign market early in order to get better credentials to acquire a profitable distribution deal. Due to geographic and cultural distance, firms tend to have less control over middlemen in international markets. Such a problem would be worsened by more dependence on the middlemen owing to obligatory legal agreements, difficulty in finding other middlemen for substitutions, and competition with the middlemen who also carry other product lines themselves. In terms of logistics, first, internationalization of firms may provoke problems with supplying inventory in foreign markets. Issues like transportation delays, uncertainty in demand, and unexpected events can pose numerous disadvantages to the firms, such as noncredible image of their goods in the overseas market, decrease in sales and profits from promising and existing clients, and excess costs for more rapid transportation channels to deliver products across borders. In this fashion, myriad firms argued that the more remote the foreign market, the more unlikely it is that firms will internationalize their business operations. Second, inadequate foreign warehousing facilities can block the flow of products to the host countries and negatively affect the delivery time and product quality (Cateora et al., 2009).

According to a case study of logistics barriers to internationalization faced by a Japanese firm in China conducted by Yu (2011), delayed delivery in procurement is a critical challenge for the case firm. The research results show that the delivery could be delayed because of the following factors: unstable weather and traffic conditions, different standards and understanding of logistics practices (between Japan and China, in this case), shortage of labor, and traffic regulations (particularly in the big cities). Moreover, while transporting products across borders, their quality can be deteriorated by insufficiency of transport vehicles and material storage, inadequacies in quality inspection systems and management systems, poor condition of containers, and instability of ocean freight. This also causes a rise in logistics cost, which further led to higher product costs. Another example is the case of Thamel.com, a Nepal-based e-commerce company (Kshetri, 2007). The CEO of the firm stated that there was a delivery barrier when the firm launched its services, as there were no street addresses in Kathmandu, India. It was difficult for delivery officers to find customers' residences, and in order to overcome this challenge, the company had to contact the municipality of the city to request access to their geographic information system to create delivery zones, which took a lot of time and money.

10.3.1.4 Informational and Knowledge-Related Barriers

Another key challenge to firms' internationalization is insufficient knowledge about foreign markets, together with complications in data collection (Messina, 2015). Morgan and Katsikeas (1997) defined informational barriers in terms of international expansion as "complications in identifying, choosing, and communicating with foreign markets owing to information deficiencies." According to Kaniya (2013), informational and knowledge-related barriers embrace problems and challenges inherent in cross-border value chain activities. A number of studies also suggested the following barriers as the most frequently cited knowledge-related barriers to firms' internationalization: knowledge about export procedures, export documentation, overseas business practices, and funds transfers and accumulation.

Based on the process of internationalization theory, which is a traditional view, knowledge-related barriers can be overcome along the learning process occurring during firms' international expansion. Nonetheless, according to the resource-based view theory, these barriers can be surpassed even before the internationalization process begins, as a few managers or owners may seize adequate knowledge before the international orientation or global attitudes initiates (Zheng et al., 2012). Moreover, Barney et al. (2001) argued that firms' experience is an inarticulate knowledge that is hard for competitors to resemble. Johanson and Vahlne (1977) also advocated that MNEs with more international experience tend to flourish organizational capabilities in overseas markets more effectively. In contrast with technological knowledge, experiential knowledge is more likely to be observable, accountable, and imitable; hence it is a strategic resource that differentiates firms in the competitive global economy (Kaniya, 2013).

In the same manner, Xie and Suh suggested (2014) that a lack of information is considered a major challenge to exporting operations, especially for SMEs whose liabilities of immaturity and scantiness are obstacles. According to the OECD (2009), insufficient knowledge of foreign markets is ranked as a top challenge to firms' internationalization. This includes limited informational and experiential knowledge to identify foreign business opportunities, choose international markets, find international market data, enter the export market, and contact customers abroad (Lakew and Chiloane-Tsoka, 2015). Crick (2007) also pointed out that it is difficult to locate or obtain adequate representation in target export markets, while Barnes et al. (2006) and Kneller and Pisu (2007) suggested that many SMEs have been obstructed by incapability to find suitable overseas market partners. Apart from the aforementioned issues, knowledge-related barriers also involve lack of understanding of foreign culture and business practices as well as lack of knowledge on the availability of export support channels (Lakew and Chiloane-Tsoka, 2015). Additionally, Suarez-Ortega (2003) labeled the following as knowledge-related hindrances to firms' international expansion: lack of awareness of export assistance and unconsciousness of economic and noneconomic benefits of export markets (as cited by Okpara, 2010).

Correspondingly, Leonidou (2004) studied and summarized the four major barriers to internationalization included in this category in detail as follows. First, inability to locate/analyze foreign markets increases the level of uncertainty embedded in the complex business environment. It is normal that SMEs tend to have limited sources of information both in domestic and international markets, and even though they are aware of and can access information, they may face difficulties with data retrieval. Second, the inability to find international market data is a factor leading to the first barrier. In many cases, firms may confront restricted research methods, low-quality data, and a lack of comparability of the gained information due to struggles in obtaining access to data sources, acquiring timely delivery of information, and dealing with high prices of certain data. Third, firms may face problems in effectively recognizing market opportunities that can increase their willingness to commence and expand internationalization. Without spontaneous orders from offshore customers or advisory assistance by external agents like governmental agencies and chambers of commerce, firms would hesitate to go global. Last, the inability to contact overseas customers refers to three troublesome situations: weak communication between sellers and buyers in overseas markets due to the huge geographic distance, halfhearted willingness to conduct systematic research in foreign markets, and limited potential customer bases.

To illustrate, the case study of Haier, which is one of the leading Chinese enterprises, showed that in order to expand its international activities, the company itself remained immensely dependent on foreign partners due to lack of technological knowledge; this also demonstrates the fact that the company was not ready to enter more sophisticated segments that require more technological advancement compared with more settled Asian MNEs like Samsung (Duysters et al., 2009). In another case study written by Dixit and Yadav (2008), case firms with Indian origin experienced different informational and knowledge-related barriers to their internationalization. For example, a firm coded "PTR" had to hire international consultants in order to enter Latin American markets, and a firm coded "LSA" also hired staff members with experience in international markets. In the same manner, Mai and Li (2008) suggested that Vietnamese firms tended to face serious shortages of essential information about goods, markets, and technologies as the newest and exclusive information sources were scarce in Vietnam, and managers' capability to seek information, especially IT capacity, was limited by many other constraints, such as government censorship policies, publishing and media controls, high costs of Internet connection, and so on. The qualitative study of Thai exporters conducted by Siawsurat and Önel (2011) also illustrated the inability to contact foreign customers of New Arriva CO., Ltd, which was established in 2005. According to the survey, the company could not get customers from the United States and Canada due to an inability to source distributors in the markets.

10.3.2 External Barriers to Internationalization

As shown in Fig. 10.1, this section classifies the external barriers to internationalization into procedural barriers, governmental barriers, and environmental and task barriers, as comprehensively demonstrated next.

10.3.2.1 Procedural Barriers

According to Leonidou (2004), procedural barriers to internationalization include incapacity with techniques and procedures, communication deficiencies, and sluggish accumulation of payments. First of all, a number of SMEs find exporting procedures and documentation (such as for customers and shipping) too complicated to manage. These problems usually arise from excessive costs, time losses, and bureaucratic practices. Even though firms can ask for assistance from consultative companies, governmental agencies, and financial institutions, it is not easy for them to operate their activities at reasonable prices at all times. Second, insufficient and infrequent communication with foreign customers due to large geographic and psychological distance between firms and customers in international markets as well as poor communication infrastructure can create serious dilemmas. It can result in misinterpretations emerging from information shared with customers across borders, weak control over foreign operations, delays in strategic decision-making, and defective feedback from business developments in host markets. Finally, slow collection of payments from host countries may result from the aforementioned problems combined with the possibility of credit facilities in which more guarantees are needed before entering a foreign market.

To elaborate, for the first two barriers in this category, countless MNEs are disturbed by insufficient cross-boundary relationships. They often lack representation or capable foreign market partners in their foreign activities as well as appropriate distribution channels to help them achieve their goals and serve their clients (OECD, 2009). These problems could be referred to as *network constraints*, based on the network theory. In spite of numerous advantages of networks for international expansion, network-type relationships can also pose risks on firms' competitiveness caused by cross-border relations. Apart from experience accumulation in foreign markets, the keys to effective networking that can augment the firms' competency are mutual relationship commitment and trust building between network members. First, network risks usually derive from the fact that each stakeholder may seek individual benefits at the cost of their partner companies. Regarding cross-cultural ties, opportunities are associated with uncertainty embedded in overseas markets and partnerships (Leick, 2011). Similarly, competence asymmetries within the network usually result in dependence on bigger or more technologically advanced partners, which would lead to risky situations as one of them may attempt to get more valuable beneficial partners outside the current network. This happens frequently with bonds constructed toward personal contacts. Second, concerning "East-West" networks, sociocultural dissimilarities between collaborative partners can be considered potential risks as well because they can diminish competitive advantages obtained through cooperative connections.

According to Coe et al. (2013a), different forms of global production networks between firms also have their own distinct disadvantages. First, fully owned subsidiaries require heavy capital investment and pose potential conflicts with host governments and local firms. This kind of networking relationship usually affects more cross-border managerial and organizational issues. Second, international subcontracting can disrupt supply chains and create other problems such as leakage of proprietary technology and intellectual property rights (IPRs), and lack of direct managerial control of production. Third, strategic alliances and joint ventures can lead to lack of control technology and IPRs, similar to international subcontracting. This type of network often generates problems in managing partners. Fourth, franchising and cooperative agreements can also infringe on IPRs and put more costs to firms in the areas of franchisee monitoring and ties management. In addition, another kind of network that can be both beneficial and harmful to MNEs in terms of internationalization is an ethnic network (Coe et al., 2013b). Even though ethnic enterprises can provide countless market opportunities, resources, and other initiatives, there are also a considerable number of negative impacts or costs for firms to watch over. In terms of entrepreneurship, ethnic networks can lead to discrimination and blocked mobility. Furthermore, due to their unique organizational structure, firms relying on ethnic networks often face excessive internal competition, high dependence, and commodification of ethnicity. Above all, with these network relationships, firms are limited by a closed ethnic market. To explain the root of these problems, it is necessary to study the concept of ethnicity and its economic importance.

To illustrate, Mazzarol (2003) argued that, in his study, case firms that were small high-technology companies in the Western Australian ICT sector affirmed that they were facing constraints to the development of joint initiatives and alliances due to lack of control of a business advantage, set-up costs, problems with suitable partner identification, lack of skills and partnership management, and difficulties in regulating overseas alliances. Conforming to the literature review section in his research, these resulted from the failed attempt to appropriately manage resources of other network partners as well as the unsuccessful attempt to interfere in the operations of their suppliers and/or distributors, including lack of trust or poor communication between network members. Lastly, the researcher also added that if the network members become exceedingly specialized and limited in terms of focus and product diversification, they would lose their ability to innovate and lose competitiveness in the long run. Another case study of Thai SMEs in East Asian networks written by Punyasavatsut (2010) showed another challenge embedded in establishing networks for internationalization. It found that, in order to engage in the networks, the sample firms had to meet various requirements and maintain their performance. More specifically, the study also concluded that Thai SMEs were confronting some difficulties in meeting the requirements demanded by larger firms in the networks and had problems matching competitors' prices. Another example of procedural barriers is the negative effects of "guanxi," or the Chinese network system based on personal relationships and trust embedded in all levels of Chinese business operations. The case study of internationalization among hotels (Zhang, 2005) shows that even though this system could help network members share scarce resources and cope with uncertainties, it could lead to management inefficiency due to difficulties resulting from extreme concentration of minority ethnic groups, particularly from language and cultural differences as well as a junior-senior hierarchical system that constrains the management style.

10.3.2.2 Governmental Barriers

Leonidou (1995) stated that lack of home government support and/or incentives as well as hostile export regulations are serious barriers to internationalization. Based on the study conducted by Leonidou (2004), governmental barriers are activities and inactivity enacted by home governments regarding domestic exporters. There are two main challenges falling under this category, which are the lack of interest and willingness to assist by the government, especially in terms of incentives provision and the limited role of the regulatory framework on foreign activity expansion management practices. Concerning the shortage of home government assistance or incentives for internationalization, many firms suffered from a lack of major promoters of foreign operations such as guaranteeing loans, export price subsidies, trade fairs and missions, interstate trade agreements, and market data publications. Moreover, there are also cases of firms not being aware of how to take advantage of them. In the same way, unfavorable home government rules and regulations are huge burdens for firms because they can lead to profit losses. For instance, restrictions on goods with national security or foreign policy significance are often noticeable, and firms are obliged to comply with these rules and regulations in order to sustain their favorable image in the home market. The prompt assistance of government agencies in other export ventures should be implemented to cope with this situation. Moreover, misguided regulations owing to political goals that would overwhelm economic efficiency may reduce the business opportunities of MNEs, and ineffective judicial systems may also lead to unreliable and unpredictable expansion of overseas operations (Cardoza and Fornes, 2013).

An example of governmental barriers faced by MNEs in the Asia-Pacific region is the case study of Vietnamese SMEs conducted by Mai and Li (2008). In Vietnam, due to the fact that criminal and civil laws were not disembodied and were often ambiguous, there were a variety of conflicts and inconsistencies found in the country's business laws and policies; thus, sustaining harmonization with mandatory regulations required long periods of time and diligence. Furthermore, because the written statements from the central government were barely specified or clearly explained, the appointed authorities were responsible for interpreting the laws themselves; this often led to corruption and time-consuming processes for doing business. Additionally, tax and customs regulations were usually designed to control rather than facilitate firms' development. In brief, the executives from the sample firms concluded that the regulations implemented by the government negatively impacted their international expansion due to the lack of access, vague formulation, various interpretations, frequent changes, and poor communication. Another example is the case of Chinese companies stated in the study conducted by Liu and Li (2002). It found that even though the Chinese government had encouraged the internationalization of Chinese firms, it had not yet implemented a facilitating policy framework for overseas business activities. According to the survey, Chinese firms tended to pursue international expansion on an experimental basis before the government adopted an approach to regulate their international initiatives, for example, giving special permission to certain MNEs in which they could invest across borders without being limited by existing policies like foreign exchange controls.

10.3.2.3 Environmental and Task Barriers

According to Tesfom and Lutz (2006), the most commonly cited environmental barriers consist of deficiency of tax incentives, extravagant union power, incoherent government policy, and inflation. Environmental barriers involve the widest range of barriers related to the economic, political-legal, and sociocultural environment of the overseas markets where the firms operate or plan to operate. These constraints are contingent on speedy changes that are highly challenging to prospect and regulate, and are often host country based. Host-based environmental barriers refer to host country characteristics like poor market infrastructure and high tariffs that lead to considerable barriers to firms' foreign market entry (Messina, 2015). There are two main kinds of host-based market barriers: disadvantageous operating conditions and offshore restrictions and regulations. Unfavorable conditions in this case comprise divergent momentum of business in host countries, unfriendly economic climate across borders, red tape and bureaucracy, political vulnerability, corruption, and threat of embezzlement and nationalization. On the other hand, overseas restrictions and regulations include general restrictions and standards, tariff and nontariff barriers, import permits and licenses, and other extra compliance-related documentation (Tesfom and Lutz, 2006). Recent phenomena negatively affecting firms' internationalization are antiglobalization movements, particularly standing in opposition to trade liberalization and the deregulation of financial markets, which are the main incentives for firms to maximize their benefits at the expense of work conditions, environmental sustainability, and national dependence and sovereignty. These organized movements have expressed concerns over unlimited expansion of MNEs' cross-border activities; therefore it is unavoidable for the multinationals to prevent themselves from being targeted by social movements (Coe et al., 2013a). Grochal-Brejdak and Szymura-Tyc (2013) also added low degree of openness to information technologies and censorship policies to the list. It can be implied from these problems and challenges that firms are required to thoroughly review international environments and protectionist policies in host countries before expanding their foreign operations.

Furthermore, the most crucial barriers in this category emerging from an economic and regulatory nature are summarized by Leonidou (2004). First, poor or deteriorating economic conditions across boundaries can demotivate the firms from internationalization because they can diminish local purchasing power and affect consumer behaviors unfavorably. For example, consumers may be confronted with serious foreign debts, high inflation rates, and high levels of unemployment due to the aforementioned uncertainties. Foreign currency exchange risks can also erode international business transactions; these can be divided into three kinds of risks: unstable exchange rates, revaluation of host and home countries' currency, and unconvertible foreign currencies (Czinkota and Ronkainen, 2001). Furthermore, political instability in foreign markets caused by different economic, social, and political factors such as large overseas debt, inflationary trends, religious fundamentalism, corruption, authoritarian regime, military control, and so on can threaten the firms' international activities in many ways, like property confiscation, activity closing or suspension, and repatriation of earnings prohibition. Strict foreign country rules and regulations can also restrict or delay the flow of goods in the market, limit the firms' profitability through price controls, and increase the export price due to special tax rates, whereas high tariff and nontariff barriers also pose a severe problem for firms aiming to expand their foreign operations. In many cases, tariffs may be not considered a crucial problem for developed countries, but tariff rates in developing countries are typically higher. On the other hand, trade restrictions that pose more challenges on international firms and that should be studied more comprehensively are nontariff barriers. Examples of dominant nontariff barriers are local content policy, certification and standards, product requirements, and so on (Alavi, 2007). Furthermore, sociocultural differences comprise not only language barriers, differences in attitudes and values, and habits and traditions, but also corporate culture, and managerial and leadership style (Meyer and Gelbuda, 2006). These can seriously affect consumer behavior, targeting approaches, and marketing programs in foreign markets. This would be even more complex in countries where many subcultures or different cultural contexts are observable (Cateora et al., 2009). To cope with these problems, managers may need to have an international outlook, participate in cross-cultural trainings and workshops, and visit the foreign markets on a regular basis.

For example, according to Isa et al. (2015), Malaysian construction companies were tremendously impacted by environmental barriers, including political, financial, cultural, and legal risks extended by the host countries. The study suggested that Malaysian contractors must acknowledge political instability, unfavorable tax policies and employment laws, and industrial safety regulations, among others, as major constraints that could affect their international performance. In the case of Malaysian construction firms, there were high risks owing to market conditions such as currency fluctuation, cultural differences, and other challenges concerning host countries' rules and regulations. Another case study conducted in Vietnam also showed the threats posed by tariff and nontariff barriers from the Vietnamese government on nonstate-owned enterprises. These problems prevented the companies from actively performing in international trade. In the research, examples of such nontariff barriers faced by Vietnamese MNEs include requirements for export and import licenses, minimum working capital, and local content in the host countries. An environmental barrier like political instability is also presented in the case study of a Thai firm called Precious Memory established in 1995 (Siawsurat and Önel, 2011). According to the survey, the company owner affirmed that political instability in his country frequently led to delays of the products and decreased the number of foreign customers at trade fairs. The same company also experienced language barriers because its employees could not explain the specifications of the goods due to a lack of knowledge of specialized vocabulary used in the jewelry industry. Another case firm used in the same study is Vanda Siam, a Thai producer and exporter of candles. The CEO of Vanda Siam declared that, throughout the past 2 years, political instability had become a major barrier for SME exporters. She stated that fewer customers and importers came to trade fairs and fewer foreigners came to Thailand; that affected about 90% of the sales in duty-free at Bangkok international airports.

Task barriers refer to problems and challenges stemming from the competitive pressures in international markets. First, different foreign customer habits and attitudes vary by geographic and climate conditions, level of consumption, level of technical knowledge, income level and income allocation, educational standards, manners and customs, and the like (Cateora et al., 2009). These factors bring about divergent product preferences and utilization patterns, levels of price acceptance, distribution systems, and communication means. Adapting the firm's strategy to these variations is contracted with greater costs and delays in operating foreign activities. Second, even though firms may possess a competitive advantage in the local market, they may simultaneously lose such an advantage and encounter more complex and challenging competitive situations once they surpass national borders. The reasons behind this phenomenon are competition from many sources (such as domestic, host country, and international markets), operations on a different base, and diverse marketing strategies from country to country (Doole and Lowe, 2001). An example of task barriers in the Asia-Pacific region can be found in the work of Deng (2012), which showed that industry competition is highly evident among Chinese MNEs. According to the study, domestic competition in China could negatively impact Chinese firms by cutthroat price wars and pressures from competitors who tirelessly and sharply investigate each other's internationalization patterns.

10.4 CONCLUSION

In conclusion, it is significant to recognize these barriers to internationalization because they affect firms' attitudes and behaviors in foreign markets remarkably. Specifically speaking, these barriers could waste the resources of firms and threaten the efficiency and effectiveness of their performance. This chapter demonstrates a set of notable internal and external barriers to internationalization faced by firms in the Asia-Pacific region, such as financial and resource-related barriers, managerial/functional barriers, marketing-related barriers, knowledge-related barriers, procedural barriers, governmental barriers, and environmental and task barriers. The reviewed literature shows that today, international expansion of MNEs, including SMEs, is exposed to the aforementioned problems and challenges due to changing market conditions and business environments. Hence firms' operations must be based on a good understanding of the external factors as well as internal factors that affect firms' preparedness to go abroad, in order to sustain and improve their effectiveness and competitiveness in international markets.

REFERENCES

Abdelzaher, D.M., 2012. The impact of professional service firms' expansion challenges on internationalization processes and performance. Serv. Ind. J. 32 (10), 1–18.

Alavi, R., 2007. An Overview of Key Markets, Tariffs and Non-tariff Measures on Asian Exports of Select Environmental Goods. ICTSD Programme on Trade and Environment Issue Paper No.4. Available at http://www.ictsd.org/downloads/2008/04/rokiah%2520alavi_maese.pdf.

Arndt, C., Buch, C.M., Mattes, A., 2012. Disentangling barriers to internationalization. Can. J. Econ. 45 (1), 41–63.

Barnes, B.L., Chakrabarti, R., Palihawadana, D., 2006. Investigating the export marketing activity of SMEs operating in international healthcare markets. J. Med. Mark. 6 (3), 209–221.

Barney, J.B., 1986. Strategic factor markets: expectations, luck, and business strategy. Manag. Sci. 32 (10), 1231–1241.

Barney, J.B., 1991. Firm resources and sustained competitive advantage. J. Manag. 17, 99–120.

Barney, J.B., Wright, M., Ketchen, D.J., 2001. The resource-based view of the firm: ten years after 1991. J. Manag. 27, 625–641.

Barreto, I., 2010. Dynamic capabilities: a review of past research and an agenda for the future. J. Manag. 36, 256–280.

Campbell, A.J., 1996. The effects of internal firm barriers on the export behaviour of small firms in a free trade environment. J. Small Bus. Manag. 34 (3), 50–59.
Cardoza, G., Fornes, G., 2013. The International Expansion of China's Small and Medium-sized Enterprises: A Review. School of Sociology, Politics and International Studies University of Bristol Working Paper No. 05-12. Available at http://www.bristol.ac.uk/media-library/sites/spais/migrated/documents/cardoza-fornes-05-12.pdf.
Cateora, P.R., Gilly, M.C., Graham, J.L., 2009. International Marketing. McGraw-Hill Irwin, Boston.
Coe, N.M., Kelly, P.F., Yeung, H.W.C., 2013a. The Transnational Corporation: How Does the Global Firm Keep It All Together? In: Coe, N.M. et al., (Ed.), Economic Geography: A Contemporary Introduction. Wiley, New York, NY, pp. 294–329.
Coe, N.M., Kelly, P.F., Yeung, H.W.C., 2013b. Ethnic Economies: Do Culture have Economies? In: Coe, N.M. et al., (Ed.), Economic Geography: A Contemporary Introduction. Wiley, New York, NY, pp. 432–462.
Crick, D., 2007. SMEs' barriers towards internationalization and assistance requirements in the UK: differences between exporters and firms employing multiple modes of market entry. J. Small Bus. Entrep. 20 (3), 233–244.
Czinkota, M.R., Ronkainen, I.A., 2001. International Marketing, sixth ed. Fort Worth Harcourt College Publishers, Texas.
Deng, P., 2012. The internationalization of Chinese firms: a critical review and future research. Int. J. Manag. Rev. 14, 408–427.
Dewan, J., Singh, A.K., 2015. Internationalization of the KARAM group of companies: experiences, imperatives and challenges. South Asian J. Manag. 22 (2), 167–190.
Dixit, M.R., Yadav, S., 2008. Motivations, Capability Handicaps and Firm Responses in the Early Phase of Internationalization from Emerging Economies: A study in the Indian Pharmaceutical Industry, No WP2008-02-05, IIMA Working Papers. Indian Institute of Management Ahmedabad, Research and Publication Department, Ahemedabad, India, pp. 1–35.
Doole, I., Lowe, R., 2001. International Marketing Strategy. Thomson Learning, London.
Duysters, G., Jacob, J., Lemmens, C., Yu, J., 2009. Internationalization and technological catching up of emerging multinationals: a comparative case study of China's haier group. Ind. Corp. Chang. 18 (2), 325–349.
Dyer, J.H., Hatch, N.W., 2006. Relation-specific capabilities and barriers to knowledge transfers: creating advantage through network relationships. Strateg. Manag. J. 27, 701–719.
Flint, D.J., 2004. Strategic marketing in global supply chains: four challenges. Ind. Mark. Manag. 33, 45–50.
Golgeci, I., Arslan, A., 2014. Internationalization of emerging economy firms to developed economies: a discussion on institutional pressures and marketing and supply chain capabilities. J. Strateg. Mark. 22 (7), 587–602.
Grant, R.M., 1996. Prospering in dynamically—competitive environments: organizational capacity as knowledge integration. Organ. Sci. 7, 375–387.
Grochal-Brejdak, M., Szymura-Tyc, M., 2013. Internationalization process of e-commerce enterprises—prerequisites, barriers and basic modes. J. Econ. Manag. 13, 40–55.
Hewapathirana, G.I., 2014. Bridging, bonding and linking global entrepreneurs: the case of Sri Lanka. Hum. Resour. Dev. Int. 17 (2), 164–182.
Hitt, M.A., Ireland, R.D., Camp, S.M., Sexton, L.D., 2001. Guest editors' introduction to the special issue strategic entrepreneurship: entrepreneurial strategies for wealth creation. Strateg. Manag. J. 22 (6), 479–491.
Holmlund, M., Kock, S., 1998. Relationships and the internationalization of the finnish small and medium sized companies. Int. Small Bus. J. 16 (4), 46–64.

Isa, C.M.M., Saman, H.M., Preece, C.H., 2015. Determining significant factors influencing Malaysian construction business performance in international markets. J. Constr. Dev. Ctries. 20 (2), 1–23.
Johanson, J., Vahlne, J., 1977. The internationalization process of the firm: a model of knowledge development on increasing foreign commitments. J. Int. Bus. Stud. 8 (1), 23–32.
Johanson, J., Vahlne, J.E., 1990. The mechanism of internationalization. Int. Mark. Rev. 7 (4), 11–24.
Kaniya, E.T., 2013. Export barriers and path to internationalization: a comparison of conventional enterprises and international new ventures. J. Int. Entrep. 11, 3–29.
Karagozoglu, N., Lindell, M., 1998. Internationalization of small and medium-sized technology-based firms: an exploratory study. J. Small Bus. Manag. 36 (1), 44–59.
Katsikeas, C.S., Morgan, R.E., 1994. Differences in perception of exporting problems based on firm size and export market experience. Eur. J. Mark. 28 (5), 17–39.
Kneller, R., Pisu, M., 2007. Export Barriers: What are They and Who Do They Matter To? University of Nottingham Working Paper No. 2007/12. Available at http://ssrn.com/abstract=968428.
Korsakiene, R., 2014. Internationalization of Lithuanian SMEs: investigation of barriers and motives. Econ. Bus. 26, 54–60.
Kshetri, N., 2007. Barriers to e-commerce and competitive business models in developing countries: a case study. Electron. Commer. Res. Appl. 6, 443–452.
Lakew, Y.D., Chiloane-Tsoka, G.C., 2015. Internationalisation barriers of small and medium-sized manufacturing enterprises in Ethiopia: leather and leather products industry in focus. Int. J. Bus. Econ. Dev. 3 (3), 68–80.
Leick, B., 2011. Barriers to co-operation and competitive advantage: cross-border business networks of Saxon and Northern Bohemian firms. J. East Eur. Manag. Stud. 16 (2), 162–184.
Leonidou, L.C., 1995. Empirical research on export barriers: review, assessment and synthesis. J. Int. Mark. 3 (1), 29–43.
Leonidou, L.C., 2004. An analysis of the barriers hindering small business export development. J. Small Bus. Manag. 42 (3), 279–302.
Liu, H., Li, K., 2002. Strategic implications of emerging Chinese multinationals: the haier case study. Eur. Manag. J. 20 (6), 699–706.
Lu, Y., Zhou, L., Bruton, G., Li, W., 2009. Capabilities as a mediator linking resources and the international performance of entrepreneurial firms in an emerging economy. J. Int. Bus. Stud. 41, 419–436.
Mai, T.T.T., Li, C.C., 2008. Born-global: the case of four Vietnamese SMEs. J. Int. Entrep. 6, 72–100.
Mazzarol, T., 2003. Strategic Networking among Small High Technology Firms: Evidence from the Western Australian ICT Sector. In: Paper presented at the ANZAM Conference 2003, 2-5 December, Fremantle WA. Available at http://www.cemi.com.au/sites/all/publications/ANZMAZZAT.pdf.
McAdam, R., Reid, R., 2001. SME and large organization perceptions of knowledge management: comparisons and contrasts. J. Knowl. Manag. 5 (3), 231–241.
Messina, L., 2015. Drivers and barriers to SME foreign expansion. InterTradeIreland 9 (28) (online). Available at http://www.intertradeireland.com/media/AIIPResearchBriefing28.pdf.
Meyer, K.E., Gelbuda, M., 2006. Process perspectives in international business research. Manag. Int. Rev. 46 (2), 142–164.
Morash, E.A., Lynch, D.F., 2002. Public policy and global supply chain capabilities and performance: a resource-based view. J. Int. Mark. 10, 25–51.
Morgan, R.E., 1997. Export stimuli and export barriers: evidence from empirical research studies. Eur. Bus. Rev. 97 (2), 68–79.

Morgan, R.E., Katsikeas, C.S., 1997. Theories of international trade, foreign direct investment and firm internationalization: a critique. Manage. Decis. 35 (1), 68–78.
Oh, N., Choi, C.J., Choi, E., 1998. The globalization strategy of Daewoo Motor company. Asia Pac. J. Manag. 15, 185–203.
Okpara, J.O., 2010. Strategic export orientation and internationalization barriers: evidence from SMEs in a developing economy. J. Int. Bus. Cult. Stud. 4, 1–10. Available at http://www.aabri.com/manuscripts/08114.pdf.
Organisation for Economic Co-operation and Development, 2009. Top Barriers and Drivers to SME Internationalisation. Report by the OECD Working Party on SMEs and Entrepreneurship. Available at https://www.oecd.org/cfe/smes/43357832.pdf.
Punyasavatsut, C., 2010. Integrating SMEs into East Asia Production Networks: Thailand. In: Vo, T.T., Narjoko, D., Oum, S. (Eds.), Integrating Small and Medium Enterprises (SMEs) into the More Integrate East Asia. ERIA, Jakarta, pp. 262–297. ERIA Research Project Report 2009-8.
Rajendran, R., 2015. Influence of information systems strategic orientation on SMEs' perception of export barriers. South Asian J. Manag. 22 (2), 120–143.
Ratajczak-Mrozek, M., 2014. Companies' simultaneous embeddedness in local, international and global networks—a conceptualization from the perspective of local enterprises and their degree of internationalization. Poznan Univ. Econ. Rev. 14 (1), 31–47.
Reuber, A.R., Fischer, E., 1997. The influence of the management team's international experience on the internationalization behaviors of SMEs. J. Int. Bus. Stud. 28 (4), 807–825.
Rogers, E.M., 1962. Diffusion of Innovations. Free Press of Glencoe, New York.
Shaw, V., Darroch, J., 2004. Barriers to internationalisation: a study of entrepreneurial new ventures in New Zealand. J. Int. Entrep. 2 (4), 327–343.
Siawsurat, D., Önel, Y.C., 2011. Internationalization Stages of SMEs Through Exporting: A Qualitative Study of Internationalization Stages of Thai SME Exporters and Their Export Barriers. Unpublished Master's Thesis, Umeå School of Business, Umeå.
Spyropoulou, S., Skarmeas, D., Katsikeas, C.S., 2011. An examination of branding advantage in export ventures. Eur. J. Mark. 45 (6), 910–935.
Suarez-Ortega, S., 2003. Export barriers: insights from small and medium-sized firms. Int. Small Bus. J. 21 (4), 403–419.
Szabo, A., 2002. Internationalization of SMEs, UNECE. (website). Available at http://www.unece.org/indust/sme/internat.htm.
Tellis, G.J., Crawford, C.M., 1981. An evolutionary approach to product growth theory. J. Mark. 45, 125–132.
Terpstra, V., Sarathy, R., 2000. International Marketing. Dryden Press, Fortworth.
Tesfom, G., Lutz, C., 2006. A classification of export marketing problems of small and medium sized manufacturing firms in developing countries. Int. J. Emerg. Mark. 1 (3), 262–281.
Vasilchenko, E., Morrish, S., 2011. The role of entrepreneurial networks in the exploration and exploitation of internationalization opportunities by information and communication technology firms. J. Int. Mark. 19 (4), 88–105.
Vozikis, G.S., Mescon, T.S., 1985. Small exporters and stages of development: an empirical study. Am. J. Small Bus. 49–64.
Winch, G., 2014. Strategic business and network positioning for internationalization. Serv. Ind. J. 34 (8), 715–728.
Xie, Y.H., Suh, T., 2014. Perceived resource deficiency and internationalization of small- and medium-sized firms. J. Int. Entrep. 12 (3), 207–229.
Yiu, D.W., Lau, C.M., Bruton, G.D., 2007. International venturing by emerging economy firms: the effects of firm capabilities, home country networks, and corporate entrepreneurship. J. Int. Bus. Stud. 38, 519–540.

Yu, L., 2011. Logistics Barriers to International Operations: A Case Study of Japanese Firm in China. In: International Conference on Economics and Finance Research, Vol. 4, pp. 374–378.
Zhang, Z., 2005. Impacts of globalisation on hotel companies' internal operation environment. Can. Soc. Sci. 1 (3), 68–71.
Zheng, C., Khavul, S., Crockett, C., 2012. Does it transfer? the effects of pre internationalization experience on post-entry organizational learning in entrepreneurial Chinese firms. J. Int. Entrep. 10 (3), 232–254.

CHAPTER 11

Concluding Remarks

N. Thirawat
Mahidol University International College, Nakhon Pathom, Thailand

Businesses can benefit greatly from free trade of goods, services, investments, and skilled labor through government arrangements. In the Association of Southeast Asian Nations (ASEAN) region, businesses are faced with relatively few limitations in accessing regional markets. ASEAN has also become a desirable destination for investment, particularly from large multinational companies. For this reason, companies in ASEAN may seek business opportunities upon commencement of the ASEAN Economic Community (AEC) and use this to their highest benefit. The ASEAN business industry will promote competitiveness and drive the regional economy as it continues to keep this mindset.

In general, economic productivity within the AEC can grow exponentially, and both strengths and weaknesses of member nations must be considered. Examples include Cambodia, Lao People's Democratic Republic, Myanmar, and Vietnam (CLMV), which are rich in natural resources and have an abundance of semiskilled and unskilled workers available at low wage rates, which is beneficial to multinational companies in establishing production bases. On the other hand, Thailand is a good representative as a host country in providing effective connectivity with its strategic geographical location, which will allow it to become an ASEAN logistics center. Thailand's logistics and tourism sector will grow, particularly in physical infrastructure on road, air, and sea. Singapore, known for being the world's financial center, is the biggest target for foreign direct investment (FDI). For this reason, businesses must adjust to the changing business environment to survive. ASEAN members can complement each other by supporting each other's strengths and weaknesses, rather than engaging in more intense competition.

Though the business world is filled with convenient infrastructure and facilities, a smooth future for ASEAN cannot be guaranteed. Labor-intensive production companies are trending toward relocating manufacturing bases to CLMV or along the border where wages are much lower; otherwise, they are faced with fierce competition as other countries

Internationalization and Managing Networks in the Asia Pacific
http://dx.doi.org/10.1016/B978-0-08-100813-3.00011-0

adjust to changing surroundings. To cope with the pressure of competition, businesses may opt to modernize production and invest in research and development (R&D) more, requiring enormous investments; for this reason, this option is not suited to all companies. R&D investments can help create innovative products and further illustrate advancement beyond a labor-intensive industry. A good example of change is South Korea, which has experienced success in technological manufacturing innovations, becoming a "creative economy" promoting global exports.

Many businesses in ASEAN, particularly large production companies, have transformed from being labor-intensive to being equipped with relevant know-how to survive in the market. Companies can compete effectively by improving their products and creating niche markets with unique offerings. Examples include products infusing different designs and traditions, which shows that companies must adapt and invest in marketing and innovations to respond to new demands. Companies within the ASEAN region should utilize business opportunities and prepare to compete outside the region.

Businesses have also gained immensely from the increasing digitalized economy within ASEAN, particularly with development in information and communications technology (ICT), which has facilitated the movement of goods and services, investments, and skilled labor. Business entities should establish regional connections to reiterate benefits from connecting and working together as an ASEAN region, eliminating the digital divide by creating strong structural foundations, expertise, and knowledge. From this, companies in ASEAN will benefit from the connectivity of systems and varying industries.

The telecommunication and mobile applications industry has not only facilitated convenience, but further improved the productivity and quality of goods and services. People, goods, and services have become more connected through modernized telecommunication systems and mobile applications, which will continue to be in the interest of businesses in the long run. For this reason, the business sector must adapt in terms of quantity and quality of products and services, as the Internet and telecommunication will continue to extend coverage, providing easier access to information at all times. The telecommunications industry has the opportunity to play a bigger role in all industries, including retail, communications, banking, education, and even agriculture.

The retail e-commerce sector within the AEC has targeted the sale of products through free trade platforms to eliminate both tariff and nontariff trade barriers, creating a free flow of goods throughout the region. The ASEAN market has become a targeted region as the government and business sector has improved Internet connectivity and speed, as well as telecommunications infrastructure, in order to reduce the digital divide and knowledge gaps within the region. This is because the rate of Internet usage is bound to increase exponentially in the near future as the middle-income population in the region increases, which will lead to more opportunities for retail e-commerce in ASEAN.

However, the growth in the electronic retail industry is dependent on the financial strength of the economy. In promoting free trade within ASEAN, online payments must be reliable in order to create trust among consumers. Apart from enhancing Internet connectivity to access more consumers, financial institutions and governments must enforce legislation to secure consumers' confidence regarding safety of private and financial information. Simultaneously, consumers can use e-payment channels to purchase goods online and pay upon receipt, which will require integration of work with numerous parties.

Banks and other financial institutions must implement continuous development. Such institutions should integrate with businesses more in order to support business growth over the Internet. Financial institutions should cover this gap by providing credible online payment channels; many banks have already established Internet and mobile banking for consumers to complete transactions on their own and at their own convenience. Banks can also benefit from global positioning systems to track the movement of consumers and use such information to determine future trends and needs.

Medicine and public health has benefited from ICT advancements and regional economic integration. Hospitals can work together with the telecommunications and mobile industry by creating infrastructure to support rural areas, connecting the center with outer provinces. The use of advanced information communication technology within the ASEAN framework will allow member nations to share information on treatments and extend medical coverage to underserved areas. The commencement of the AEC will create opportunities for companies and facilitate their growth internationally, also enhancing product standards. The disappearance of barriers in the private sector will allow for more convenient cross-border movement, benefiting the tourism and medical tourism industries from increased senior populations, which will tend spend more on medical treatment.

Transportation is another industry in which the Internet and its tools have enhanced businesses opportunities. The innovation has improved convenience and safety for its users. Transportation companies can coordinate with government units and use the collected traffic information to improve services. Many airlines use communication technology to help their customers, such as providing online payment gateways, self check-in, and in-flight entertainment.

Business organizations can benefit from many other Internet technologies through connections with other equipment and tools. There has been much worry in the agricultural and energy industry about food safety, as resources become limited and the surrounding environment becomes depleted. Smart farms will require stable telecommunication structures, which are often an obstacle for rural areas in the ASEAN region.

Education is another area of great impact, reiterating ASEAN's goal and vision to integrate collaboration on e-ASEAN and the ASEAN ICT Masterplan. The general public should be more aware of how Internet technology and mobile devices can impact their daily lives, whereby ASEAN can become a more knowledge-based economy by using modernized communication technology in schools, preparing the younger generations for the future change, which is similar to medical communication devices. Modern technology will help reduce the digital divide by connecting schools in rural areas with central institutions. Distance learning can be the future of education through the creation of stable foundations. In addition to this, technological training could be implemented in the education system in order to eliminate the divide in access to technology and knowledge. However, all of this will require effort from schools and relevant government units, as well as telecommunication companies in creating stable foundations for a regional digital economy.

As discussed in Chapter 3, all ASEAN member countries have given great importance to the formulation and implementation of direct foreign investment promotion policies as they become more aware of the benefits of FDI. This is particularly true for developing markets such as ASEAN. In general, policies implemented among ASEAN member nations are relatively similar, such as reduction on corporate income tax, personal income tax, and tax on customs; special economic zones; liberalization of investment regulations; and facilitation in other forms of investment. Though some policies promote positive competition, other policies such as tax reductions can also cause friction with other member countries. To date, investment promotion policies among the member countries still lack cooperation.

In the future, the heart of successful investment promotion in the ASEAN region will be a common plan that encompasses flexibility to respond to the individual needs of each country. The different benefits gained through investment in each country should align with each other, further enhancing the attractiveness of ASEAN as a region for international investors. There should also be integrative projects to invite third-party investors to improve the region as a whole, such as investing in logistical and connecting infrastructure.

It is recommended that each member nation have policies to promote investment and attract quality investors to sectors that contribute to economic growth. Member countries should also specify targeted industries based on their individual competitiveness. Apart from this, countries should be aware of other factors on investment, such as guarantee on the share of technological know-how, gaps allowing multinational enterprises (MNEs) to avoid taxes, responsible investment promotion, and environmental friendliness. Countries must also beware of coordinating investment promotion policies on a regional level, ensuring that policies do not exceed what is necessary in the region. ASEAN member nations can avoid unnecessary cross-border competition by collaborative policy planning, and together, attract direct investments that suit development needs.

This book also discusses literature on internationalization theories and relevant research on network and institutionalization theories, resource-based theories, and case studies of numerous Asia-Pacific companies that have internationalized. Case study companies include Creative Technology, Daewoo Motor, Constellation New Zealand, Charoen Pokphand Foods, Siam Cement, Lion Group, Toyota Group, Sri Lankan Small Business Entrepreneurs, Li & Fung Group, Pohang-Yeongil Port, Boost Juice, and Indian Pharmaceutical Multinational. Chapter 4 illustrates findings from first-generation researchers that discuss international growth of multinational companies using models such as the Uppsala model and Dunning's eclectic paradigm; this contributes greatly to internationalization theories, whereas theories on networks and institutions help cover other aspects that internationalization theories cannot explain sufficiently. Revisiting literature on internationalization of MNEs in the Asia Pacific can be used as a foundation in formulating internationalization frameworks for other companies in the region.

Chapter 5 revisits internationalization strategies, covering the definition of internationalization strategies, relevant literature, and internationalization strategies in numerous dimensions (e.g., market entry, R&D, sharing of technological know-how, distribution of investment, pricing, and branding). Internationalization strategies are further separated by type of business (i.e., regional exporter/importer, international exporter/importer, multinational competitors, and design and production companies for different brands). This chapter also discusses alternate strategies and the structure of MNEs for internationalization. Examples in this chapter show internationalization strategies adopted by MNEs, mostly based in the Southeast Asian region, comprising Frase and Neave, Krungsiam Beverage, PETRONAS Trias Sentosa Tbk PT, Air Asia, Proton, Thoresen Thai Agencies, and Thai Smile Airways. In choosing successful internationalization strategies, companies should opt for those that align with the business strategy, comprising long-term growth plans, risk management and disaster mitigation, socially responsible investments, and strong organizational culture. Internationalization strategies adopted by multinational companies in ASEAN discussed in this chapter provide insight as to the companies' development over time and their adaptations to maintain competitiveness.

Current global dynamics and the changing environment not only present countless business opportunities, but also simultaneously create problems and obstacles to businesses. Many companies have redirected their interest to supply chains with strong cooperation in order to experience successful competition in the global market. Working together effectively in a chain requires units to share valuable and accurate information. As discussed in Chapter 6, the advancement of communication technology today can promote effective cooperation in the supply chain, allowing for a clearer view for cooperation and preparation among cross-border parties; this is particularly the case in Asia. The variety opens up gaps for new forms of businesses and provides an understanding of business trends in Asia for the future.

Chapter 7 focuses on the role of networks in the Asia-Pacific region in helping companies internationalize. Networks provide insight and information relevant to internationalization, such as market information, working procedures, rules and regulations, and connections, such as potential clients and stakeholders. Networks also provide information, and understanding of the market and skills that assist companies in achieving internationalization successfully.

The study of business relationships and the correlation with networks illustrates the development of businesses through close relationships, spanning from business to personal networks, and from stakeholders to friends, which makes the issue a topic of interest. Friendships in particular are highly regarded and trusted relationships within networks.

Networks are at the backbone of businesses in Asia. The concept of cultural networks is of particular interest, such as the guanxi network in

China and Singapore. This chapter also explores the role of networks in Thailand and Malaysia, where it is found that personal networks play an exponential role in the Asian business world.

Chapter 8 investigates the connection of small and medium enterprises' (SMEs) external networks, comprising external investors, advisory boards and accountants, and the possibility of companies' internationalization. The research findings suggest that networks from external investors and advisory boards play an important role in SMEs' internationalization process.

The research also discusses relevant theories on internationalization and looks at how companies are able to connect with external parties to assist with the internationalization process. Furthermore, the research reveals the likelihood and ways in which the three forms of external networks could support SME internationalization. This research contains components to support internationalization of SMEs as previously mentioned. While SME owners become aware that external investors can contribute resources, networks, and knowledge to facilitate internationalization, significant obstacles between SMEs and external investors can present themselves. This research illustrates that there may be gaps in knowledge and awareness of how SMEs can benefit from external accounting parties effectively in the internationalization process. From a positive perspective, a valuable role that advisory boards can play in internationalization is acting as a bridge between SMEs, external investors, and/or external accountants in promoting necessary skills for internationalization. However, SMEs generally do not have advisory boards, illustrating the perception that other stakeholders are important to them (e.g., policy makers, business associations, and industry associations) in helping gain knowledge and establish advisory boards.

In Chapter 9, I evaluate the importance of networks and their impact on the success of the internationalization of multinational companies. The variety of networks include MNEs, SMEs, general businesses, formal businesses, informal businesses, intrafirm and interfirm global production networks, as well as preclusterization, ethnic businesses, and clusters. According to the concept of topics and principles in both classical and contemporary organizations, networks benefit their members by providing in-depth information and insight on cost reduction. Case studies of Asia-Pacific companies are evidence of different forms of networks and their application, such as in India, Thailand, Japan, China, New Zealand, Australia, the Philippines, Singapore, and Malaysia. The findings in this chapter will contribute to formulating a theoretical framework for future research.

As elaborated in Chapter 10, we should give importance to awareness of obstacles posed upon internationalization, as such will impact the attitude and behaviors of companies in international markets. Such barriers can also result in a loss of resources, a loss in productivity, and reduced working efficiency. This chapter illustrates internal and external barriers to internationalization faced by various Asia-Pacific companies, such as financial and resource constraints, management and operational barriers, marketing and knowledge limitations, process constraints, and governmental and environmental issues. Existing literature shows that to date, multinational as well as SMEs' internationalization reveals instances of the aforementioned limitations and challenges as a result of changing market and business conditions. For this reason, companies must rely on an understanding of external and internal factors that affect the company's readiness for internationalization in order to improve and perfect their internationalization strategies.

INDEX

Note: Page numbers followed by *f* indicate figures, *t* indicate tables, and *np* indicate footnotes.

K

L

M